SUSTAINABLE FUTURE
Dynamics of Environment and Disaster Management

ABOUT THE EDITORS

Prof. Suresh Misra is currently with the Indian Institute of Public Administration as Professor of Public Administration and Chair Professor Consumer Affairs. He holds his Master's in Political Science from Jawaharlal Nehru University, New Delhi, Masters in Human Resource Management from Pondicherry Central University, D.Phil. from Allahabad Central University and Post-Graduate Diploma in Journalism and Mass Communication from Calcutta.

He had his advance training in Corporate Governance at AOTS, Tokyo, Japan; in Total Quality Management at UK Civil Service College, Sunningdale, UK; and in Public Policy Management at Development Study Centre, Rehovot, Israel. He participated in the Public Administration programme for senior officers at ENA, Paris, France and also attended advance Training of Trainers Programme on Training Techniques and Methodology at Thames Valley University, Slough, UK.

He has authored/edited 25 books and contributed more than 80 research papers in journals of repute. He is the co-editor of the book *Environmental Laws in India: Issues and Responses* published in 1996. Recently, he organised a National Seminar on Sustainable Consumption, Climate Change and Consumers—Towards a Better Future. He is also the Secretary General of Sustainable Development Foundation, a non-profit organisation working in the area of sustainable lifestyles.

Dr. Shyamli Singh is working as Assistant Professor in Indian Institute of Public Administration and is the coordinator of the Centre for Environment, Climate Change and Drought Administration. Dr. Singh has her Ph.D. in the ambit of Environmental Management. She has been awarded Gold Medal in M.Sc. from Guru Gobind Singh Indraprastha University, Delhi. She has a wide experience in research and teaching and has had affiliation with several institutes of international repute such as Indian Agricultural Research Institute, New Delhi, TERI, IIM-Rohtak, Delhi Technological University, New Delhi. She has published several research papers and chapters in national and international journals. She has designed the course module on Green Federalism and Disaster Risk Reduction catering to Government officials of different departments. Dr. Singh has authored textbook for B. Tech. Students in Environmental Studies and discussion and research paper on Climate Change.

She has organised and conducted several national and international seminars and capacity-building programmes sponsored by different Ministries. She has been a panelist and advisor in Environmental Safeguards in the Regional Plan 2021 hosted by INTACH & PEACE. She is a lead coordinator of several prestigious projects sponsored by various Ministries of Government of India.

SUSTAINABLE FUTURE
Dynamics of Environment and Disaster Management

Essays in Honour of

Prof. Vinod K. Sharma

Edited by
Suresh Misra
Shyamli Singh

CONCEPT PUBLISHING COMPANY PVT. LTD.
NEW DELHI-110059

ISBN-13: 978-93-86682-16-1

First Published 2018

Published and Printed by:

Concept Since 1974

Concept Publishing Company Pvt. Ltd.
A/15-16, Commercial Block, Mohan Garden,
New Delhi-110059 (INDIA)
T : +91 11 25351460, +91 11 25351794
E : publishing@conceptpub.com, *W* : www.conceptpub.com

Cataloging in Publication Data--Courtesy: D.K. Agencies (P) Ltd. <docinfo@dkagencies.com>

Sustainable future : dynamics of environment and disaster management : essays in honour of Prof. Vinod K. Sharma / edited by Suresh Misra, Shyamli Singh.
pages cm
Contributed articles.
Includes bibliographical references and index.
ISBN 9789386682161

1. Environmental management—India. 2. Environmental management. 3. Emergency management—India. 4. Emergency management. 5. Sustainable development—India. 6. Sustainable development. I. Sharma, Vinod K., honouree. II. Misra, Suresh, editor. III. Singh, Shyamli, editor.

LCC GE320.I5S87 2017 DDC 363.700954 23

Preface

Gandhiji said that "Earth provides enough to satisfy every man's needs, but not every man's greed." This aptly sums up what sustainable development and sustainable consumption leading to sustainable future is all about. We need to preserve earth resources for future generations and the effort for the last two-three decades has been towards this endeavour. The UN has played a major role in promotion of sustainable development.

The UN Conference on Environment and Development (the Earth Summit) in Rio de Janeiro in 1992 adopted a declaration calling for a comprehensive programme of action throughout the world towards achieving a more sustainable pattern of development for the twenty-first century and beyond. Despite significant progress since the concept of sustainable development entered international debate, the problems discussed at Rio still endure. Unsustainable trends in relation to climate change and energy use, land use, threats to public health, poverty and social exclusion, and biodiversity loss still persist, while new challenges have emerged. At the Millennium Summit in September 2000, world leaders adopted the UN Millennium Declaration, committing their nations to a new global partnership to reduce extreme poverty and setting out a series of time bound targets, with a deadline of 2015 that have become known as the Millennium Development Goals. The year 2016 presented an unprecedented opportunity to bring the countries of the world together to embark on a new path to improve the lives of people everywhere. Countries have adopted a new sustainable development agenda and a global agreement on climate change.

Climate change is now affecting every country in every continent. It is disrupting national economies and affecting lives, costing people, communities and countries dearly today and even more tomorrow. But climate change is a global challenge that does not respect national borders. Emissions anywhere affect people everywhere. It is an issue that requires solutions that need to be coordinated at the international level and it requires international cooperation to help developing countries move toward a low-carbon economy.

To address climate change, countries adopted the Paris Agreement at the COP21 in Paris on 12 December, 2015. In the agreement, all countries agreed to work to limit global temperature rise to well below 2 degrees Celsius, and given the grave risks, to strive for 1.5 degrees Celsius. Implementation of the Paris Agreement is essential for the achievement of the Sustainable Development Goals, and provides a roadmap for climate actions that will reduce emissions and build climate resilience.

Our Sustainable Future sets out the challenges facing us and how we might address them in making sure that quality of life and general well-being can be improved and sustained in the decades to come. It also charts progress achieved since sustainable development became the global focus of attention over twenty years ago and the roles played by the United Nations (UN) in advancing the environmental and sustainable development agendas globally. Ultimately, we have to meet the challenges, our success or failure will depend on our efforts to protect our natural environment and preparedness to protect it. Sustainable development is about us. While the vision may seem ambitious, even daunting, it is achievable. We need to accomplish this because we must. The challenge is to mobilise all stakeholders and work together to protect our natural environment now and into the future, in tandem with the essential economic and social progress on which our national well-being is dependent.

Our Sustainable Future contains a range of measures to address the key challenges and priorities which will deliver change and support the delivery of a sustainable development agenda. The global environment is changing rapidly. If we are to harness the opportunities associated with implementing sustainable development policies, ensuring that governance and institutional arrangements act as drivers rather than barriers to progress, is key. The essays in this volume essentially focus on this.

It is our privilege to bring out this volume in Honour of Prof. Vinod K. Sharma a well-known expert in the area of Environment and Disaster Management. Prof. Sharma has done pioneering work in this area and contributed immensely to its development. Many of his friends and well-wishers felt that it is time to honour the man for his contributions and by bring out this volume we are only echoing the sentiments of a large number of his friends and well-wishers.

We are grateful to the contributors who agreed to contribute chapters for this edited volume in spite of time constraint. Out thanks are due to Deepa Rawat of the Centre for Consumer Studies for her secretarial help.

We would also like to thank Shri Ashok Kumar Mittal, Director, Concept Publishing Co. (P.) Ltd., New Delhi for readily taking up this publication and bringing it out in a record time.

New Delhi

Suresh Misra
Shyamli Singh
Editors

Contents

Abbreviations

ACGIH	American Conference on Governmental Industrial Hygienists
ADI	Acceptable Daily Intake
AMCDRR	Asian Ministerial Conference on Disaster Risk Reduction
ASTAAG	Asia Science Technology Academia Advisory Group
ATSDR	Agency for Toxic Substance and Disease Registry
BMTPC	Building Material Technology Promotion Council
CBSE	Central Board of Secondary Education
CDA	Contractor-driven Approach
CGI	Corrugated Galvanised Iron
CMRHM	Chief Minister's Rural Housing Mission
CPSC	Consumer Product Safety Commission
DCA	Departmental Construction Approach
DCB	Delhi Cantonment Board
DDMA	District Disaster Management Authority
DRH	Disaster Reduction Hyper-base
DRMP	Disaster Risk Management Programme
DRR	Disaster Risk Reduction
EPA	Environmental Protection Agency
EU	European Union
FAO	Food and Agriculture Organization
FDA	The Food and Drug Administration
GHI	Green House Impact
GoI-UNDP	Government of India-United Nations Development Programme
GPA	Global Programme of Action
HELI	Health and Environment Linkages Initiative
IAEE	International Association of Earthquake Engineering
IDNDR	International Decade for Natural Disaster Reduction
IDRC	International Disaster Risk Conference
IETS	International Education and Technology Service Limited
IFCS	Intergovernmental Forum on Chemical Safety

IL&FS	Infrastructure Leasing and Financial Services
ILO	International Labour Organization
INC7	7th Session of the Intergovernmental Negotiating Committee
IOMC	Inter-Organization Programme for the Sound Management of Chemicals
IPCS	International Programme on Chemical Safety
IPH	Instant Prefabricated Housing
ISDA	International Strategy for Disaster Reduction
IUTOX	International Union of Toxicology
MCD	Municipal Corporation of Delhi
MDGs	Millennium Development Goals
MGNREGA	Mahatma Gandhi National Rural Employment Guarantee Act
MIS	Management Information System
MSK	Medvedev–Sponheuer–Karnik Scale
NCR	National Capital Region
NDMA	National Disaster Management Authority
NDMC	National Delhi Municipal Corporation
NGOs	Non-Governmental Organizations
NIOSH	National Institute of Occupational Safety and Health
NOEL	No Observed Effect Level
NSSP	National School Safety Project
ODA	Owner Driven Approach
OSHA	Occupational Safety Health Association
POP	Persistent Organic Pollutant
RCC	Reinforced Concrete Cement
REDRH	Reconstruction of Earthquake Damaged Rural Houses
RMDD	Rural Management and Development Department
SAICM	Strategic Approach to International Chemical Management
SDMP	School Disaster Management Plans
SEEDS	Sustainable Environment Ecological Development Society
SFDRR	Sendai Framework for Disaster Risk Reduction
SNS	Social Networking System
SPS	Sandwich Plate System
SSA	Sarva Shiksha Abhiyan
STA	Science and Technical Advisors
STAG	Science and Technology Advisory Group
TCDD	2,3,7,8-Tetrachlorodibenzodioxin
TMI-2	Three Mile Island
ToT	Training of Trainer
TSCA	Toxic Substance Control Act
UNDP	United Nations Development Programme
UNEP	United Nations Environment Programme
UNIDO	United Nations Industrial Development Organization
UNITAR	United Nations Institute for Training and Research
WHO	World Health Organization

List of Contributors

Mr. Bhandari, R.K, Chairman, Forum on Engineering Interventions or Disaster Mitigation of The Indian National Academy of Engineering. Email: rajmee@yahoo.com

Dr. Chadah, Sapna, Assistant Professor (Administrative & Constitutional Laws), Centre for Consumer Studies, Indian Institute of Public Administration, I.P. Estate, Ring Road, New Delhi-110002. Email: sapnachadah@yahoo.com

Dr. Davis, Ian, Visiting Professor in Lund, Kyoto and Oxford Brookes Universities, E-mail: ian.robert.davis@gmail.com

Donka, Pema, Development Professional, Rural Management and Development Department, Government of Sikkim, Gram Vikas Bhawan, Gangtok, Sikkim-737101. E-mail: pema_donka@yahoo.com

Dr. Gupta, Anil K., Head, Division of Policy Planning, National Institute of Disaster Management (Ministry of Home Affairs, Government of India), New Delhi, India. E-mail: envirosafe2007@gmail.com, anil.nidm@nic.in

Dr. Kaushik, A.D., Sr. Faculty, National Institute of Disaster Management, Ministry of Home Affairs, IIPA Campus, I.P. Estate, Ring Road, New Delhi-110002. E-mail: adkaushik@gmail.com

Dr. Khan, Amir Ali, Assistant Professor, National Institute of Disaster Management, 5B, I.P. Estate, IIPA Campus, New Delhi. E-mail: alikhanamir@gmail.com

Prof. Misra, R.P., Former Vice Chancellor, Allahabad University, Allahabad and President Sustainable Development Foundation, Vasant Kunj, New Delhi-110070. E-mail: sdf.misra@gmail.com

Dr. Misra, Suresh, Chair-Professor (Consumer Affairs) & Coordinator, Centre for Consumer Studies, Institute of Public Administration, I.P. Estate, Ring Road, New Delhi-110002. E-mail: drsureshmisra@gmail.com

Prof. Pandey, K.K., Professor, Institute of Public Administration, I.P. Estate, Ring Road, New Delhi-110002. E-mail: kpandey_2000@hotmail.com

Pradhan, Sarika, Development Professional, Rural Management and Development Department, Government of Sikkim, Gram Vikas Bhawan, Gangtok, Sikkim-737101. E-mail: saree18@gmail.com

Rana, S.V.S., Toxicology Laboratory, Department of Zoology, Ch. Charan Singh University, Meerut-250004. E-mail: sureshvs_rana@yahoo.com

Sharma, Anshu, Co-Founder and Chief Mentor of SEEDS, a network that works for disaster response and risk reduction in the Asia region. E-mail: anshu@seedsindia.org

Dr. Shaw, Rajib, Adjunct Professor, Kyoto University and Co-chair, Asia Science Technology Academia Advisory Group. E-mail: rajib.shaw@gmail.com

Dr. Singh, Shyamli, Coordinator & Assistant Professor, Centre for Environment and Climate Change, Institute of Public Administration, I.P. Estate, Ring Road, New Delhi-110002. E-mail: shyamli.env@gmail.com

Prof. Tambe, Sandeep, Professor, Indian Institute of Forest Management, Nehru Nagar, Bhopal, Madhya Pradesh. E-mail: jointsecy@gmail.com

Dr. Varshney, C.K., Emeritus Professor, School of Environmental Sciences, JNU, New Delhi-110067. E-mail: ckvarshney@hotmail.com

Vijendran, R., Group Captain, Indian Airforce. E-mail: r.vijendran@gmail.com

Profile of Professor Vinod Kumar Sharma

Prof. Sharma was born in a small village Nala of District Muzaffarnagar (Uttar Pradesh). After his primary education in village, he did schooling from Hindu Inter College, Kandhla, graduation and post-graduation from D.A.V. (PG) College, Muzaffarnagar. He joined B.H.U. Varanasi in 1968 and did PG Diploma in Resource Ecology followed by Ph.D. in Forest Ecology. The three years stay at BHU transformed his personality apart from subject knowledge and academic degrees, he got international exposure and interest in area of Ecology and Environment.

Prof. Sharma started his academic career as 'Lecturer of Botany' in D.A.V. (PG) College Muzaffarnagar (Meerut University). He was consultant in a research project of US Forest Service in Delaware State College, Dover, Delaware in USA and worked for two summers in 1977-1978. He served as "Visiting Faculty of Sulaimaniyah University, Iraq" (which later on become Salahadeen University and shifted to Erbil) from 1978-1982 on deputation from his college. He got another foreign assignment in Garyounis University, Banghazi, Libya and served there as Associate Professor of Ecology and Environment from 1985-1990. He returned back to India because of Gulf War in 1990 and joined Khadi and Village Industries Commission (KVIC) as advisor for short time till he was appointed 'Associate Professor of Environment' in the Indian Institute of Public Administration in July 1992.

Prof. Sharma was instrumental in setting-up of 'National Centre for Disaster Management' (NCDM) in the Indian Institute of Public Administration supported by Government of India in 1995 and became its founder coordinator. He nurtured this centre for one decade till it was upgraded as National Institute of Disaster Management in 2004. As one of thc pioneer in the subject of Disaster Management, he served in most of the important National Committees on Disaster Management. The most important one was the High Powered Committee set-up by the former Prime Minister of India in 1999 (before Orissa Super Cyclone). He was specialized in the capacity building of Disaster Management and did following important trainings in India and abroad –

- Health Emergency in Large Populations (HELP) 2001, Centre of Excellence, Hawaii, USA.
- Environmental Management and Sustainable Development (1996), University of Edinburgh, Scotland, UK.
- Training of Trainers Programme on Rehabilitation and Resettlement (1994) World Bank/ASCI Hyderabad.
- Direct Trainers' Skill (DTS), 1993, British Council, UK / L.B.S.N. Academy, Mussoorie.

He started working in area of Disaster Management, when this subject was not very popular and known only for 'Relief Management'. With the support of Government of India, he developed the concept of Disaster Preparedness, Mitigation and Linkage of Development with Disaster Risk Reduction. He organised more than 100 training programmes for senior and middle level officers, NGOs and assist Government in setting-up small Disaster Management cells in all the states of the country. He developed training modules, prepared case-studies and documented almost all major natural disasters in India after the setting of NCDM. This became the course material for training in India and Asia. Prof. Sharma's contribution in disaster education, public awareness, policy planning and even in response is significant. He is one of the few top Disaster Management specialists in Asia.

Prof. Sharma was deputed to NSET Nepal (2003-2007) to head one of most prestigious 'Programme for Enhancement of Emergency Response (PEER)' funded by USAID/OFDA. The project aims for capacity-building of first responders during disasters in five countries, *viz*. India, Nepal, Bangladesh, Philippines and Indonesia, prone to Earthquakes and other natural and man-made disasters. The project was basically to train various stakeholders (Government and Non-governmental Organisations) in Collapse Structure Search and Rescue (CSSR), Medical First Responders (MFR), Training For Instructors (TFI) and Hospital Preparedness for Emergencies (HOPE) and to establish a coordinating network of emergency and medical response and training institutions and individuals in these countries that can ensure the continuation of the PEER process and further promote its evolution. The programme was implemented by National Society for Earthquake Technology in Nepal in partnership with IRG, John Hopkins University and Safety Solutions Inc. of USA. India was also highly benefited by this project as it developed Master Trainers in four para-military forces and in NDRF.

He served in a number of committees of National Disaster Management Authority and National Institute of Disaster Management. Prof. Sharma was nominated as Vice Chairman, Sikkim State Disaster Management Authority (2012-till date), where he is responsible for making State Policy and Plans; District, Block and Village-level Plans for Disaster Management and their implementation in the different levels. We have State public awareness and capacity building plan for the Disaster Management. The state is having school and hospital safety programme, Urban risk reduction programme, which are closely monitored by him. Sikkim is preparing disaster plans up to Village Panchayat level. The state is using science and technology for early warning system at most vulnerable places in the state by putting sensors. The project is being taken by Amrita University with SSDMA.

Apart from his academic contribution in IIPA, he served in many other national and international institutions in "Honorary Capacity" and with consent of his parent organisation –

- Visiting Professor, Kyoto University, Japan; February/March 2013
- Adjunct Professor, Disaster Management, Amrita University, India (2015-2017)
- Member, UN ISDR Asia Scientific, Technology and Academic Advisory Group (2015-2020)
- Member, Executive Committee of SPHERE India (GO-NGO coordination body in DRR) (2015-2017)
- Founder Chairman, SEEDS India since 1995 till date.

Consultancies

- Consultant with Khadi and Village Industries Commission on Human Resource Development and Livelihood issues (Ministry of Small Scale Industries, GoI).
- Restructuring of KVIC (Ministry of Small Scale Industries, Government of India).

- Peoples' Participation in Ganga Action Plan (Ministry of Environment and Forests, Government of India).
- Capacity Building of local NGOs of Orissa for Drought Mitigation (Action Aid-India).
- Lessons Learned from relief work of Orissa Super Cyclone (CARE-India).
- Lessons learned from relief work of Gujarat Earthquake (CARE-India).
- Programme for Enhancement of Emergency Response (Primary data collection for two states – Delhi and Maharashtra) – ADPC, Bangkok.
- Training of Senior and middle-level officers in Disaster Planning in India, ADPC, Bangkok.
- Reducing Urban Risk, India (Technology Development and Research – TDR) in collaboration with Oxford Centre for Disaster Studies and SEEDS – India, funded by DFID, UK.
- Urban Risk Reduction (Knowledge and Research – KAR) in collaboration with CARE India, CARE-Nepal, DMI, Ahmedabad and SEEDS – India.
- Need Assessment for REDD (Reduced Emission from Deforestation and Forest Degradation) in India sponsored by USAID, 2009.
- Incident Command System – Institutionalization Strategy in India (USAID), 2010.
- Development of tools for mainstreaming Disaster Risk Reduction in Environment Sector, NIDM (Ministry of Home Affairs and UNDP, 2011.
- Guidelines for Safety from Natural Disasters for Schools and other Educational Institutions, Edcil India Ltd., 2012.
- Impact assessment Study of the initiatives implemented under the aegis of investor education and protection fund. Sponsored by the Ministry of Corporate Affairs, Government of India, 2012.
- Pilot Project on Capacity Building of IAS and officers of all India service officers for Disaster Management by LBSNAA, Mussoorie, India 2015 (sponsored by NDMA).
- Multistate Earthquake scenario building in Himachal and Haryana and UT of Chandigarh by IIT Mumbai (2015).
- Evaluation of Research on Soil Piping in the highlands and foot-hills of Kerala to avoid disaster (2015).

- Evaluation of "Preparation of Upgraded Earthquake Hazard Maps" 2015.
- Evaluation of Pilot Project on "Capacity Building on Disaster Management of Government officials", representatives of Panchayati Raj Institutions and Urban local bodies in the areas of Disaster prevention, preparedness, mitigation, response and recovery (2015).
- Evaluation of Pilot Project on "Advance Trauma Life Support Project," at J. P. N. Apex Trauma Centre, AIIMS, New Delhi, India (2015).
- Impact Assessment of 8.7 Shillong 1897 Earthquake Scenario: NE Multi-State Preparedness Campaign Project, NDMA (2016).

Countries Working Experience

India, Nepal, Bangladesh, Philippines, Indonesia, Sri Lanka, Iraq, Libya and USA.

Publications in the Area of Disaster Management

Books

- *Proceedings, Symposium on Advancement of Ecology*, 1979
- *Progress of Ecology*, Vols. 3 & 4, Today & Tomorrow Publications, New Delhi, India
- *Disaster Management* (1994) (Proceedings of UNDP workshop of Natural Disaster Management) Published by UNDP/Indian Institute of Public Administration, New Delhi (Reprinted in 1995-1997 – 1999-2001).
- *Disaster Management* (New Edition) 2013
- *Culture of Prevention*, IIPA, New Delhi, 1999
- *Cyclones in Andhra Pradesh* (Oxfam, Hivos and IT, 2000)
- *India : IDNDR and Beyond* (IIPA, New Delhi, 2000)
- *Manual on Natural Disaster Management* (IIPA, New Delhi, 2001)
- *Orissa Super Cyclone*, 1999 (IIPA, New Delhi, 2001)
- *Drought of Gujarat* (IIPA, New Delhi, 2001)
- *Drought of Rajasthan* (IIPA, New Delhi, 2001)
- *Gujarat Earthquake* (IIPA, New Delhi, 2002)
- *Sustainable Rural Development for Disaster Mitigation* (Concept Publishing Company (P) Ltd., New Delhi, 2004)

- *Global Warming – Its impact on India* (Indian Institute of Public Administration Publication) 2008
- *Knowledge Management* (2014) (ed.) Usha Munshi and Vinod K. Sharma.

Research Papers

1. Sharma, V.K. (1996) Natural Disaster Mitigation and Government Interventions – An overview. INCODIM – 96. In Role of Universities in Natural Disaster Reduction at Anna University. Madras. P.C1-6.
2. Sharma, V.K. (1996) Natural Disaster preparedness, mitigation and reduction: Efforts in India during IDNDR. In Disasters, Environment and Development (ed., R.B. Singh) Oxford & IBH, New Delhi, pp. 93-104.
3. Sharma, V.K. and Amir Ali Khan (1996) Earthquake Disaster – Management and Administrative Issues. Symp. on Earthquake effects on structures, Plant & Machinery. ISET Delhi Chapter: IX - 5.1-5.12.
4. Sharma, V.K. (1996) Environmental Conservation and Sustainable Development, a case of NCT of Delhi. 'National Capital Territory of Delhi' Landmarks in Delhi Administration Post-Independence era (1947-1997) (eds.) S.C. Vajpeyi and S.P. Verma) Gyan Books, pp. 296-311.
5. Sharma, V.K., A. Sharma, A. Bagley, M. Jain and M. Gupta (1997) Risk in Cities – A case of Delhi and an outline Risk Assessment Methodology. *Jour. Ind. Buildings Congress* 4 (1): 164-69.
6. Sharma, V. K. (1997) Natural Disaster Administration in India. In Governing India Public Policy, Institutions and Administration. (ed., O.P. Dwivedi *et.al.*) B.R. Publishing Corp., Delhi, pp. 303-42.
7. Sharma, V.K. (1997) Functioning of disaster management organisation and methodology to cope with disasters in India. Indo-US Seminar on Disaster Relief, New Delhi, pp.1-12.
8. Sharma, V.K. (1997) Strengthening Vulnerable Communities for Natural Disaster Reduction. Workshop on "Understanding Vulnerability: A South Asian Perspective" (August 21-22, 1997) Colombo, Sri Lanka.
9. Sharma, V. K. (1997) Earthquake Disaster Mitigation and

Preparedness in India. Workshop on Earthquake Disaster Preparedness, University of Roorkee (October 13-14, 1997), pp.89-96.

10. Sharma, V. K. (1997) Natural Disaster Management in India. *IJPA*, Vol. XLIII (3), pp. 764-74.
11. Sharma, V. K. (1997) National Policy and Planning for Emergency Response in India. International Disaster and Emergency Response (IDER) Conference, Hague, The Netherlands (October 7-9, 1997) (Paper selected for special presentation in the opening session).
12. Sharma, V. K. (1997) Roles and Responsibilities of Health Sector in Disaster Situation in India. *Medico Friend Circle Bulletin*, OXFAM (India), July-August, pp. 7-8.
13. Sharma, V.K., Gupta, M. and Sharma, A. (1997) Science and Technology in Disaster Risk Reduction. International Conference on Habitat, Institution of Engineers (India), New Delhi.
14. Sharma, V.K. (1997) Preparedness for Natural Disasters in Urban Areas. Golden Jubilee Conference on Natural Hazards in Urban Habitat, New Delhi, November 10-11, 1997.
15. Sharma, V.K., Gupta, M., Sharma, A. (1997) Environmental Considerations in Urban Development. *Nagarlok*, Vol. XXIX, April-June 1997 (2), pp. 63-68.
16. Sharma, V.K. and Amir Ali Khan (2000) Post-Earthquake reconstruction and rehabilitation in Jabalpur. XI Symposium on Earthquake Engineering organised ISET at Roorkee University, Roorkee (17-19, December 1988), pp. 132-42.
17. Sharma, V.K. (1998) Comparative Analysis of Andhra Cyclones of 1977 and 1996, UNIDNDR Conference on Early Warning Systems, Potsdam, Germany.
18. Sharma, V.K. (1999) Use of GIS related technologies for managing disasters in India : An overview. GIS@Development. May-June, Vol. III (3), pp. 26-30.
19. Sharma, V.K. (1999) Status of preparedness planning in India for disaster mitigation, *Shelter,* Special issue – World Disaster Mitigation Day, October 13, 1999, A HUDCO-HSMI Publication, pp.13-15.
20. Sharma, V.K. (2000) Scope of Business Partnerships towards Disaster Management in India, Conference on Building a Disaster Resistant Asia – Managing for twenty-first century, April 2-5, 2000. (Organized by U.S., T.D.A. at Honolulu, Hawaii, U.S.A.).

21. Gupta, M.C., Sharma, V.K. (2000) Orissa Super Cyclone: Administrative Issues, Conference of Relief Commissioners, Pune, India, May 2000: 4-20 (Mimeo).
22. Sharma, V.K. & Amir Ali Khan (2000) Orissa (India) Super Cyclone: Impact and Emergency Management. Proceedings International Millennium Conference on Village Infrastructure to Cope with Environmental Hazards, Dhaka (November 24-25, 2000) pp. 135-49.
23. Sharma, V.K. (2001) Institutional set-up and Disaster Response Mechanism in India. Seminar on Earthquake in Built Environment (May 24-26, 2001) *Journal of Indian Buildings Congress*, Vol. 8 (1): 290-99.
24. Sharma, V.K. (2001) Food availability & vulnerability to Natural Disasters (workshop on "Towards Hunger free India" organised by Planning Commission, Government of India).
25. Sharma, Vinod K. & Tanu Priya (2001) Development Strategies for Flood Prone Areas: Case Study Patna, India, *Disaster Prevention and Management : An International Journal*, Vol. 10, No. 2: 101-109.
26. Sharma, Vinod K. (2001) Managing Disaster in the New Millennium. In Disaster Mitigation, Experiences and Reflections (ed. Pradeep Sahni *et.al.*), Prentice-Hall, India, pp.15-21.
27. Sharma, Vinod K. (2001) Disaster Management in India – Past Experiences, Seminar on Disaster Mitigation Strategy in India, organised by Fire Engineer, New Delhi, Vol. 26, No. 3A Special Issue September 2001, pp. 11-26.
28. Sharma, Vinod K. (2003) Disaster Management – Approach and Emerging Strategies in India. *Vision : The Journal of Business Prospective*, January-June 2003, pp. 135-44.
29. Sharma, V.K. (2004) National Policies Relating to Disaster Care. Disaster Mental Health in India (eds.) Dr. Rashmi Lakshminarayana, Dr. R. Srinivasa Murty and Dr. Joseph O. Prewith Diaz), pp.70-81.
30. Dixit, Amod M., Vinod K. Sharma and Damodar Adhikari (2004) Programme for Enhancement of Emergency Response (PEER): An initiative towards self-sufficiency in responding to large scale disaster in Asia. World Congress on Natural Disaster Mitigation, New Delhi, February 19-22, 2004, (Vol. 2), pp. 413-19.
31. Sharma, V.K. (2004) Disaster Management Strategies in India In "Coping with Natural Hazards: Indian Context", (ed.) K.S. Valdiya), Orient Longman, pp. 250-56.

32. Sharma, V.K. (2004) Psychological Support within Disaster Management Plan International (India) Newsletter, 4 (4): 7-8.
33. Sharma, V.K. (2005) Capacity Building in Emergency Response in Five Asian Countries. DMISA Conference, South Africa.
34. Sharma, V.K. (2006) Linking Development with Disaster reduction – A case of Surat Floods 2006. First India Disaster Management Congress, Vigyan Bhawan, New Delhi, November 2006.
35. Sharma, V.K. (2006) Programme for Enhancement of Emergency Response (PEER) – An Initiative of USAID in Six Asian Countries. First India Disaster Management Congress, Vigyan Bhawan, New Delhi, November 2006.
36. Sharma, V.K. (2007) Recent Developments in Disaster Management in India. Lessons from Natural Disasters: International Roundtable on Policy issues and mitigation strategies, organised by Centre for Science & Technology of the Non-aligned and other developing countries, New Delhi and Centre for Disaster Mitigation and Management (CDMM), Vellore Institute of Technology, Vellore, India (January 8-12, 2007).
37. Sharma, V.K. (2008) India's Planned National Approach for Disaster Risk Reduction. South Asia Disaster Reduction Report, Duryog Nivaran, Sri Lanka.
38. Sharma, V.K. (2008) Drought Risk Management, South Asia Disaster Reduction Report, Duryog Nivaran, Sri Lanka.
39. Sharma, V.K. (2008) Global Warming – Its Impact on India, Theme paper of Annual General Body Meeting of Indian Institute of Public Administration. Indian Institute of Public Administration Publication, New Delhi.
40. Sharma, V. K. (2009) Climate Change Adaptation – Governance Issues, "Governance for Climate Security Business Innovation, Social Change and National Security" (ed.) Lt. Gen. J. S. Ahluwalia) pp. 272-83.
41. Sharma, V. K. and Kaushik, A.D. (2009) Natural Disaster Management – An Overview. *World Focus*, 371-78.
42. Sharma, Vinod K. (2009) Drought Risk Management, In Disaster Management – Global Challenges and Local Solutions (ed.) Rajib Shaw and R.R. Krishnamurthy, University Press, pp.77-85.
43. Sharma, V.K. (2010) Disaster Management in India – New Initiatives. Paper presented in EROPA Seminar at Kathmandu,

Nepal, 21-25 November 2010. (Indian Institute of Public Administration Publication).

44. Anil K. Gupta, Sreeja Nair and Vinod K. Sharma (2011) Environmental Knowledge for Management of Hydro-meteorological disasters. In Environmental Knowledge for Disaster Risk Reduction, pp. 106-17.
45. Kaushik, A. D. and Vinod K. Sharma (2012) Flood Management in India, *Ind. Jour. of Public Administration*, Vol. LVIII (1) : 119-36.

Introduction

Environment protection has since the mid-1970s assumed a progressively greater importance and in India is regarded as being as important as world peace, and development. It has been recognized that as a consequence of economic growth and new production methods, but also as a result of consumer behaviour, the environment suffers damage exceeding matters regeneration capability thus endangering the foundations of life. Therefore, environmental planning is needed. Environmental planning may be defined as the control and development of interaction between natural environment and social development or as the regulation of inter relationship between nature and society to optimize the interdependencies between the natural basis of the society and the structure of social activities and production. Environmental planning should be designed to develop interaction between social and natural environment leading to a sustainable development of the society.

The worldwide exploitation of raw-materials and destruction of the environment are revealing with increasing urgency that our planet earth is virtually an integrated system. Its natural resources are limited. The overall system of our eco-sphere consists of hierarchically organized sub-system with varying degrees of interchanges and interrelationship. The human race is obliged to fit itself into the system and place its actions within the general context.

Until recently, it was felt that human beings did not have sufficient power to seriously affect the environment for better or worse. It would appear that natural limitations, as opposed to moral limitations would more than suffice to protect the environment from human destruction. However, a re-examination of human history and pre-history from an ecological perspective reveals a long-standing, but changing pattern of anthropogenic environmental destruction, paleolithic hunter gatherers armed with stone topped spears and arrows, traps and not least fire caused local extirpation and in some cases global extinction of other animal species and profoundly altered the character of biotic communities. Neolithic, ancient, medieval and modern agriculturalists caused soil erosion, siltation of surface waters deforestation, salination of both arable lands and fresh waters and desertification. This has now been replaced by the industrial civilization which has polluted the environment with synthetic toxic chemicals and radioactive elements, as well as intensified the kinds of destruction already apparent in the activities of pre-industrial man.

Now-a-days, nature is called the life supporting and self-sustaining system. So, a development prospect which is built on the destruction of life supporting and life sustaining system is bound to be counterproductive and this is what is happening. This realization has made us think that we can no longer ignore environment, we can no longer say that environmental problems are the disease of the rich.

Although simple, even obvious, the point that all environmental problems are human problems, in the sense that they are defined by people in terms of their effects on themselves, is not without significance. It means that environmental problems are not acts of gods or plagues visited on us by nature. Generally, the situations arise out of anthropogenic activities, and it is we who designate them as problems. Given that we are rational there might be a contradiction here in that we are creating problems for ourselves.

This decade is a critical period for setting environmental policy, as well as the socio-political and scientific agenda, for the new generation. Promoting environmentally sound policies concerning our planet's natural resources must become a top priority of national and international agencies and organizations, both Governmental and private. The task is now more important in the developing countries. Least able to afford expensive environmental protection measures, the nations of the Third World find themselves under pressure both at home and abroad to trade the protection of irreplaceable natural resources for economic development. Sadly the earth's greatest diversity is found in the countries least able to pay to protect it. The destruction of these natural resources, moreover, has dire consequences far beyond the borders of the individual nations.

Global Concerns for Environmental Problems

Perhaps the global concern for environmental problems can be traced to the seminar on Development and Environment at Founex, Switzerland in 1972 organised by the Secretariat for the United Nations' Conference on the Human Environment. The Seminar concluded that environmental problems do not wrongly result from the development process itself, but also from the very lack of development. Poor water, inadequate housing and sanitation, malnutrition, disease and natural disaster, were cited as important examples. The term, "pollution of poverty" was later used to describe this aspect of the environmental question. Consequently, it was suggested that environmental goals provide a new dimension to the development concept itself requiring an integrated approach to environment and development.

There are a number of reasons cited for environmental crises. In the book *The Third Revolution;* Paul Harrison says that the environmental crisis of the 1970s and 1980s is the outcome of population explosion during the two decades. Environmental impact in any place depends on three factors; population, consumption of each person and technology which determines how much space and resources are used and how much waste is produced. His book also focuses on the question of hyper urbanization in the Third World countries. The 2014 revision of the *World Urbanization Prospects* by UN DESA's Population Division notes that the largest urban growth will take place in India, China and Nigeria. These three countries will account for 37 per cent of the projected growth of the world's urban population between 2014 and 2050. By 2050, India is projected to add 404 million urban dwellers, China 292 million and Nigeria 212 million. The urban population of the world has grown rapidly from 746 million in 1950 to 3.9 billion in 2014. Asia, despite its lower level of urbanization, is home to 53 per cent of the world's urban population, followed by Europe with 14 per cent and Latin America and the Caribbean with 13 per cent. Of today's 28 mega-cities, sixteen are located in Asia, four in Latin America, three each in Africa and Europe, and two in Northern America. By 2030, the world is projected to have 41 mega-cities with 10 million inhabitants or more.

In the Third World, environment has deteriorated as the population living in the cities has increased manifolds. Poor housing, sanitation and health is the most visible problem with typical Third World cities turning into islands of concrete, steel and glass, surrounded by an ocean of wood, tin and plastic. Urban water needs are still poorly provided for and sanitation is in for worse shape with road gutters, open ditches and canals serving the purpose.

Further in their bid to ape the West, the developing nations have indulged in continued exploitation of the natural resources without any concern for the consequences. Thus, developing countries too in the long run will contribute immensely to global environmental pressures and risks. But more importantly the developing countries need to do a bit of soul searching. Industrialization causes immense pressure on land and resulting in destruction of tropical forests for, e.g. tropical forests are being destroyed at a rate of at least 8 million hectares or 31,000 square miles a year. That's an area the size of the State of South Carolina or the Czech Republic that is chopping down every year. Millions of indigenous people live in tropical moist forests which cover some 3.6 million square miles in 70 countries. This has let not only to environmental problems but also to the creation of a large pool of landless labourers. The beneficiaries are often the large industrial groups and other such powerful lobbies.

Extent of Environmental Degradation

In fact the problem of environmental degradation is so acute that on a trip to the hills one's fantasy image of the hills get shattered. Patches of Green hills turned into ashes, *deodar* trees axes to half and other debarked tall trees present a haunting sight. Most trees wear a deathly look. The forests are denuding at a faster rate than one could ever imagine. Forest fire is partly to be blamed for deforestation, besides illegal felling. Every year, wildfires destroy millions of hectares of forest woodlands and other vegetation, causing the loss of many human and animal lives and an immense economic damage, both in terms of resources destroyed and the costs of suppression. There are also impacts on society and the environment – for example, damage to human health from smoke, loss of biological diversity, release of greenhouse gases, damage to recreational values and infrastructure. It is estimated that 90 per cent of the forest fires are manmade. The uncontrollable fires are no doubt destroying forests and the environment.

There is no doubt that rural and urban economy is intimately connected with forestry. The post-independence population explosion and thrust on economic growth in both villages and towns, have made increasing demands on forests for fuelwood, fodder, minor forest produce, industrial raw-material and land for income-generating activities such as agriculture, dams and mining.

There is no doubt that deforestation is one of the main causes of climate change and one of the important contemporary global challenges facing us, with implications for food production, water supply, health, energy, etc. and ultimately may be the very existence of mankind and of life. The earth resources such as air, water, soil and other natural resources are being depleted and one of the reasons for that is the consumerism of the present era. There has been destruction of ecosystems and the extinction of wildlife leading to degradation of the environment. Economic policies that have yielded significant growth are destroying its support system. The gap between what we need to do, to arrest both wasteful resource use and the environmental deterioration of the planet and what we are presently doing continues to widen. Somehow we have to turn the tide. The need is to promote sustainable lifestyles and reduce the impact on environment. India through ages has believed in sustainable consumption and we need to balance man-nature relationship through sustainable consumption.

Promoting Sustainable Consumption

The concept of sustainable consumption is easily understandable in terms of the statement of Mahatma Gandhi that "The Earth has resources for meeting man's every need, but not his every greed". Sustainable consumption can be seen both as a challenge and an opportunity. Ever increasing and irresponsible consumption is putting a major strain on the environment, by using up resources many of which are finite and not easily renewable; by causing pollution and global warming induced by climate change; by adversely affecting the ecosystem; and by undermining sustainable lifestyles. Promoting sustainable consumption and production are important aspects of sustainable development, which depends on achieving long-term economic growth that is consistent with environmental and social needs. A key issue in such a scenario will be not just reducing the volume or quantity of goods and services consumed, but also the extent to which improvement in environmental quality and in human lives can be achieved through the substitution of more efficient and less polluting goods and services.

No doubt it is essential that governments and other stakeholders should commit to implementing policies that will guide us towards a sustainable course. However, it is equally essential that people are empowered to act in relation to sustainable consumption, and they assume their rights and responsibilities in this respect. People are the key to the widespread behavioural shifts needed. They are the key to driving sustainable consumption and production and thus to playing a central role in sustainable development.

Even the international instruments recognize sustainable consumption as need of the hour. Way back in 1999, the UN General Assembly revised the *United Nations Guidelines on Consumer Protection* to include sustainable consumption in the Objectives and General Principles as well as in a specific new section of the guidelines. The UN Guidelines now encompass conducting sustainable consumption research, promoting recycling and sustainable government practices, encouraging life-cycle thinking and eco-products, and developing standards for regulating and verifying environmental claims. The new section on "Promotion of Sustainable Consumption" (Section G) encourages governments "*to create or strengthen effective regulatory mechanisms for the protection of consumers, including aspects of sustainable consumption*".

Today globally people are concerned about climate change and its effects and many of them want to act in ways consistent with the necessary reduction in emissions. In spite of global awareness about the problems, there is a lack of effective action. Sustainable consumption is a balancing act. It is about consuming in such a way as to protect the environment, use natural resources wisely and promote quality of life, while not spoiling the lives of future consumers. It is not surprising that industry and governments, as well as consumers themselves, struggle to understand sustainable consumption and fail to agree on the best way of achieving it. With climate change now commonly identified as one of the most urgent and critical issues for the global community to address, there are greater efforts than ever before to promote policies for sustainable consumption at international, national and local levels.

Although environmental awareness is increasing, most people find it difficult to relate their personal consumption habits to large scale problems such as climate change. And this is a major cause of concern. We, as individuals, as individual citizens fail to link our individual as well as group action with such macro-phenomenon as climate change and think that it is something which is impacted only by actions of say large MNCs or of government. However, it is individual action, individual consumption decisions which ultimately add-up and affect the region, the country and ultimately the world. Hence, each individual is important. In this respect, it is the consumer and citizen who is the driver of all activity. It is the consumer/citizen who is king. Fundamental changes are needed in how natural resources are extracted, the way products are produced, distributed, used and disposed of. Action is needed at all levels of society – from individuals, industry, Governments at Central, State and local levels, and civil society organizations; in order to reverse current trends and to ensure that we live within ecological limits. Action to address better products and smarter consumption, leaner production and availability in the markets of sustainable products and services are required. To reverse the current unsustainable trends, people need to be well informed, empowered and to realize and feel that their actions make a difference. People need clear and better information about which changes in their spending and consuming habits will have the biggest impact. They need to know which are the best-performing products, how to make the most efficient use of them and the cleanest ways to dispose of the resultant wastes.

It has now become clear that a holistic, cooperative multilateral and partnership approach is needed to be taken relating to the multifarious aspects of our natural ecosystems. We need social and technological innovation, appropriate policies, public and private investments, multi-stakeholder cooperation, and improved private-sector management practices all of which can be significantly affected by peoples' behaviour.

In encouraging sustainable patterns of consumption the corporate sector also has an important role to play. Business and Industry needs to make concentrated efforts if people are to be provided with sustainable solutions. Often sustainable consumption has been taken as a limitation on business. Whereas addressing today's consumption challenges should be thought of as a way to create competitive advantage, not solely as a way to mitigate risk. Companies that will embrace this new frontier in sustainability will be the winning companies of tomorrow. Though people may be in the driver's seat when it comes to choices about products and use, but companies can give people the keys to more sustainable behaviour by embedding sustainable options into products and services and giving consumers simple, accessible information about how to use their products in more sustainable manner.

It is every citizen's obligation to protect the earth and its resources and to contribute in his own small way to help save the environment. Thus, there is need for a new paradigm for sustainable consumption leading to sustainable development. Some of the principle ingredients of this are minimizing the depletion of renewable resources by recycling or by substitution of products, maintaining the carrying capacity of the earth's ecosystem with the use of alternative eco-friendly technologies, preservation of the life support systems and bio-diversity with the use of renewable resources etc. The change in the personal attitudes and practices can play an important role in conservation of the ecosystem. Unless public opinion is aroused, and the proper conservation of the natural and human resources of every country regarded as a moral duty, then the earth's fertility will not be able to continue to sustain her rising population. Further, we need to encourage the local communities to care for their environment by encouraging socially valuable actions through their own institutions and community-based organizations.

Climate has acquired importance in global agenda. The Global climate is being polluted on ground of prosperity for increasing GDP propelled by consumption. The problem with all of us is that we only take into account and care for those resources for which we pay and we do not take into account the resources which we get free from the environment. This is leading to pressure on earth's resources and increasing pollution. The development which the globe is celebrating has its environmental consequences. Climate change is the result of changes in weather patterns due to increases in the Earth's average temperature.

Climate change will alter both global and regional climates. Climate change has the potential to adversely affect our environment; our communities and our economy unless we take action now to reduce our greenhouse gas emissions and prepare for the impacts. The Copenhagen Summit did highlight the problem of climate change and environment degradation, but did not achieve much to solve the problem. Climate change and unsustainable consumption is a global problem. Thus, there is a need to take action at global, national, regional and local levels. Local institutions capacity needs to be built for them to play the required role in environment protection and to encourage sustainable consumption patterns. Further, it is every citizen's obligation to protect the earth resources by contributing in his own small way to help save the environment. Conservation of natural resources should be regarded as a moral duty. Further, there is a need to encourage the local communities to care for their environment through community-based organizations. The governments have to also act quickly. The national Action Plan on Climate Change which was given to the concerned Ministries and Departments to prepare their own plan for climate change mitigation and adaptation needs to be effectively implemented. Recently, the NGT has issued notice to Delhi Government as to why the plan has not been prepared. Some states have taken measures and prepared state specific plans for climate change and disaster mitigation.

Community response is the key to solving the problem of environment pollution and degradation as most of the products and services are targeted to the peolpe. So, people's acceptance, response and behaviour can really bring about change which can solve the problem. To prevent the adverse effects on the environment, the consumers can play an important role by adopting sustainable patterns of consumption or what we call as green lifestyle as it can bring a change in the situation. The sustainable consumption on which we are deliberating today requires adoption of sustainable practices like recycling of products, walking, use of bicycle and public transport, keeping thermostats low, and avoid too much of meat eating. There is an urgent need to reduce carbon footprint and this needs to receive increased attention.

Today, the developing and developed countries are blaming each other for such a situation. Per capita consumption may be less in developing countries; however, the large population in these countries makes the amount of total gases released quite high as opposed to excess per capita consumption as compared to the population in the West. Time has come for developing countries to cease the population growth and then reduce population. Climate Change is leading to disasters like floods, shortage of water, glacial melts, coastal cyclones, declining health, increased mortality and threat to food security.

Disaster and Disaster Risk Reduction

During the past four decades, natural hazards such as earthquakes, volcanic activity, landslides, tsunamis, tropical cyclones and other severe storms, tornadoes and high winds, river floods and coastal flooding, wildfires and associated haze, drought, sand/dust storms, and insect infestations have caused major loss of human lives and livelihoods, the destruction of economic and social infrastructure, as well as environmental damage. There has been a tenfold economic loss during this period. In recent years, floods in Algeria, Bangladesh, Ethiopia, Guinea, India, Mozambique, Nigeria, Sudan, Thailand, Venezuela and Vietnam, volcanic eruptions in Ecuador, Democratic Republic of Congo, Indonesia, Montserrat, and the Philippines, and earthquakes in Afghanistan, El Salvador, India, Indonesia, Japan, Peru and Turkey, have created widespread social, economic and environmental destruction. Some cases, witness the amplification of manmade services or *vice versa*, as epitomized by the drought, earthquakes and unfolding events.

While no country in the world is entirely safe, lack of capacity to limit the impact of hazards remains a major burden for developing countries. An estimated 97 per cent of natural disaster related deaths each year occur in developing countries and, although smaller in absolute figures, the percentage of economic loss in relation to the Gross National Product (GNP) in developing countries far exceeds that in developed countries. While the world has witnessed an exponential increase in human and material losses due to natural disasters, there is an ongoing debate about the increase of the frequency and intensity of extreme hydro-meteorological events due to, in particular, climate change. For these geological hazards, the reasons for increased losses are found in the global rise of people's vulnerability, induced by currently determined paths of development. The effects of climate change and the risks posed by the increasing degradation of the environment, epitomized by deforestation, loss of biodiversity and associated knowledge, reduced water supply and desertification, can only contribute to increased concern on these issues.

Disaster risk reduction is basically about choices. It is a concept and practice of reducing disaster risks through systematic efforts to analyse and reduce the causal factors of disasters. Reducing exposure to hazards, lessening vulnerability of people and property, wise management of land and the environment, and improving preparedness and early warning for adverse events are all examples of disaster risk reduction. Disaster Risk Reduction (DRR) is an integral part of social and economic development, and is essential if development is to be sustainable for the future. A risk-informed and resilient Post-2015 development agenda can only be achieved through partnering with groups, communities and the private sector. This is recognized by the Sendai Framework for Disaster Risk Reduction. Throughout the last decade, the interrelation between DRR and sustainable development is continuously strengthened. Reducing disaster risk and increasing resilience to natural hazards in different development sectors had multiplier effects and accelerate achievements of the MDGs, established at the Millennium Development Summit in 2000. It is also understood in the recent past that Disaster risk reduction is everyone's business. It includes disciplines like disaster management, disaster mitigation and disaster preparedness, but DRR is also part of sustainable development. In order for development activities to be sustainable they must also reduce disaster risk. On the other hand, unsound development policies will increase disaster risk – and disaster losses. Thus, DRR involves every part of society, every part of government, and every part of the professional and private sector.

A transformative plan of action for people, planet and prosperity implementable by all countries and all stakeholders should be chartered highlighting the need for disaster risk reduction across a number of sectors in line with the understanding that disaster risk reduction is cross-cutting and requires a multi-sectoral approach. Going forward, the ongoing development of indicators to monitor the SDGs and the Sendai Framework for Disaster Risk Reduction will support coherence and align implementation. A call for a revitalized global partnership echoing Sendai Framework's call for building disaster risk reduction partnerships across sectors and stakeholders to meet the post-2015 international agreements should be addressed recognizing and reaffirming the importance of reducing the risk of disasters in the future.

About the Volume

March towards the goal of sustainability requires fundamental changes in human attitudes and behaviour. Advancement in this direction is critically reliant on education and community awareness. The concept of sustainable development – as suggested through the chapters of this book – is not humble; there is no prescribed road map on how one should proceed. The period is diminutive, and we are called upon to act without further deferral. We must move ahead, in a spirit of investigation and research and with the broadest possible range of partners, so as to contribute through education towards the search of various facets of sustainable future and dynamics of environment and Disaster Management.

The book "*Sustainable Future: Dynamics of Environment and Disaster Management*" is being brought out in honour of Prof. Vinod K. Sharma a well-known expert in the area of environment and disaster management. Popularly designated as *Bhishma-Pitamah* of Disaster Management for his relentless service to the discipline. He has worked for nearly four decades in this area and has devoted his academic career for advancement of the study of environment and disasters. A pioneer who advocated that there is a need to humanize disaster management.

The book is a collection of fourteen chapter written by well-known experts and attempts to stimulate discussion. The book cruises through different realms starting from Indian viewpoint of environmental crisis reflecting the search for a paradigm shift to get over the issues of environmental degradation. The chapter implores the potential of Indian worldview ensuring development without adverse effect on the environment. It also advocates against aping the Western culture. It emphasises the possibility to promote welfare without adversely affecting environmental quality, only if science and technology can be welded to spirituality. Development should not be seen through the lens of material progress, but should be measured in terms of increasing spiritual consciousness embracing the concept of "*Vasudhaiva Kutumbakam*".

The book then reflects to the daunting challenge for sustainable development and human welfare. The approach to disaster risk reduction and disaster resilient development should be holistic and ecosystem based with a focus on transition from emergency response to risk reduction; better risk assessment and communication; strengthening of disaster preparedness and strong institutional bias for implementation and governess. Integration of climate change adaptation and disaster risk reduction into planning and budgeting should be prioritised. The book further envelopes the consumption facet which is an important aspect of sustainable development as all the environmental problems including water scarcity, land degradation, deforestation, loss of biodiversity and pollution are all connected with the consumption and production patterns. The chapter emphasises on the need for innovative, concerted efforts to decouple economic growth from natural resource extraction and environmental degradation.

One of the major highlights of the book is dissemination of training and promoting education for community sensitization to achieve excellence in Environment management and disaster research including school safety programmes. The chapters of the book give ample notion in this direction.The mainstreaming of disaster risk reduction approach, which has been talked about for quite some time, is possible only if there is capacity across all sectors to be able to understand, formulate programmes, and implement and manage them towards effective disaster management. With the new global frameworks in place for development, disaster risk reduction and climate change adaptation, more synergistic approach is required. The initiative mentioned above is the first step to make systematic efforts of bringing science into decision-making and bridging science policy people gap. This would need support from different stakeholders, including national, local governments, civil society, private sectors, media etc.

The book then ventures through a few case studies giving examples of large scale reconstruction of Sikkim, providing a lateral analysis factoring vulnerability attributes of risk, emergency response and recovery sustainability in Nepal Earthquake. The sections also explore India's quest for freedom from landslide. The Chemical disaster which have occurred in recent past have also been overviewed and the management of the same is also one of the flavour of the book.

Social Media and Social Networking has been an uptrend in the modern times keeping this in as the backdrop of the chapter has been attributed to the usage of social media as a disaster management tool. Last, but not the least, the chapter on extra budgetary resources for sanitation in India flags the much talked about Clean India Mission and discusses about the extra budgetary resources for improved sanitation are a must to achieve national policy agenda on rapid pace of economic development and structural readjustment.

The book will surely help the community at large to think in terms of embracing sustainable development and making it inclusive in their lifestyle, thus leading to a disaster resilient society.

1
Indian Worldview and Environmental Crisis

R. P. Misra

Environmental crisis is no longer impending. It is already here. Those concerned with it are growing in number. And they come from all age groups, walks of life, and regions of the world. Search for a paradigm and policy to get over the problem and ward-off any further deterioration in our living environment has been on for quite some time, but the success is limited, if at all. Economic development still is the top priority and if in the process of economic growth, ecology suffers; it must be treated as an opportunity cost, so goes the thinking. Economy and ecology are two sides of the same coin, but not in the Western model of development. It believes in analysis, in specialization and in linear growth. The search for a way out is still on within the framework of Western thinking.

The dominant groups in all countries of the world still subscribe to the view that human ingenuity will triumph and man would one day have complete control over nature. Science and technology would help man get over whatever hurdles come in the way of material advancement. They also believe that progress has inbuilt opportunity costs. Humanity has always paid a price for progress. How else man could come out of his animal existence? The environmental crisis that has gripped the world today is nothing but the cost of progress. Man cannot avoid it, but he can certainly minimize it. So, goes the thinking.

This chapter explores the potentials of the Indian worldview, which ensures development without adversely affecting the environment. It does not consider development and ecology as antithetical to each other. It is possible to promote material welfare without adversely affecting the environmental quality.

Indian Worldview

India's written history goes back to over 5000 years. Archaeological records take this culture further back to several millennia. Its philosophy, grand narratives, religion, history, values and ethical standards are marked with reverence for all that exists in nature so much so that it evolved the concept of *Vasudhaiva kutumbakam* (the whole world constitutes a family). This cultural dictum was accepted not only by the Hindus, but also by the other co-religionists. Even the religions, which originated outside India were deeply influenced by it. "Live and let live" has been the core belief of Indian culture. The question is: Can the Indian worldview as evident from its cultural heritage be used as a paradigm to create what Gandhi called modern civilization, a civilization, which treats nature as a source of not only livelihood, but also of life.

Indian culture as it evolved during the last several millennia is deeply rooted in two different, but interdependent traditions. The Aryan tradition had its sway in the Indus and Upper Ganga valleys while the Dravidian tradition, south of the Vindhyas. The cultures ultimately merged to produce the well-known Indus Civilization and thereafter, the Vedic and Post-Vedic civilizations of India. Some of the statuettes and seals found in Mohenjo-daro and Harappa, now in Pakistan, and parts of Gujarat and Rajasthan in India point to the fact that some of the basic ingredients of Indian civilization as we notice in later periods were present in their incipient forms even then. The statuette of Mother found in Mohenjo-daro points to a concept that gave rise to the concept of Mother Earth or *Shakti*, *Kali* and *Durga*.

Let us explore more deeply the continuity of the main currents of Indian civilization from ancient most times to this day.

Origin of Life

All life found on the earth has a common source, i.e. God. There is 'One without the second' say the *Upanishads*. The source of life is one and one alone. "All this is *Brahma*, *Brahma* is devoid of any attribute. Nothing can be positively postulated about Him. He can be indicated only by "not this, not this." Hence, He is perceived by different people differently depending upon past experiences. When these various perceptions are concretized into thoughts they give rise to different philosophical and religious traditions. Religions are nothing but different paths to arrive at the same reality. No religion is therefore superior to the other. All are in search of the same reality. Religions should, therefore, unite all the peoples irrespective of their origin, mode of expression, and rituals. Since, God is indivisible, the creations of God should also be indivisible. And hence the concept of *Vasudhaiva kutumbakam*, which unites all that, exists in the universe into a common bond.

The *Brahma* reveals Himself in two forms: in the unconscious, non-Self (*achetan*) form that we call matter and conscious, Self (*chetan*) form that we call *Atma* or soul. The non-Self is transitory; the Self is eternal. The non-Self ends to re-emerge in other forms, the Self remains indestructible for it is the part of the Universal Self or *Paramatma*. It cannot be reduced or expanded, nor can it be destroyed.

Unity of life is one of the basic tenets of Indian civilization. It is not only the human life. All life forms, from single cell amoeba to human beings, are united; they have a common origin and a common destiny even if they were born differently as:

> *Jarayuja* (viviparous),
> *Andaja* (oviparous),
> *Udbhija* (germinating), and
> *Swedaja* (generated by heat and moisture).

The *Jarayuja* are born of placenta like human, beings and animals; the *Andaja* are born of eggs like birds and reptiles; the *Udbhijas* sprout through the soil; and *Swedjas* are born of heat and moisture like bacteria. The inorganic matter (*Jada*) does not fall in any of the above four categories for it only forms the base for the creation of life. Indian civilization considered plants as living species, and the same was confirmed by modern science in twentieth century.

The creation, according to Hindu thought, is not accidental nor it is purposeless. The Brahma did not create the universe; He is Himself the universe for He is a *Shakti*, a Cosmic Law, which has all the ingredients of the universe in Him. Just as a small seed, gives rise to a huge tree, so does Brahma gives rise to the universe. The size, shape and structure of the tree and its each leaf and twig is ingrained in the seed; so also the size, shape and structure of the universe is inherent in Brahma's *Shakti*. Gandhi called this *Shakti* the Cosmic Law.

Like the universe, life too is not purposeless. It entered first into a single cell bacterium, which evolved in due course of time to become *Homo sapiens* with a brain of a size and complexity that could produce a self-energized and propelled super-computer. The journey from bacterium to *Homo sapiens* was long and tortuous but the goal appears to have been set, i.e. to bring into a being a super-conscious creature able to know its Creator.

Concept of Progress

The concept of progress envisaged by Indian civilization is different from the one in vogue today. Progress in modern sense essentially means material advancement and all that goes with it. It is often measured in terms of how much money one has. A progressive society is one, which promotes material development. It is presumed that the economically well-off would be a satisfied and happy people. So, more wealth one has, the more happy he is. And since man has eternally been in search of happiness, it is the duty and responsibility of all societies, peoples and nations to work to accelerate the growth of Gross Domestic Product, which in turn accelerates the growth of per capita income. All those who have more income would be more happy. As the GDP grows, more of the people would have more income, and thus all the people would be happier than before and there would be no unhappiness in the world. So, goes the logic.

There are two flaws in this argument. First, happiness is the function of the state of mind, not the amount of goods and services consumed. How else can one explain increasing rates of suicide among the rich people in the world – the people who have all the physical comforts and luxuries for body welfare. Material development alone is not enough to be happy. And second, man is not a machine; he is the most evolved species among the living things. He has body, mind and soul. The first is essentially natural like the body of any other living thing. Being formed of material substances, it decays through time and ultimately gets recycled in the earth of which it is a part. The mind helps the body to perceive the environment, both physical and spiritual. It is invisible but knowable. It stores experiences and knowledge and gives meaning to one's life and the world in which it lives. The soul, i.e. *Atma*, links the body, which encases the mind, to its Creator (*Paramatma*). It is a part of the Creator, which is none other than a Cosmic Law or Truth as Gandhi proclaimed. Various religions give this Law a name: God, *Bhagawan*, *Khuda*, and so on. The Soul exists or not is a question that is difficult to answer for it cannot be seen; it is beyond material body and logical mind to know. To know the Soul one has to transcend the material and psychic to achieve higher level of consciousness. One has to merge into the whole. Religion would lose its meaning if the existence of soul is denied. Material advancement improves body welfare; logic perfects the mind to analyze, but neither of them, jointly or individually, knows the soul as long as they are self-centred. Soul is beyond material existence as also beyond logic. It is all pervading; it is present in all that lives and all that lives has a common origin. And hence, all life is one.

Indian culture has different concepts of progress or development. It is called *Kushala* and *Mangalya*. *Kushala* means body welfare; *Mangalya* conveys the meaning of bliss, i.e. inner happiness. Together, they mean blissful material advancement of all. Development is complete only if the whole environment in which man lives is harmonious. Not only are individuals satisfied; others around them should also be satisfied. If others are unhappy, the happiness of a single individual is meaningless. It lays emphasis on collectivity. The collective includes not only the human beings, but also the animals, birds and plants.

The modern concept of development is man centred. It is greed based and hence each one tries to enhance his welfare often at the cost of others. Development pitches man against man, man against animals and man against nature. To secure development, people are prepared to kill and maim their fellow beings and other life forms. Species after species of animals and plants are going extinct. Wars are fought to protect rights over properties. People have gone so wild that they indulge in terrorism to revenge the alleged wrongs done to them; and that too in the name of religion.

Development has let loose a situation in which some are winners and some losers; some are tormentors and some tormented; and some are rich and some are poor. The strong are winners and weak are losers. Development has destroyed nature to the extent that it is no longer able to sustain life in its pristine exuberance and health. There is a lurking fear that climatic change caused by development may destroy all that development has given to man. In fact, it may herald the end of life on planet earth.

The Indian concept of development calls for a win-win situation, a situation wherein all cooperate to live harmoniously and blissfully. The evolution of species leading to the emergence of man was possible because of cooperation and sacrifice for a cause, which was ingrained in each cell of each living being. And further evolution of man from the conscious to super-conscious stage will be possible only through cooperation and sacrifice, not through competition and killing spree.

Indian culture is thus not human centred; it is life centred to begin with. As such nothing should be done that would jeopardize life on planet earth. It does not prohibit the use of nature; in fact it encourages its use but in a form that keeps it healthy, i.e. its vitality is not sapped. A farmer, for example, can cut trees provided that he plants more trees. It is the duty of the farmer to plant trees; the right to cut emanates from the duty to plant. Other life forms use only that much of the plants as to meet their basic needs. Man alone uses them for comforts and luxuries and very often to satisfy his greed for money.

Systems View of Nature

"Yatha pinde tatha brahmande", say the *Upanishads*. The nature functions like a set of systems that ranges from the universe to a single cell and its constituents like minute organelles and bio-machines. In between are biosphere, species like *Homo sapiens*, individual human beings, the organs of which their bodies consists of, tissues and finally the cells. Each of them constitutes a subsystem of a larger system, all of them interlinked horizontally as well as vertically to each other forming a web of millions of connections. Nothing stands alone and the only way everything can prosper and play its assigned role is to follow the Cosmic Law, which consists of the following seven principles that constitute the bedrock of all stable organic systems:

1. Change beyond the Threshold Limit is controlled by Negative Feedback;
2. Efficient Functioning and Physical Growth Go Together. They are Interdependent;
3. Nature is not marked by Specialization. Interdependence is the Law;
4. Conservation of Energy. The Force Applied from outside is diverted, not combated;
5. Production without Waste – Everything is Recycled;
6. Symbiotic Relationship, both Vertical and Horizontal; and
7. Biology of Nature and Man go together.

All that exists in nature is essential for life. Had nature not evolved the way it has, life would have not been possible on planet earth in the form we see it today. All that exists in nature is therefore sacred; it has to be preserved. Modification can and must be made, but they must be within the threshold limits. Ocean has given the poison as well as the nectar; Himalaya is the abode of Lord Shiva who represents welfare of all (through the control of the climatic forces) as well as destruction (earthquakes, floods and droughts); Ganga is the mother for it has given so much for life to prosper; cow and certain trees are sacred, for all that is living is essential for human life. The concepts of *Kamadhenu* and *Kalpa Vriksha* (the animal, and the tree that provides everything man desires) is there not only in Indian culture but in other cultures too.

If we study the *Dashavatara*, we find that God came in different forms. *Gita* proclaims that God is like Banyan among the trees. His first *Avatara* was *Matsya* (fish) for life emerged in water first and fish is the first life form, which had developed enough brain to think and feel. Next came the Tortoise, (*Kurma*) which lived in water, but came out on the land too. Boar (*Varaha*) which lived on land but enjoyed water too was next to follow. Half-lion and half human form (*Narasimha*) came next. *Vamana*, he measured the whole world in three steps. And then came *Parashurama* who used weapons to set things right. He was followed by *Rama* who was the embodiment of a person who cared for all irrespective of his social or economic status and who symbolized sacrifice in order that others may live happily. *Krishna* was the embodiment of Love, and *Buddha* of non-violence. The last God's Tenth *avatara* would be *Kalki*. They all showed the way to evolve into what we may call super-human beings, not in physical but, in spiritual terms.

Modern civilization, proud as it is of its scientific and technological achievements, is ever engaged in developing methods and processes to uncover the secrets of nature and to use the knowledge so gained to control the nature. But nature is elastic only to a certain limit; beyond the limit, it is brittle. Once it breaks, it becomes devastating. The *Rig Veda*, the ancient most written treatise, calls it *R'ta*.

"The processes whose perpetual sameness or regular occurrence gives rise to the representation of order, obey *R'ta* or their occurrence is *R'ta*", says Maurice Bloomfield. "We read in the Vedas that rivers flow *R'ta*. According to the *R'ta*, the light of the heaven born morning has come.... The year is the Path of *R'ta*. The gods themselves are born of the *R'ta* or in the *R'ta*; they show by the acts that they know, observe and love the *R'ta*. In man's activity, the *R'ta* manifests itself as the moral law." (*Rig Veda*)[1]. Gandhi called it the Cosmic Law, which in human terms is the law of *Dharma* or Truth.

To enjoy the privileges of nature's bounties, man must obey the *R'ta*: "for one who lives according to the Eternal Law the winds is full of sweetness, the rivers pour sweet. So, may the plants be full of sweetness for us" says Rishi Atharva, the first deep ecologist of the world. We have polluted the air, contaminated the water and cleared the plants. We can now see the consequences of our deeds.

The concept of the Eternal Law is found in Buddhism and several other religions. When the Lama turns the prayer wheel in motion, he reminds us the *R'ta*. As Jane Harrison wrotes, "He finds himself in sympathetic touch with the Wheel of the Universe when he performs the act of '*Dharmachakrapravartana*' (Setting the Wheel of Justice in Motion). He dare not turn the wheel contrariwise, lest that were to upset the whole order of the nature."[2]

Raphael Patai in *"Man and Temple in Ancient Jewish Myth Rituals"* says: "The fact that primitive man draws no strict line of cleavage between the animal, vegetable, and mineral kingdoms on the one hand and human beings on the other, has been so often emphasized that it can be regarded as anthropological commonplace." And Jane Harrison in *"Themis: A Study of the Social Origins of the Greek Religion"* says "To man in the totemistic stage of thinking, Dike and Themis, natural order and social order, are not distinguished not even distinguishable. Plants and animals are parts of this group, a factor in his social structure. It is not that he takes them under his protection; they are his equals, his fellow tribesmen; naturally they obey the same laws."[3]

Unlike the other cultures, Indian culture had no interruptions and hence the concept of nature as a living system was never abandoned. No wonder then that Indian culture is considered *Sanatana*, never ending. According to the Indian cultural tradition all that exists in nature is formed by the following five ingredients (*panchabhutas*): Land, Water, Fire (energy), Air, and Space (ether).

And after death or destruction everything gets converted into these very ingredients. Our bones constitute the Earth, the blood, the Water, the oxygen we breathe in represents the Air, the food represents Energy and the influence of the outer space on us represents the Space.

Concept of Mother Earth

The *Prithivi Sukta* of *Atharva Veda* is devoted to Earth. When the disciple asks the nature of relationship between us, the human beings and the earth, which sustains us, the Rishi Atharva says:

Mata bhumih putroham prithivyaha (Earth is the Mother and we are her Children).[4]

When the pupil asks about the nature of the Earth, the Rishi says, "The Earth has hills, snow covered mountains, it has dense forests and soils of different colours; it is the mother of herbs, it has fire inside and also gets energy from the son; it produces a special odour, which enriches all that exists and grows on it. ... To protect us from all that is evil, the Earth contains pure water. It purifies all that is impure. It produces good harvest for us. It cleans everything that goes in it. Earth is real purifier of all that is undesirable and unclean. Let us not hurt its vitals and its heart. Let us use it judiciously. "[5]

And he adds: "the Earth is full of variety; it contains people speaking different dialects and speeches and diverse religious customs; each living according to what they think is right. Earth contains innumerable valuable things. It bears different varieties of trees and plants. We should pay homage to that Earth."[6]

> *Jana vibhrati bahudha vivasharsam*
> *Nana dharmanam prithivi yathokasam*
> *Sahasra dhara dravinasya methudham*
> *Dhruven dhanuren parasphuranti.*

The *Prithivi Sukta* of *Atharva Veda* represents the main current of Indian thought on man's relations with the earth. The post-Vedic literature, especially the Jain and Buddhist literature, is imbued with reverence, love and compassion for nature, unity of life and unity of living (*chetan*) and non-living (*jada*). The *Svetasvatara Upanishad* has captured the essence of this unity and integration when it tells the people to salute the God who exists in everything – in fire, in water, in medicines, in vegetation and in the whole universe.[7]

> *Yo devo agne yo apmu yo vishvam bhuvanamavi vesa,*
> *Ya aushadhishu yo vanaspatishu tasme devaya namo namah.*
> (God who is fire, who is in water, who pervades the whole universe, who is in the medicines, who is in vegetation, we salute that God.)

Indian culture treats the earth as a living system governed by certain bio-cybernetic laws. While developing the economy man has to follow these laws, so that, the future of the generations to come is not jeopardized. Soil conservation methods used then remain unmatched to this day. Crop rotation, intercropping, green manuring, barn manuring, ploughing, irrigation and other agricultural practices were so designed that the soil remained ever fertile. There were innumerable ponds and lakes, which captured the rainwater containing humus and minerals necessary for soil fertility. In summer the tanks were excavated and the new soil deposited was taken back to the land to enhance soil fertility. And thus the cycle continued.

Water, the Purifier

Pure and uncontaminated water commanded a very high value in Indian culture. No ceremony, from conception to death, was complete without *Ganga Jal* – the water from River Ganga. The story of the decent of River Ganga from heaven is an excellent allegorical presentation of the concept of hydrological cycle. As the sunrays fall on the sea, the water evaporates. The vapour is carried by the winds to the North to form clouds that rain snow on the Himalaya. The snow flows through the glaciers from which are born Rivers like Ganga. But for the Ganga and its tributaries the land between the Himalaya and the Vindhyas would have not nurtured such a great variety of life.

India has the unique distinction of developing a unique system of irrigation as early as 5000 years ago, which conserved and replenished surface and groundwater and improved the living environment even in deserts. Rural areas all-over India, but more so in peninsular India, are dotted with small and large tanks and lakes, most of them manmade, provide excellent examples of how man can improve the environment while using the natural resources for greater productivity. But for these tanks, Deccan plateau would have been a barren land. The annecuts (shallow dams) that our forefather built across various rivers in South India and the wells they constructed to harness the surface and groundwater point to the environment sensitivity of our culture.

Forest, the Abode of Gods

Forest constituted an inseparable part of Indian culture. Most of our ancient books – the *Vedas*, the *Upanishads*, the *Brahmanas*, the *Aranyakas*, *Puranas*, *Ramayana*, and *Mahabharata* were written by the wise men living in *ashramas* dotted in forests all-over the country. One finds references to three types of forests:

Mahavana,
Tapovana, and
Shrivana.

Mahavana was a dense and virgin forest found in the hills, mountains and low-lying areas unsuitable for human habitation. They were devoid of human habitation. Rich in bio-diversity (both plants and animals), these forests were the main source of medicinal herbs. Lord Shiva was the presiding deity of these forests and hence no one dared to interfere with them.

The *tapovana* was the forest where the wise men (*rishis*) build their *Ashramas*, which were the main centres of education. These forests were also protected, not by law, but by tradition and mutual consent. It is here that the great religious and spiritual books were written. It is pertinent to note that the *tapovanas* were also marked with rich biodiversity. No one cut the trees or killed the animals, because doing so was against moral code of conduct, *Dharma*. Most of these forests were destroyed during the last 1000 years.[8]

The *Shrivanas* were local village forests. They were managed by the village-community. *Shrivanas* had trees of local variety to meet the needs of the community. They abounded in fruit trees. They were not protected forests; felling of the trees was permitted provided that those cutting the trees compensated the loss by planting more trees. Within the *Shrivana* were sacred groves with a temple or shrine. They were also called *Panchavatis*, the groves of five trees. Each village had a sacred grove or *Panchavati*.

The *Panchavatis* had at least five species of trees. These were:

Banyan,
Peepal,
Ashok,
Bela, and
Harad.

All these trees are known to be environment friendly. Banyan is a tree that gives shade; it is everlasting unless felled; it attracts birds of various kinds. It is associated with fertility and longevity of life. *Peepal* (*Ficus religiosa*) is the abode of Lord Shiva. It is said to give oxygen for 20 hours a day. It is healthful and medicinal. *Ashok* is a pain killer apart from being shady. *Bela* (*Aegle marmelos*) is a medicinal tree. Almost every part of it is used to cure various diseases. The last of the five trees was *harad* (*Myrobalan terminalia chebula*) is well-known as a medicinal plant.

All the villages had *panchavatis* but the species of trees differed from region to region. It is the local trees that predominated. The trees of the *Panchavatis* were never cut. The *Shrivanas* and Sacred groves offer an excellent example of social forestry, which we are now trying to revive at the instance of the World Bank.

Indian and Western Worldviews Compared

According to Richard Saint Barbe-baker, "this generation may either be the last to exist in any semblance of civilized world or it will be the last to have the vision, the bearing and the greatness to say "I will have nothing to do with this destruction of life; I will play no part in this devastation of land; I am determined to live and work for peaceful construction for I am morally responsible for the world of today and the generations of tomorrow."[9] Had he been aware of what Indian civilization stands for, he would have quoted from the *Vedas* in support of his point.

Baker was addressing the man intoxicated by modern industrial civilization and who "has lost his way in the jungle of chemistry and engineering and will have to retrace his steps, however, painful this may be. He would have to discover where he went wrong and make his peace with nature. In so doing, perhaps he may be able to recapture the rhythm of life and love of the simple things of life which will be an ever unfolding joy to him."[10]

Many others have expressed similar views from time-to-time, but those who think that science and technology would resolve all problems including ecological and environmental are not in minority. In fact, the ruling elites the world over subscribe to this view and no amount of evidence against it would induce them to change their perspectives. They would change only when the ruling paradigm has changed. They tend to flow with the current.

Thus, the Indian worldview cannot stand the test of modernity, a product of the Western worldview. The whole structure and superstructure of the society is built on the foundation of this paradigm. A shift from this would be painful. And a society, which is in search of pleasure, would not like to invite pain. But then, a time comes when the meaning of pleasure and pain changes. Suffering to relieve others' pain becomes a source of pleasure.

The world in which we live today is buoyant in terms of economic and technological progress. Sky is the limit. But then what would happen in the future is full of uncertainties. A series of crises loom large: ecological crisis, moral crisis, social crisis, political crisis, economic crisis, and many other crises. Who could imagine just a couple of decades back that our own deeds would take us to a watery grave if we do not stop tinkering with our environment? The economic crisis constitutes a great dilemma for us. More we progress more poor we have amongst us. What about the social crisis? We live under the shadow of the gun. None is safe. The political crisis is no less disturbing. One third of the members of the parliament of the largest democracy of the world are proclaimed criminals. The lawbreakers have become law-makers.

While many pin their hopes in science and technology, small popular movements have sprung up all-over the world to counter these trends. They have also started networking with each other to create a global movement. In India too a rethinking has begun and the urge to go to our cultural roots to recover the values that make scientific and technological development eco-sensitive and ethics-sensitive, has become apparent. Ecological destruction has invited unexpected climatic change and ethical degradation has made life so insecure that development tends to lose its meaning.

Gandhian Paradigm of Development

India was fortunate to have Gandhi under whose leadership the country fought for independence using the means, which had the sanction of Indian civilization. He taught to follow the path of truth and non-violence and be ready to sacrifice even one's life for a right cause. Gandhi's greatest contribution lay not in freeing India but in inculcating the values that go with the concept of *Vasudhaiva kutumbakam*. He taught us that science and technology must be welded into spirituality so that development is seen not just in terms of material progress, but also and more importantly in terms of increasing spiritual consciousness of human beings. The roots of the ills modern civilization suffers from are deeply rooted in the minds of the people. New law and institutions to handle them attack the symptoms, not the roots. The remedy therefore lies in changing the mindset of the people. Unless it is imbued with truth and non-violence; love and affection; and the spirit of sacrifice for others, nothing substantial can be gained. Human values must guide the life and living of the people.

Gandhi's genius encompassed all religious traditions. He found among them more unity than diversity in so far as the fundamentals were concerned. The rituals might differ, but the goal was the same and so was also the message. He outlined an alternative civilization, different from modern industrial civilization, which was life centred and eco-sensitive; and warned

India that political freedom would have no meaning so long as man behaved like animals. Man must become truly human and his attitude towards his fellow human beings, irrespective of the caste, creed, race or place of origin, and towards nature must be imbued with love and compassion.

> "God forbid that India should ever take to industrialize after the manner of the West. The economic imperialism of a single tiny island kingdom is today keeping the world in chain. If an entire nation of 300 millions took to similar economic exploitation, it will strip the world bare like locusts."[11]

Elsewhere he said: "Earth has enough to meet everyone's need but not everyone's greed."[12] One of the dictums of Gandhi was simple living and high thinking. He wanted the seven basic needs – food, clothing, shelter, education, health, security and self-esteem – of each and every individual to be me equitably me. He was against luxuries for luxuries promoted inequity and had very adverse effects on natural and social environment.

Education Is the Key

The inculcation of time honoured human values in the people from early childhood is the only solution to the problems we face today. Gandhi developed the concept of new education (*Nai Talim*) to make children knowledgeable about the environment in which they would spend their life; to train them to acquire skills, which would help him earn his livelihood; and to sensitize him to become loving instead of hating, compassionate instead of cruel, and cooperative instead of competitive human being. He advocated the concept of learning while earning.

Somehow the concept of *Nai Talim* otherwise known as Basic Education was never put into practice in India. The British system of education was not only retained, but also allowed to supplant the other innovative systems. The Sriprakash Committee, set-up by the Government of India in 1959 said:

> "Many ills that our world of education and our society as a whole is suffering today resulting in widespread disturbances and dislocation of life are mainly due to the gradual disappearance of the hold of basic principles of religion on the hearts of the people. ...The only cure it seems to us, is in deliberate inculcation of moral and spiritual values from the earliest years of our life."[13]

Moral and Ethical Education is Inclusive of Ecological and Environmental Education

The Commission on Education chaired by Professor D.S. Kothari was more vocal on the issue when it said:

> "Modernization did not mean, least of all in our national situation, a refusal to recognize the importance of or to inculcate necessary moral and spiritual values and self-discipline. While a combination of ignorance with goodness may be futile, that of knowledge with a lack of essential values may be dangerous".

The weakening of social and moral values in the younger generation is creating many social and ethical conflicts in Western societies and there is already a desire among great Western thinkers to balance the knowledge and skills which science and technology bring with the values and insights associated with ethics and religion at its best, viz. a search for the knowledge of self, of the meaning of life, of the relationship of man to other human beings and the ultimate reality. In the situation that is developing, it is equally important for us to give a proper value orientation to our educational system.

India has a unique advantage with her great tradition of duty without self-involvement, un-acquisitive temperament, tolerance, and innate love for peace and reverence for all living things. Too often are these precious assets forgotten and we tend to relapse into woods of pessimism, fears and forebodings, discard and destructive criticism. A new pride and deeper faith expressed in living for the noble ideals of peace and freedom, truth and compassion are now needed.[14]

Several other commissions, committees, seminars and conferences have since then repeated the above views but not much has been done to implement them. In 1976, the Constitution of India was amended to insert certain fundamental duties that would go with the fundamental rights guaranteed to all citizens of the country. The following five duties are relevant to ecological and environmental issues:

- To promote harmony and the spirit of common brotherhood amongst all the peoples of India transcending religious, linguistic and regional or sectional diversities to renounce practices derogatory to the dignity of women.
- To value and preserve the rich heritage of our composite culture.

- To protect and improve the natural environment including living creatures.
- To develop scientific temper, humanism and the spirit of enquiry and reform; and
- To safeguard public property and to abjure violence.

The incorporation of the above duties was inspired by the Stockholm Conference on Environment wherein Srimati Indira Gandhi, the then Prime Minister of India played a leading role.[15] The National Education Policy Statement, 1986 included the above points and suggested a national curriculum framework which among others included:

> "The history of India's freedom movement, the Constitutional obligations and other contents are essential to nurture national identity. These elements will cut across subject are areas will be designed to promote values such as India's common cultural heritage, egalitarianism, democracy and secularism, equality of sex, protection of the environment, removal of social barriers, observance of small family norms and inculcation of scientific temper."[16]

The Ramamurthy Committee while reviewing the working of the 1986 policy said:

> "The hidden curriculum as distinct from the explicit ones obtaining in the classroom situation, is much more important for the development of a balanced personality amongst the students. It is also the role of value education to bring about the integration of the hand, head and the heart to ensure that education does not alienate the students from the family, community and life. One of the key roles of education should be creation of a work culture at all stages of education so that the individual develops into a socially and economically a useful human being with respect for the welfare of all living beings "*sarva bhoota hitaya*". Above all else, critical appreciation and concern for the cultural and artistic heritage of the country has to be instilled amongst the students. It is this package of values, which will help the creation and sustenance of an enlightened human society in the country."[17]

Echoing the above feeling, the Seventh Five Year Plan of India (1985-90) stated: Value orientation should constitute a special thrust in the Seventh Plan, teacher education particularly being oriented for this purpose. Earlier in 1981, a seminar on value education held at Shimla recommended among other things, that:

> "There should be an integrated approach in the value oriented education programme. Instead of tackling piecemeal with such areas as awareness of ecology, environmental protection, community development, productivity, population stabilization, national integration and international understanding etc., they should be handled in a comprehensive manner under the broad spectrum of social responsibility and inner development of human personality."[18]

Each Five Year Plan of India allocates funds for environmental protection. Recently, a course of environment has been introduced at the secondary level to sensitize students about the emerging problems. Eighteen Crores of rupees were spent on cleaning the Ganga, but Ganga is dirtier than ever before the project was completed. The story of the environmental protection in India is a sordid story of utter failure. There are some success stories as the introduction of CNG operated public transport in Delhi to check air pollution. But we have yet to tackle the root causes. We are still dealing with the symptoms.

The issue is much broader than environmental. It is the issue of inculcation of human values in us from early childhood. Unfortunately, the educational system of the country has so far failed to respond to the ever-growing need of value education. Humanity is facing serious challenges of survival and development but the political leaders who call the shots continue to close their eyes as if by not seeing the problems, the problems would find their own solutions.[19]

In the growing darkness, one can see some light; a hope in hopelessness. Several institutions in the country have brought value education in their curricula and have become role models for other institutions. Let us, therefore, not be perplexed; let us follow the *Upanishadic* exhortation which calls upon each of us "to get-up, wake-up, and learn from the wise. It is painful to walk on the righteous path as it is painful to walk on the razor's edge."[20]

The right path of environmental conservation is spiritual. What is spiritual is also ecological and environment friendly. It is a difficult path but it is the only path for human survival and development.

Notes

1. Maurice Bloomfield (2009), *The Religion of the Veda, the Ancient Religion of India: From Rig-Veda to Upanishads.*
2. Raphael Patai (1947), *Man and Temple in Ancient Jewish Myth and Rituals*, London: Thomas Nelson & Sons, p. 227.
3. John Harrison (1912), *Themis: A Study of the Social Origin of Greek Religion.*
4. Griffith, Ralph T.H. (1895-96), *Hymns of Atharva Veda*, see *Prithivi Sukta.*
5. *Ibid.*
6. *Ibid.*
7. *Ibid.*
8. *Ibid.*
9. Richard, St. Barbe-Baker (Man of the Trees), *The New Earth Charter.*
10. *Ibid.*
11. M.K. Gandhi, *Harijan*, 20-12-28, p. 422.
12. *Ibid.*
13. Sriprakash Committee (1959), *Report on Religious and Moral Education.*
14. Kothari D.S. (1967), *Report of Commission of Education.*
15. Stockholm Conference on Environment, 1972; see also Brento, T. (1994), *The Greening of M : The Evolution of International Environmental Politics*, pp. xvi and 282.
16. *National Education Policy Statement*, 1986.
17. Ramamurthy Committee Report, 1990.
18. *Ibid.*
19. *Report of Seminar on Value Education*, New Delhi: Manager of Publications, 1981.
20. "Learning without Burden", Yashpal Committee Report, 1993.

2
Climate Change and Natural Disasters

C.K. Varshney

Climate change and increasing number of disasters present a daunting challenge for sustainable development and human welfare. Any change in the climate system exacerbates societal vulnerability and enhances disaster risk. The climatic hazards seriously impact communities, livelihoods, businesses, and biodiversity and ecosystem services. Recent studies have shown that climate change has had, and will continue to have, varying impacts in different regions, and societies with different vulnerabilities. Climate change will disproportionally hurt poor or otherwise vulnerable communities. Climate change is predicted to have a range of serious consequences depending on regional and local vulnerability, weather conditions, topography and socio-economic conditions. While recognizing the importance of predicted consequences of climate change the 'extreme weather events' have been responsible for serious disasters. They include:

- Extreme temperature highs – heat waves, drought, forest fires.
- Storms, including windstorms, cyclones etc.
- High levels of precipitation, unseasonal rains and associated flooding.
- Lack of precipitation, reduced number of rainy days during rainy season and associated drought.

The impact of these climatic events in turn trigger a range of 'secondary' effects, e.g., avalanches, landslides, rock falls, water scarcity, flooding and land subsidence having devastating consequences.

Growing Risks and Vulnerabilities

According to a recent report of WMO, the world is already nearly five times as dangerous and disaster prone 20as it was in the 1970s, because of the increasing risks brought by climate change. The first decade of the twenty first century saw 3,496 natural disasters including floods, storms, droughts and heat waves. That was nearly five times as many disasters as the 743 catastrophes reported during the 1970s and all of those weather events are influenced by climate change. Analysis of decades of disaster risk data shows more than 226 million people globally are affected on an average by disasters associated with natural hazards every year. These include both geo-physical events (e.g., earthquakes, tsunamis, volcanoes) and hydro-meteorological events (e.g., floods, cyclones, droughtes). Weather-related disasters comprise about 81 per cent of all events, causing 72 per cent of all economic losses and 23 per cent of fatalities. An international team of scientists examined 28 weather extremes on all seven continents to see if they were influenced by climate change or were just normal weather. On the basis of their studies, they concluded that at least 14 extreme weather events last year bore the fingerprints of human-induced climate change. The frequency of natural disasters in South Asia is increasingly showing an upward trend. According to recent regional assessments by UNEP, Asia-Pacific region continues to be the world's most disaster prone region. Approximately 41 per cent of all natural disasters reported over the last two decades occurred in the region. The number of record-breaking rainfall events increased in the region by 56 per cent over the 1981-2010 periods (GEO-6, 2016). Over 49 per cent of the total South Asian populations are at "relatively high mortality risk" from natural disaster (World Economic Forum, 2016).

NASA and the National Oceanic and Atmospheric Administration (NOAA) have announced that the year 2015 is the new global temperature record for hottest year since record keeping began in 1880. Both NASA and NOAA separately analyzed the global temperature data and arrived at the same conclusion (Schmidt, Gavin A. & Thomas R. Karl, 2016). As the ambient temperature is rising heat waves are an emerging new killer. Heat waves were not even recognized as a threat in the 1970s. However, by 2010 they were one of the leading causes of deaths in natural disasters along with storms. In Russia alone, more than 55,000 people died as a result of heat wave in 2010 (EM-DAT, 2016).

In urban areas, a combination of climate change and Urban Heat Island (UHI) can greatly exacerbate the impact of heat waves on sensitive populations, such as children and older adults. The Centres for Disease Control and Prevention estimates that from 1979–2003, excessive heat exposure contributed to more than 8,000 premature deaths in the United States (CDC, 2006). The starkest impact of climate change was in the form of the 32 major droughts that were recorded globally in year 2014, the number of recorded major droughts have doubled in 2015 (UNISDR, 2015). The year 2015 was really a year of drought, and the drought situation may get worse in 2016, and may also be bad in 2017 (Debarati Guha-Sapir, 2015). The annual average number of people affected by droughts between 1995 and 2015 according to the UNISDR report was 34.4 million while in 2015 it was 50.5 million – well above the average. Data indicate that disasters have not only become more frequent, they are striking new areas (UNIDSR, 2015).

Disasters can have devastating impacts on food security – not only in the short term, but also long after they have occurred. They destroy crops, food stocks, cattle and transportation routes, and therefore above all the livelihoods of those depending on agriculture. However, the reverse is true as well. It is not unusual for extreme natural events to turn into disasters because the population affected is particularly vulnerable due to a poor food situation. In the worst case, the combined effect of disasters and food insecurity leads to a fatal downward spiral, with the people shifting from one crisis into the next.

The Indian Scenario

Developing countries are by far the most vulnerable to disasters. The effect of climate change and the accompanying disaster risk is disproportionately high in tropical areas and more so, for India, on account of the burgeoning population growth, poverty and overstressed ecosystems. The impact of climate change exacerbated disasters is being felt in various parts of India in a variety of ways and at different scales. India was among the top three most disaster-hit countries in 2015. There were 19 events of natural disasters, including floods, droughts and heat waves in 2015, with whopping economic damages worth $3.30 billion revealed by a new analysis released by the UNISDR (2015). Recent natural disasters in India have made top headline news about record setting high summer temperatures breaching 50°C mark, heat waves, droughts, acute shortage of water caused by extreme weather events. The deadliest heat wave on record in India is the 1998 one in which 2,541 people died (see Table 2.1).

Table: 2.1: Heat wave Deaths in Different Countries

	Country	*Year*	*Estimated Deaths*
1.	Europe	2003	71,310
2.	Russia	2010	55,736
3.	Europe	2006	3,418
4.	India	1998	2,541
5.	India	2015	2000+
6.	US, Canada	1936	1,693
7.	US	1980	1,260
8.	India	2003	1,210
9.	India	2002	1,030
10.	Greece, Turkey	1987	1,030

Source: EM-DAT, CERD, Brussels.

Heat wave has killed the most number of people in Andhra Pradesh and Telangana, while affecting many more in other parts of the country. As the death toll in the current heat wave crossed the 2,000 mark, this has become the fifth deadliest ever heat wave in the world and the second deadliest in India, according to an international database of disasters (UNISDR, 2016). In future, heat waves are projected to be more intense, have longer durations and will occur at a higher frequency than in the earlier years. A multi-year rainfall deficit, prolonged drought and acute shortage of water in Latur, a city in the state of Maharashtra, led to the imposing of Section 144 to prevent water stealing and violence for water. The situation deteriorated to such an extent that many families were forced to migrate to other areas. The UNISDR study also warned of severe droughts globally in 2016 as well. The intensification of heat waves might lead to severe heat stress and increased mortality (Pai *et. al.*, 2013; Meehl, Gerald A. & Claudia Tebaldi, 2014). Record setting temperature, heat waves, drought, incessant rains, storms and floods have far-reaching consequences on ecological resource base, economy and well-being of people. The number of record-breaking rainfall events increased significantly over past three decades.

In the year 2013, Uttarakhand suffered from a major catastrophic natural disaster in the form of huge and deadly cloudbursts. Sudden, heavy rains caused dangerous flesh floods and multiple landslides, killed 5,700 people and thousands were reported missing. Over 1,00,000 pilgrims to the Kedarnath shrine were trapped and suffered their worst nightmare. The torrential rainfall in Kashmir in September 2014 caused unprecedented floods killing over 500 people. Hundreds of people were trapped in their own homes for days, without food and water. Around 50 bridges were damaged across the state, and the damage of properties was estimated between Rs. 5000 crore and 6000 crore. Destruction of bridge and roads and other infrastructure, vitally important for the economy and well-being of communities far away from the disaster site suffer from abrupt snapping of transportation and communication to and from the disaster affected site, resulting in economic losses and enormous hardship to the far away communities. Loss and sufferings of such distant communities are rarely assessed and included in disaster loss estimates. In 2005, Mumbai was lashed by highest ever over 900 mm of rainfall in a 24 hour period – almost half the average rainfall it receives in an entire year (SREX, 2012). Hundreds of people died from the ensuing flooding that paralyzed the city, killed hundreds of people and caused serious economic losses. Mountainous regions like Uttarakhand and J & K are the most vulnerable to such events, and the future threatens to carry even greater risks.

Developing countries have low adaptive capacity to deal with climate change and disaster impacts, because a larger proportion of population is dependent on climate-sensitive sectors like agriculture and forestry. Regional and local differences result in a wide variation in resilience and adaptive capacity of different regions and communities. In addition, poor infrastructure, overstressed ecosystems and a lack of effective disaster reduction strategy further complicate and seriously undermine societal resilience and capacity to recover. For instance, irrigation coverage is about three-fourths of the total cultivated area in Punjab, while in Odisha about a quarter of the cultivated area is irrigated (Mahapatra, 2006). Consequently, farmers in Odisha are more dependent on the monsoon than others, thus more vulnerable to weather related disasters. Odisha for over a long time has been suffering from one extreme weather condition to another; from heat waves to cyclones, drought to floods. The state is highly vulnerable to climate perturbations and has been declared disaster-affected for 95 of the last 105 years (Gupta, 2008).

The Human Cost of Weather Related Disasters

Over the last twenty years, the overwhelming majority (90% of disasters) have been caused by floods, storms, heat waves and other weather-related events. In total, 6,457 weather-related disasters were recorded worldwide by EM-DAT, the foremost international database of such events. The weather-related disasters during this period claimed 6,06,000 lives, an average of some 30,000 per annum, with an additional 4.1 billion people injured, left homeless or in need of emergency assistance. During the period from 1970 to 2008, over 95 per cent of deaths occurred from natural disasters in the developing countries.

Asia is the biggest sufferer from weather-related disasters, with more frequent events and greater numbers of people killed and affected than any other continent (EM-DAT, 2016). This is mainly due to Asia's large and varied landmass, including multiple river basins, flood plains and other zones at high risk from natural hazards, plus high population densities in disaster-prone regions. In total, 2,495 weather-related disasters struck Asia between 1995 and 2015, affecting 3.7 billion people and killing a further 3,32,000 individuals, frequent events and greater numbers of people killed and affected than any other continent (UNISDER, 2015). The year 2015 had smashed all records and was declared by the World Meteorological Organization as the hottest year since reporting began 136 years back. Extreme temperatures played havoc worldwide with France registering 3,275 heat wave deaths, India with 2,248 deaths and Pakistan with 1,229 deaths. Overall, 7,346 deaths were recorded and 1.2 million people were affected by the record high temperatures in 2015. Heat waves contributed to major deaths in India which accounted for 30 per cent of the heat wave deaths globally (Shreerupa Mitra-Jha, 2016).

According to UNISDR (2016) India and China in the past two decades were most affected by weather-related disasters. Between 1995 and 2015, these two nations account for 3 billion disaster-affected people accounting for 75 per cent of the global total of 4.1 billion people (UNISDR, 2016). As is often the case, the poor people face some of the greatest risks.

There is a close nexus between climate and global water cycle. In a changed climate scenario water cycles will be altered in every possible way from global to local level, creating problems of more water, no water and polluted water. Water scarcity or water in the wrong place are going to be major issues engaging our attention in this century and beyond. Extreme wet and dry spell within the monsoon period has increased since 1980 and this change represents one of the important manifestations of climate change (Singh, *et al.*, 2014). Floods have been the most common type of natural disaster making up for 43 per cent of the total global natural disasters, followed by storms, earthquakes, extreme temperatures, landslides, droughts, wildfire, and volcanic activity. Globally, 27.5 million people were affected by 152 floods across the world that claimed 3,310 lives in 2015. India, accounted for nearly 60 per cent of people affected by floods globally. Children and women are relatively more vulnerable and suffer the most. About one in four of the world's 2.3 billion children live in areas where floods are extremely frequent, almost 160 million live in areas where droughts are particularly severe, and more than 115 million children are in areas with a high to extremely high risk of tropical cyclones – known as hurricanes, typhoons or cyclones, depending on the region (UNICEF, 2015).

Coastal Cities

Coastal areas have long attracted human settlement because of their economic advantages and aesthetic appeal. Sea level rise is the growing risk to coastal cities posed by climate change. Many of the fastest developing cities are coastal cities, meaning that more people, infrastructure, and buildings are vulnerable to the flooding caused by storm surges or cyclones and enhanced by sea level rise. Often floodplains and wetlands have been drained and colonized to accommodate growing urban population. Data released by NASA show that sea level is raising by 3.27 mm per year (satellite sea level observation, relative to 1993-2010). Latest measurements show that the average sea level is currently 50 mm higher than in 1993. According to a United Nation's forecast, sea levels are likely to rise by up to 60 cm by 2100 due to global warming. It is going to be a major disaster for Maldives, with an average land level of 1.5 m above sea level, may disappear if the global warming continues unabated. For example, around the Bay of Bengal alone there have been an estimated 1.3 million cyclone related deaths over the past 200 years (Small and Robert, 2003). More than 10 million people each year, most of them in Asia, experience some flooding due to storm surges (Mimura, 2013). Major recent coastal floods include the 1991 flood in Bangladesh when 1,40,000 persons were killed and 10 million made homeless; and the 2007 flood in Myanmar when 1,46,000 persons were killed as a result of storm surges up to 6 metres in height and which reached inland some 30 km causing an estimated economic toll of US$ 17 billion. Storm related floods in recent years have inundated 70-80 per cent of both Jakarta and Manila displacing many hundred thousands of inhabitants. It has been estimated that by the year 2100, even with a sea level rise of only 59 cm, a 100 year storm surge could inundate areas in Asia with a population of 362 million, 10 per cent of the total projected population (Mimura, 2013).

Coastal cities of Asia face an ever growing risk of future catastrophic loss brought by climate change and rapid urban growth in low elevation coastal zones. Global warming is leading to a rise in sea level, resulting from thermal expansion of ocean water and the melting of glaciers and ice sheets. Moreover, a number of record-breaking rainfall events have increased significantly. By the 2070s, the top Asian cities in terms of population exposure to coastal flooding will be Bangkok, Dhaka, Guangzhou, Kolkata, Mumbai and Shanghai, threatening hundreds of millions of people with displacement (Vermeer & Rahmstorf, 2009).

Disasters are Getting More Costly

Economic losses due to disasters are steadily increasing. Data indicate that disasters have not only become more frequent, the overall cost of natural disasters on social and economic systems is substantial. However, there are few empirical studies that seek to quantify the uncertainty and establish confidence intervals surrounding natural disaster cost estimates (Smith & Matthews, 2015). In 30 years, the average annual loss due to disasters has gone up 27 times. Disasters were about 5.5 times more expensive by 2010 than they were in the 1970s, and most of that was because of the rising losses due to floods. The cost of disasters rose to $864bn (£505bn) in the last decade (WHO, 2016).

The U.S. has sustained 188 weather and climate disasters since 1980 where overall damages/costs reached or exceeded $1 billion (including CPI adjustment to 2015). The total cost of these 188 events exceeds $1 trillion. In 2015, there were 10 weather and climate disaster events with losses exceeding $1 billion each across the United States. Overall, these events resulted in the deaths of 155 people and had significant economic effects on the areas impacted. Losses from disasters show significant increase over the years (NOAA, 2016).

Floods in Kashmir valley during September 2014 took a heavy toll as 300 people died and another flood in 2015 further devastated the valley. Apart from human loss, the floods damaged crops, horticulture, houses, roads, bridges, loss of tourism, businesses and livelihoods of people in the valley as well affected their business partners in other parts of the country.

Disasters and Internal Displacement Climate-related displacement is already a global reality. Every year, the lives of millions of people are affected when they are displaced by the impacts of weather and climate hazards. The International Displacement Monitoring Centre has estimated that since 2008, an average of 26.4 million people have been displaced by disasters each year equivalent to one person every second. Developing countries account for over 90 per cent of weather hazard-related displacement recorded since 2008. In 2014, for example, the 10 largest events, all of which were related to either storms or floods in Asia, each displaced around 5,00,000 to 3 million people in the Philippines, India, Pakistan, China, Japan and Bangladesh (IDMC, 2015). Post-disaster rehabilitation of displaced families and persons is frustratingly slow, seldom satisfactory and complete.

People Displaced by Disasters

Significantly more people are living in hazard-prone areas such as coastal and river floodplains than ever before, due to their proximity to livelihood opportunities or the lack of land in safer areas. The global population has grown by 96 per cent since 1970 and average urban populations have grown twice as fast. Taken on their own, urban populations in developing countries have grown 326 per cent. Mainly because this growth is often unplanned and poorly managed, vulnerability is also increasing. Policy and actions that aim to decrease exposure and vulnerability through ecosystem conservation, climate adaptation and disaster risk reduction, are important in averting or minimizing displacement risk.

Disasters, Conflict and Political instability

Climate change is expected to make the climate warmer, wetter, and wilder. It is predicted that climate change will increase the severity and frequency of climate change influenced disasters like heat waves, droughts, floods, surges, cyclones, and severe storms. The frequency of such disasters has risen sharply over the last decades, and the increase is expected to continue due to both climate change and demographic changes. Disasters invariably result in sharp decline in the availability of accessible resources, supplies and services cause serious and sudden societal disruption to the point of increasing the conflicts and civil war. Majority of the disaster affected people live in fragile areas where underdevelopment is intractable and capacity to manage disaster risks is weak. In many instances, it is observed that weather related disasters significantly increase the risk of violent conflicts in short and medium term, specifically low and middle-income societies suffering from inherent inequality and sluggish economic growth. Recent drought in Latur is an example where local administration has to impose Section 144 and institute armed security guards around water sources, water tankers and water distribution centres to prevent potential water riots and conflicts. Climate change can indirectly increase risks of brutal conflicts in the form of civil war and inter-group violence by amplifying well-documented drivers of conflicts such as poverty, deprivation and ineffective law and order machinery. Given the likelihood that the climate change will escalate natural disasters, more attention should be given to mitigating the social and political risks posed by disaster episodes (Nel & Righarfts, 2008).

Climate change is expected to increase rates of violent conflict.The Intergovernmental Panel on Climate Change's Fifth Assessment Report (2014) affirms that the impact of climate change on human well-being, peace and security will worsen, especially for the poorest members of society. Majority of the disaster affected people live in fragile areas where underdevelopment is intractable and capacity to manage disaster risks is weak. Climate change interacts with other features of the social, economic and political landscape; there is a high risk of political instability and violent conflict.

Road Ahead

Climate change and disaster risk are fundamental threats to sustainable development and for eradication of poverty. Detrimental impacts of disaster events on development have been seen over and over, resulting in the destruction of lives and livelihoods, setting back development progress and increasing levels of poverty – or forcing new groups into poverty. In future, weather and climate change related disasters are going to increase in intensity, magnitude and geographical spread with the progressive intensification of climate change. Climate change and its consequences will extend over many centuries in future even after CO_2 emissions are stopped completely. In this regard climate change and disasters accentuated by climate shift represent a substantial multi-century climate change adaptation and disaster risk reduction challenge. There is an increasing recognition that action on climate change and disaster risk reduction is a prerequisite for achieving sustainable development. This fast emerging challenge requires a proper understanding of the nature and magnitude of disaster risk for pro-active action to eliminating and or minimising misery and loss to the people. Disaster risk reduction, resilience building and risk preparedness should receive high priority in planning for sustainable future. Government and civil society both need to respond to climate and weather induced disaster risks through greater coordination, commitment and focus. Ecological conservation and environmental improvement strengthen disaster preparedness for effective response, and in helping post-disaster recovery and rehabilitation.

It is increasingly recognized that the disaster risk reduction strategy should be prospective and preventive as against a reactive approach. The Sendai Framework for Disaster Risk Reduction 2015–2030 places emphasis on recognition of underlying social causes of hazard, exposure and vulnerability (arising out of the deliberations at the Third UN Conference) on Disaster Risk Reduction. Accordingly, the approach to disaster risk reduction and disaster resilient development should be holistic and ecosystem based with a focus on transition from emergency response to risk reduction; better risk assessment and communication; strengthening of disaster preparedness and strong institutional bias for implementation and governess. Integration of climate change adaptation and disaster risk reduction into planning and budgeting is a practical and cost-effective strategy for reducing poverty and for promoting resilient future.

References

Birkmann, J. and Mechler, R., (2015) Advancing climate adaptation and risk management. New insights, concepts and approaches: what have we learned from the SREX and the AR5 processes? *Climatic Change*, 133 (1): 1-6.

CDC, (2006) *Extreme Heat: A Prevention Guide to Promote Your Personal Health and Safety*. Part-1, Centre for Disease Control and Prevention (CDC), USA.

Debarati Guha-Sapir, Philippe Hoyois and Regina Below. (2015), *Annual Disaster Statistical Review 2014—The numbers and trends*. Centre for Research on the Epidemiology of Disasters (CRED) Institute of Health and Society (IRSS) Université catholique de Louvain – Brussels, Belgium.

EM-DAT, (2016). Emergency Events Database, maintained by the Centre for Research on the Epidemiology of Disasters (CRED) based in Brussels.

GEO-6. (2016), *Asia and the Pacific Regional Assessment*, UNEP, Nairobi.

Gupta, K.R. (2008), *Encyclopaedia of Environment, Global Warming*, Vol. VI, Atlantic Publishers and Distributors (P.) Ltd., New Delhi, p. 159.

SREX (2012), *Managing the Risks of Extreme Events and Disasters to Advance Climate Change Adaptation*. A Special Report of Working Groups I and II of IPCC [Field, C.B., V. Barros, T.F. Stocker, D. Qin, D.J. Dokken, K.L. Ebi, M.D. Mastrandrea, K.J. Mach, G.K. Plattner, S.K. Allen, M. Tignor, and P.M. Midgley (eds.)]. Cambridge University Press, Cambridge, UK, and New York, USA, p. 582.

International Displacement Monitoring Centre (IDMC), (2015). *Global Estimates 2015: People Displaced by Disasters*, IDMC, Norwegian Refugee Council Chemin de Balexert 7–9, CH-1219 Châtelaine, Geneva.

Mahapatra, Richard, (2006), *Disaster Dossier: Impact of Climate Change on Orissa. InfoChange News*.

Mechler, R. & Bouwer, L., (2014), Understanding trends and projections of global disaster losses and climate change: Is vulnerability the missing link? *Climatic Change*, 133(1): 23-35.

Meehler, Gerald A. and Claudia Tebaldi, More Intense, (2014), More Frequent, and Longer Lasting Heat Waves in the twenty first Century. *Science*, 305 Issue, 5686,994-997.

Mimura, Nobuo (2013), Sea-level rise caused by climate change and its implications for society, twenty first, *Proc. Jpn. Acad. Ser. B. Phys. Biol. Sciv.* 89(7); July 25.

Nel, P. and M. Righarts, (2008), Natural disasters and the risk of violent conflict. *International Quarterly*, 52: 159-185.

NOAA, (2016), *Billion-Dollar Weather and Climate Disaster: Overview*. National Centre for Environmental Information, National Oceanic and Atmospheric Administration, USA.

Pai, F.D.S., Smitha Nair and A.N. Ramanathan, (2013), Long term climatology and trends of heat waves over India during the recent 50 years (1961-2010). *MAUSAM*, 64, 4, 585-604.

Singh, Deepti, Michael Tsiang, Bala Rajratnam and Noah, S. Diffengurgh (2014). Observed changes in extreme wet and dry spells during the South Asian summer monsoon season. *Nature Climate Change*, 28 April.

Shreerupa Mitra-Jha, (2016). Natural disasters cost India $3.30bn in 2015: Here's why we should be very worried. *First Post*, February 12.

Schmidt, Gavin A. & Thomas R. Karl, (2016) NOVA/NASA Annual Global Analysis for 2015. NESDIS strategic communication. http://www.nasa.gov/sites/default/files/atoms/files/noaa_nasa_global_analysis_2015.pdf

Smith, A.B. and Jassica L. Matthews, (2015). Quantifying uncertainty and variable sensitivity within the US billion dollar weather and climate disaster cost estimates. *Nat Disasters*, 77: 1829-1851.

UNICEF, (2015). *Unless We Act Now: The impact of Climate Change on Children.* The United Nations Children's Emergency Fund, New York, p. 81.

UNISDR, (2015). *The Human Cost of Weather-Related Disasters 1995-2015.* United Nations Office for Disaster Risk Reduction (UNISDR), Bioccoa, Milan, Italy.

Vermeer, Martin and Stefan Rahmstorf (2009), Global sea level linked to global temperature. *PANS*: 1-6.

WCDRR, (2015). Proceedings Third UN World Conference on Disaster Risk Reduction 14-18 March, 2015. Sendai, Japan. Sendai Framework for Disaster Risk Reduction 2015-2030. A/CONF.224/CRP.1

World Economic Forum, (2016), *The Global Risks Report*, 11th Edition. World Economic Forum, Geneva.

WMO, (2015), likely to be warmest on record, 2011-2015 warmest five year period. World Meteorology Organisation (WMO), Geneva.

3
Human Induced Disasters and Environment

A.D. Kaushik

Introduction

The environment may be viewed in its totality, which comprises the whole set of natural or biophysical, and man-made or socio-cultural system in which human and other organisms live and interact. In ecology, environment means all factors, which affect the survival and reproduction of living organism (Napoleon, 1980).[1] The transformation of forested lands by human interventions represents one of the great forces in global environmental change and one of the great drivers of biodiversity loss. The impact of human has been and continues to be profound. Forests are cleared, degraded and fragmented by timber harvest, conversion to agriculture, road-building, human-caused fire, and in myriad other ways. The effort to use and subdue the forest has been a constant theme in the transformation of the earth, in many societies, in many lands, and at most times. Deforestation has important implications for life on this planet. In India where the population explosion is too high, the problem of environmental pollution is further being aggravated by both poverty and underdevelopment as well as by the negative effects of the very process of development. In other words, malnutrition, lack of sanitation, massive industrialization, mechanization, motorization and chemicalization of agriculture have added new dimensions to the problem of environmental pollution *vis-à-vis* its protection and control. The two important documents, i.e. Stockholm Declaration of 1972[2] and Charter of Economic Rights and Duties of States, 1974 show the deep concern of the international community for taking preventive steps to protect the environment (The Charter—Article 30).[3]

The Sixth Five Year Plan (1980-85)[4] attached a great importance to the protection of environment. In this plan, it had clearly been emphasized that environment should form a crucial guiding dimensions for planning and development. Environment management has to take note of the impact on health and integrity of our natural resources and soil, water, forests, wildlife, etc. But the environment conservation is really, the very basis of all development. The Seventh Five Year Plan established the Ganga Authority[5] for cleaning the water of the Ganges and the surrounding slums was a step in the right direction. The Environment (Protection) Act, 1986,[6] was enacted to tackle major environmental issues related to atmospheric and water pollution and the increasing concentration of CO_2 in the atmosphere.

Environmental Degradation and Disasters

Owing to various other factors, the deterioration of the overall environmental condition is the major cause for increase in both physical as well as socio-economic vulnerability of a country towards disasters. Environmental degradation increases the intensity of a natural disaster and is often the factor that transforms a natural hazard or climatic extreme into a disaster. In the recent past due to so-called developmental activities, particularly in disaster-prone regions, the environment had been very adversely affected resulting into exponential increase in fragility of land mass as occurred recently in the form of major disasters in Himalayan regions of Indian States of Uttarakhand in 2013 and Jammu & Kashmir in 2014, respectively. Though there had been many factors responsible for the present bad shape of the environment, the deforestation and degradation of the forests during the last 50 years is the most prominent and one among them. The elites, government officials or traders, all exploit the natural resources in a very inefficient way. The forests are axed ruthlessly. The mining is very unscientific. As a matter of fact, the exploitation of natural base is highly characterised by indiscipline and inefficiency. The approach to nature, from all points of view, is however, wasteful and responsible for the degradation of environment. Hence, Environmental Degradation affects Water Bodies, Soil, Air, Plants, Wildlife and Aquatic life.

Environmental Degradation is the aftermath of the impact of human activities as well as natural causes during which the natural environment is compromised in some way, biological diversity is minimised and the health of the environment deteriorates drastically. Environmental

Degradation has now become a global problem due to lack of proper awareness on the deleterious impacts of constant alteration of the natural habitat on the environment in general.

When there is exploitation of natural resources, whether forest, flora, fauna or water, it must understand that the environment which we find today is of very fragile nature. Environmental resources are extremely fragile. A tree has to be cared for, especially if it is a multipurpose tree which not only provides wood, but also fruit or fodder. A pond is also a fragile resource because its catchment must be brought under a good land-use system otherwise it will silt up very fast. Loss of biodiversity is an important aspect of environmental degradation. Biologists agree that species are becoming extinct at an alarming rate. Biodiversity is also being lost at the ecosystem level due to environmental degradation. Tropical forests are recognized as the most diverse ecosystems on Earth and are experiencing the highest rate of ecosystem loss, but temperate habitats are also suffering degradation. Because the temperate parts of the world were settled first, the loss of biodiversity has been greatest there. This care cannot be provided by Government officials. It can only be provided by the village community themselves. The major causes of environmental degradation are as follows:

Population Explosion

In India, the tendency of population explosion is one of the main causes of environmental degradation. As a result of it, pressure of population on land has increased very much and land is being exploited ruthlessly. Population explosion has caused deforestation at large-scale to make use of the land for agriculture, construction of houses for urban population and construction of river-valley projects for irrigation and power supply.

Increasing Number of People

Number of persons living below the poverty line is very large in India Mostly these people cut trees for their subsistence and thereby deplete natural resources.

Increasing Urbanization

Tendency of urbanization has gained momentum after independence. As a result, demand for houses and other public amenities have increased tremendously. To meet this increasing demand, land and other natural resources are still excessively being exploited.

Modernization of Agriculture

Consequent upon modernization of agriculture, effect of chemical fertilizers and pesticides has increased very much. It has also contributed to the rise in pollution.

More Rapid Industrialization

After independence, Indian economy has witnessed rapid industrialization which has added to air pollution, water pollution and noise pollution.

Multiplicity of the Means of Transport

Increasing multiplicity of the means of transport, in the wake of independence, has also been another main cause of the problem of environment. It has resulted air and noise pollution at large-scale.

Discard of Civic Norms

General public in India is not a respecter of civic norms. People abuse it. For instance, no cleanliness on roads, littering of roads with rubbish, burning of litter, drains remaining choked with silt and refuse, excessive use of loud-speakers etc. All these factors add to environmental pollution. In short, whereas on the one hand, environment has degraded as a result of rapid industrialization and urbanization and on the other, due to neglect of civic norms by the people, the process of pollution has assumed a permanent character.

Effects of Environmental Degradation

1. *Impact on Human Health*: Human health might be at the receiving end as a result of the environmental degradation. Areas exposed to toxic air pollutants can cause respiratory problems like pneumonia and asthma. Millions of people are known to have died of due to indirect effects of air pollution.
2. *Loss of Biodiversity*: Biodiversity is important for maintaining balance of the ecosystem in the form of combating pollution,

restoring nutrients, protecting water sources and stabilizing climate. Deforestation, global warming, overpopulation and pollution are few of the major causes for loss of biodiversity.

3. *Ozone Layer Depletion*: Ozone layer is responsible for protecting earth from harmful ultraviolet rays. The presence of chlorofluorocarbons, hydro chlorofluorocarbons in the atmosphere is causing the ozone layer to deplete. As it will deplete, it will emit harmful radiations back to the earth.
4. *Loss for Tourism Industry*: The deterioration of environment can be a huge setback for tourism industry that relies on tourists for their daily livelihood. Environmental damage in the form of loss of green cover, loss of biodiversity, huge landfills, increased air and water pollution can be a big turn off for most of the tourists.
5. *Economic Impact*: The huge cost that a country may have to borne due to environmental degradation can have big economic impact in terms of restoration of green cover, cleaning-up of landfills and protection of endangered species. The economic impact can also be in terms of loss of tourism industry.

Deforestation and Disasters

Deforestation, clearance or **clearing** is the removal of a forest or stand of trees where the land is thereafter converted to a non-forest use. Examples of deforestation include conversion of forestland to farms, ranches, or urban use. Tropical rainforests is where the most concentrated deforestation occurs.[7] Almost 30 per cent of the world is covered by forests, excluding water mass.[8]

In developed countries, deforestation most commonly occurs as the result of clearing land for agriculture. In this case, most of the deforested land will be at or near wetlands due to the extremely fertile soils found in them. While the wet areas themselves may not be particularly forested, the highland forests surrounding them are often cleared to make way for the farmland. While in developing countries, forests are cleared for a number of different reasons. Low income members of the population often cut down immense tracts of forests to burn for heating and creating charcoal. The forests are also cut down to make way for mining operations in a way that is inconsistent with the higher regulatory standards of more developed nations. Also, the popularity of exotic hardwoods in western markets has further strained this problem.

Deforestation occurs for many reasons: trees are cut down to be used or sold as fuel (sometimes in the form of charcoal) or timber, while cleared land is used as pasture for livestock, plantations of commodities and settlements. The removal of trees has resulted in damage to habitat, biodiversity loss and aridity. It has adverse impacts on biosequestration of atmospheric carbon dioxide. In India, at the time of independence, 22.74 per cent of the total geographical area of the country was covered by forest representing nearly 2 per cent of the world's forest area, which reduced to 19.39 per cent in 1999. The loss to forest has been very high during the mid-1970s to 1980s. Though this degradation of forest has somewhat slowed down after the promulgation of the Forest Conservation Act, 1980[9], but it still remains a cause of concern and alarm. Between 2000 and 2012, 2.3 million km^2 (8,90,000 square miles) of forests around the world were cut down.[10] As a result of deforestation, only 6.2 million km^2 (2.4 million square miles) remain of the original 16 million km^2 (6 million square miles) of forest that formerly covered the earth. Deforested regions typically incur significant adverse soil erosion/landslide and frequently degrade into wasteland.

According to the United Nations Framework Convention on Climate Change (UNFCCC)[11] secretariat, the overwhelming direct cause of deforestation is agriculture. Subsistence farming is responsible for 48 per cent of deforestation; commercial agriculture is responsible for 32 per cent of deforestation; logging is responsible for 14 per cent of deforestation and fuelwood removals make up 5 per cent of deforestation, respectively.[12] Many Experts however, do not agree on whether industrial logging is an important contributor to global deforestation. Some argue that poor people are more likely to clear forest because they have no alternatives, others that the poor lack the ability to pay for the materials and labour needed to clear forest. One study found that population increases due to high fertility rates were a primary driver of tropical deforestation in only 8 per cent of cases.[13]

In 2000, the United Nations Food and Agriculture Organization (FAO) found that "the role of population dynamics in a local setting may vary from decisive to negligible and that deforestation can result from "a combination of population pressure and stagnating economic, social and technological conditions".[14] The large-scale deforestation in the country along with faulty development and management practices have resulted a serious environmental degradation. Deforestation has increased the frequency and intensity of various cataclysmic disasters like soil-erosion, landslides, floods, droughts, desertification, etc. The large scale damage to soil in Shiwalik range, the Chos of Punjab, parts of Haryana and the ravines of Madhya Pradesh, Uttar Pradesh, Uttarakhand and Rajasthan is largely due to deforestation. It has also very adversely affected the eco-balance resulting into various problems, ultimately leading to increase in vulnerability of the society and the land to various forms of natural disasters. In ecologically more sensitive and destabilized areas like Himalaya and other hill regions like Western Ghats, the impact of deforestation has been more severe.

A 2005 report by the United Nations Food and Agriculture Organization (FAO) estimates that although the Earth's total forest area continues to decrease at about 13 million hectares per year, the global rate of deforestation has recently been slowing.[15,16] Still others claim that rainforests are being destroyed at an ever-quickening pace.[17] Mexico, India, the Philippines, Indonesia, Thailand, Burma, Malaysia, Bangladesh, China, Sri Lanka, Laos, Nigeria, the Democratic Republic of the Congo, Liberia,Ghana and the Ivory Coast, have lost large areas of their rainforest.[18,19] Several countries, notably Brazil, have declared their deforestation a national emergency.[20,21]

The world's tropical forests are disappearing at an alarming rate. A recent estimate is that about 1,00,000 km^2 are deforested each year, and another 1,00,000 km^2 are degraded. Estimates are constantly improving, based on satellite imagery, and deforestation rates change in response to social and economic conditions, as well as quality and accessibility of remaining forest. NASA's Land sat (satellite) cannot see below the forest canopy, and so cannot detect below-canopy clearing, whereas radar remote sensing can detect, e.g., a coffee plantation beneath overstory trees. Tropical forests once occupied 16 million km^2, today about 8-9 million km^2 remain. It is estimated that Latin America and Asia have already lost 40 per cent of their original forest; Africa a little more than half. In many countries, the rate of deforestation is accelerating. For example, most of the forested areas of Bangladesh, India, the Philippines, Sri Lanka and parts of Brazil's rainforest could be gone by the end of the century.

While on one hand the deforestation lead environmental degradation has increased the intensity and frequency of natural disasters, on the other hand, it has also enhanced the people's vulnerability to natural hazards (increasing both the risk and exposure to disasters). The deforestation and destruction of other natural resources have compelled the people from the rural areas to migrate in search of new livelihood in urban areas, resulting into unplanned settlement even in highly risk zones like seismic zones, steep hillsides and flood-prone areas of the various metropolitan cities of the country, as a consequence of this unplanned development, are at maximum risk to natural disasters.

Poverty and vulnerability are inextricably linked and mutually reinforcing each other. The poor for their survival are dependents on natural resources, mainly forests. This dependency of the poor on forests has caused tremendous loss to forest resources. While this dependency leads to environmental degradation and increases the intensity and frequency of natural disasters, simultaneously, it enhances the people's vulnerability to natural hazards as well.

The worst impact of deforestation is the manifold increase of soil erosion and landslides. The mountains consisting of fragile rocks either due to mineral composition or due to fractures or frequent frequency of earthquakes and shears are worst affected by deforestation. The loss of tree cover loosen the soil and rock material, otherwise bound by the roots of the trees disallowing it to be eroded by water and wind. The problem has become very serious in some parts of Himalaya, where due to deforestation and soil erosion/landslide, a major portion of the fertile topsoil is lost and the areas are approaching desertification. The natural appearance of xerophytic plants in some Himalayan areas is certainly a matter of concern for the country.

The calamity of the Indian Ocean tsunami provides an opportunity to reassess the role of forests in natura! disaster risk reduction. It also presents a policy space to make significant progress in the global commitment to environmental conservation. Rather than waiting for the next disaster to remind the world of the true value of forests, forest conservation must become a central part of disaster resilience and human security strategies.

Impacts of Deforestation

Overgrazing

Forests and grasslands provide much needed fodder for animals. During the rainy season, there is plenty of growth and animals get enough fodder. But during the long dry period, there is shortage of fodder and the grass is grazed to the ground and torn out by the roots by animals. This leads to lose structure of the soil and the soil is easily washed away by heavy rains. Moreover, soil is pulverized by the hoofs and teeth of animals, especially by sheep and goats and thus proves detrimental to top soil when heavy showers fall on it. Soil erosion/landslide due to overgrazing is a common site in the hilly areas of Himachal Pradesh, Jammu & Kashmir and Uttarakhand and in the dry areas of Andhra Pradesh, Chhattisgarh, Rajasthan, Madhya Pradesh, Maharashtra, Karnataka and Telangana.

Faulty Methods of Farming/Agriculture

Much of the soil erosion/landslides in Indian hills is caused by faulty methods of agriculture. The most outstanding are wrong ploughing, lack of crop rotation and practice of shifting cultivation. If the fields are ploughed along the slope, there is no obstruction to the flow of water and the water washes away the top soil easily. In some parts of the country, the same crop is grown year after year which spoils the chemical balance of the soil. This soil is exhausted and is easily eroded by wind or water. Another outstanding example of faulty method of agriculture is the shifting cultivation practised in some areas in the north-eastern states of Arunachal Pradesh, Assam, Meghalaya, Manipur, Nagaland, Tripura, and Mizoram as well as in Orissa. It is sporadically practised in Andhra Pradesh, Madhya Pradesh, Chhattisgarh, Maharashtra, Kerala, Karnataka and Tamil Nadu. In this method, a piece of forest land is cleared by felling and burning of trees and crops are grown.

The removal of the forest cover leads to the exposure of the soil to rains and sun which results in heavy loss of top soil, especially on the hill slopes. Thus the soil becomes unfit for cultivation and the tribes move to another piece of land after 2-3 years, returning to the earlier one after a gap of 10-15 years. In this way, the whole of the forest area is adversely affected by shifting cultivation resulting in intensive soil erosion/landslides in vast areas.

Climate Change Impact on Environment

Climate change is likely to have a significant impact on the global environment. In general, the faster the climate changes, the greater will be the risk of damage. Forests, deserts, rangelands, and other unmanaged ecosystems would face new climatic stresses. As a result, many will decline or fragment and individual species will become extinct. Large scale industrialization, deforestation and non-sustainable overuse of other natural resources have increased population leading to global change in the environment. This human induced climate change has increased the overall global temperature resulting excessive melting of glaciers in the Himalayas, causing water and climate related disasters. The main reason for this climate change or increase in temperature is the excessive burning of fuels (coal, petrol diesel), large-scale deforestation and forest fires resulting into substantial increase of carbon dioxide and other harmful gases in the atmosphere. This increased carbon dioxide, which prevents the heat rays returning back to the atmosphere. Thus, a part of the heat energy absorbed by the earth and carbon-dioxide and its objects, partially remains in the atmosphere, causing increase of the overall global temperature. This phenomenon called "Green House Effect" along with excessive snow melting also cause many other adverse impacts on the environment and society. The global warming is also up to an extent responsible for annual maximum daily rainfall and its variation, accelerating desertification and land degradation (Sharma, 2008).[22] Loss in agriculture production (particularly rain-fed), human and cattle health deterioration, scarcity of water resources are other adverse impact of this phenomenon on society. All these factors have a compound effect on the impact and frequency of various disasters. Besides escalating the intensity and frequency of various disasters, they also increase the vulnerability of the society, particularly in the sensitive zones, like Himalayas and the coastal areas.

Box 3.1 : Uttarakhand Forest Fire 2016

In 2016, forest fire has been detected at more than 1,200 places in Uttarakhand State. Almora, Chamoli, Nainital, Pauri, Rudraprayag, Pithoragarh, Tehri and Uttarkashi have been declared the worst affected areas. With the Air Force team, NDRF, SDRF joining the fire-fighting operations in Uttarakhand State, it is time to have a look at the facts surrounding this tragic incident. Over the last three months, the raging fires destroyed nearly 3,000 acres of forest cover and claimed seven lives. In the last three months of forest fire, 922 incidents have occurred with 1890.79 hectares of green cover getting blighted. Among the possible causes, there are some natural reasons for the forest to catch fire. Dry weather and increase of very high temperatures due to climate change, as well as windy conditions are certainly fanning the fire and helping it to spread in Uttarakhand region. The government has decided to study the reasons behind major fires, especially in summer, and prepare an action plan accordingly.

Source: http://www.mapsofindia.com/my-india/india/uttarakhand-forest-fires-facts-you-should-know

Box 3.2 : Modern Indian refugees

"It is not a war or insurgency, but fleeing of farmers from their farmlands growing barren from years of drought due to climate change impact".

Many farmers from drought-hit areas like Latur and Beed have been fleeing from their villages to nearby cities in Maharashtra due to lack of drinking water and their lands have grown parched and hence they have no livelihood. In Ghatkopar area of Mumbai, a dumping ground has become a refugee camp for hundreds of drought-hit farmers from Latur and Nanded. Away from their dry agricultural lands, they have been migrating to cities and living in deplorable conditions for months, in search of water and work. Most of migrants live in the dumping ground at Ghatkopar. They are in the city to make enough money, and maybe go back home once a year. Most of the women work as household helps in the adjoining middle-class neighbourhood. An income, regular food, may be an education for their children takes priority over a dwelling, may be farmland that's been barren for three summers now. Or emotional attachments back home. The families are seasonal refugees. Every time the monsoon fails, they sell their cattle, leave the old and cripple in villages, and travel in overcrowded trains, hoping the city will help them survive. It often does, but with little dignity.

According to IBN News, around 33 crore people in 256 districts of 10 states are affected due to drought, the Centre told the Supreme Court on Tuesday, i.e. 19.4.2016. The Centre also informed that it has released Rs. 19,555 crore out of the total amount of Rs. 38,500 crore allotted under Mahatma Gandhi National Rural Employment Guarantee Act (MNREGA) in the current financial year to drought-hit states.

Source: http://www.msn.com/en-in/news/newsindia/farmers-fleeing-latur-drought-end-up-at-dumps-in-mumbai/ar-BBs1Tpv

Box 3.3 : Increasing Flood Frequencies

There is evidence from climate models and hydrological impact studies that flood frequencies are likely to increase with global warming, which may produce changes in the frequency of intense rainfall (IPCC, 1995). In temperate regions, more floods are caused by changes in the magnitudes of snowmelt and rain on snow. Impacts of climate change are expected to be greater on Tundra lands and alpine regions. Deglaciation on temperate mountains would increase sediment loads in alpine rivers and accelerated sedimentation in lakes and artificial reservoirs. Lakes dammed by landslides, moraines and glaciers may drain suddenly and produce floods or debris flows of an order of magnitude larger than normal stream flow. Loukas (2003) examined the effect of the increased storm intensity due to climate change on the frequency and magnitude of floods in the region of coastal British Columbia. The results showed that annual maximum daily rainfall and its variation would increase for the three climate change scenarios affecting the frequency and magnitude of floods as occurred recently in Uttarakhand flood 2013, J&K flood 2014 and Chennai flood 2015 in India.

Unscientific Development

Unscientific development practices adopted in the country have been yet another major factor causing immense loss to environment. The fragile and sensitive eco-systems like Himalayas have been most adversely affected by such practices. Development projects, i.e., road construction, hydropower, irrigation, railway tracks etc., have also caused irreparable losses to the environment of the region increasing the risk of human society towards natural hazards.

Urbanization is one of the indicators of development. As per 2011 census, India has 6.41 lakh inhabitant villages. After India embraced globalization as its new economic *Dharma* in 1991, urbanization is gaining momentum. In 1901, only a mere 11 per cent of India's population lived in urban areas, it reached 17.6 per cent by 1951, which rose to 25.8 per cent in 1991; from there urbanization raised enormously adding 160 million in 20 years, which increased to 31.16 per cent by 2011. In another twenty years, Urbanization is expected to add another 250 million to its existing 377 million, taking the urban population to over 627 million. The major factors such as natural increase of population in towns, migration of people from rural to urban areas, cities encroaching the surrounding villages and growing as bigger towns, Government policies on industrialization in some designated places under the establishment and development of industrial areas programme have boosted the trend of urbanization in India (Table 3.1).

Table 3.1: Trends of Urbanization in India

Sl. No.	*Year*	*Urban Population (in millions)*	*Urban as % of Total Population*	*No. of Towns*
1.	1901	26	11	1627
2.	1951	62	17.6	2843
3.	1961	79	18.3	2365
4.	1971	109	20.2	2590
5.	1981	160	23.7	3378
6.	1991	217	25.8	3768
7.	2001	285	27.8	5161
8.	2011	377	31.16	7936

Source: S.R. Keshava (2013), Indian Urbanization under Globalization; Development or Delusion!, *Shiv Shakti International Journal in Multidisciplinary and Academic Research (SSIJMAR)*, Vol. 2, No. 1, January-February (ISSN 2278–5973).

The Urban Ministry, Urban Planning department miserably failed to foresee the growth and plan for the future urban growth as urban areas in India grew in haphazard and unscientific manner without proper planning (Keshava, 2013).[23] But population grew and vehicles too. The net result is that majority of Indian cities are already choking under its own weight. Lack of urban infrastructure has lead to roads which is good for traffic jams and congestion. There is acute shortage of housing, water, power, sanitation, public transportation facilities, inadequate playgrounds and recreational facilities. Today, one third of population of India is living in urban area and is generating more than two third of the country's solid waste.

The socially and economically weaker sections are still unable to afford the houses in urban areas and hence live in slums. It is estimated that 158.42 million are living in the India's urban slum by the mid of 2011. It means that 42 per cent of urban population in India lives in slums, i.e., 50 per cent in New Delhi and 60 per cent in Mumbai, respectively. Further, the unfortunate thing is a sizable population which does not get space even in slums and compelled to live on pavements, railway platforms, under flyover etc. But urban planning never includes them in their scheme of housing.

Dams and Reservoir Construction

Dam construction, obstructing the natural water flow, considerably affects the ecological balance in an area. This disturbance along with creating environmental degradation of the area also increases its vulnerability to many forms of natural disasters. The normal flow pattern, in equilibrium with the ecosystem is upset. The geological conditions are affected and the riverine and geo-hydrological ecosystems are altered due to dam construction in that area.

Building a dam in a river causes great changes within the river and leads to great changes in the river systems, leading to habitat loss, which is the biggest cause of extinction. The structure of the dam itself acts as a barrier preventing fish populations from migrating along the river. Dams are used to provide a store of water for agriculture, industrial uses, household uses for thousands of years. Hydroelectric dams, additionally, act as an alternative to non-renewable energy resources that constitutes the majority of the world's energy.[24] In the twentieth century, over $2 trillion was spent on making dams around the world.[25] However, dams have drastic damaging effects on the environment and on the populations that live near the dams and so have become the subject of great scrutiny, with organizations concerned with environmental health such as World Wildlife Fund (WWF) and International Rivers advocating the removal of old dams and the use of alternatives.[26, 27] Today the dams all-over the world did not meet their initial goals often had failures at the management or organizational level rather than structural or engineering deficits as reported by World Commission on Dams (WCD).[28]

Reservoirs can act to prevent floods downstream by holding and regulating the flow during major flood events. Reservoirs can also be used to balance flow during different weather conditions, such as decreasing the flow by holding water back during heavy rainfall and releasing more water during droughts.[29] Human activity/intervention upstream can increase the nutrient level in the reservoir and may lead to eutrophication, which eventually leads to the loss of most species in the reservoir.[30] According to the WCD, if the area being flooded during the reservoir filling is not cleared out, the amount of greenhouse gases such as methane and carbon dioxide produced could be higher and can affect the environment of the area. Reservoirs have large open surfaces that facilitate water loss by evaporation, and much more water is lost in the same period of time from reservoirs than was originally lost from the river that flowed in its place. This evaporation can affect the microclimate of the area as it reduces fluctuations in the extremes temperature[31] and may change the nature and type of the vegetation and ecosystems that can suited to the two extremes of temperatures. It has been known that the filling of reservoirs of large dams has triggered seismic activity because of the physical change incurred in the area where the reservoir was filled, and the activity of the dam as observed in case of Sichuan earthquake (2008) of 7.9-magnitude, which killed 80,000 people linked to the construction of the Zipingpu Dam, and is possibly the most serious earthquake caused by a dam.[32] In addition, the worldwide construction of dams and reservoirs causes social effect on people by displacing them and affecting their health at the construction area.

Mitigation measures for reducing the impacts of Human Interventions on Environment

Interaction among Environment, Development, Society and Governance

Environmental governance is a process, which advocates sustainability (sustainable development) as the supreme consideration for managing all human activities – political, social and economic. Governance includes government, business and civil society, and emphasizes whole system management. According to International Union for Conservation of Nature (IUCN), Environmental Governance is the "Multi-level interactions (i.e., local, national, international/global) among, but not limited to, three main actors, i.e., state, market, and civil society, which interact with one another, whether in formal and informal ways; in formulating and implementing policies in response to environment-related demands and inputs from the society; bound by rules, procedures, processes, and widely accepted behaviour; possessing characteristics of 'good governance'; for the purpose of attaining environmentally – sustainable development (ICUN, 2014)".[33]

The climate models suggest that the changes in temperature and sea level can be the causal effects of human activities such as consumption of fossil fuels, deforestation, increased agricultural production and production of xenobiotic gases.[34] There has been increasing actions in order to mitigate climate change and reduce its impact at national, regional and international levels. Kyoto protocol and United Nations Framework Convention on Climate Change (UNFCCC) plays the most important role in addressing climate change at an international level.[35]

Environmental governance for protecting the biodiversity has to act in many levels. Biodiversity is fragile because it is threatened by almost

Box 3.4 : Paris: Climate Conference 2015

The UN says that over the past 30 years, one of every $3 spent on development for countries was lost because of recurring crisis. A total of $3.8 trillion has been lost. It is not just an economic loss these countries suffer from natural disasters, but social and environmental as well. This affects 217 million people every year. The UN warns that failure to manage water resources hurts attempts to reduce poverty and reach goals to sustain resources. The U.S., China and India account for about half of the world's emissions of carbon dioxide. That is the gas that traps heat in the atmosphere, and scientists say it is a leading cause of the rising global temperatures. The U.S. President Obama highlighted India's work with a group to provide affordable clean energy to developing countries. Leaders at the U.N. Climate Summit also worked on an agreement to keep global temperatures from rising more than two degrees Celsius above levels of the pre-Industrial Revolution (1760-1840) time.

France will give African countries $2.1 billion over the next four years. The money will help countries in Africa develop renewable energy sources and replace fossil fuels. Those are the fuels blamed for climate change.

Source: http://learningenglish.voanews.com/a/paris-climate-summit-update/3085038.html

all human actions. To promote conservation of biodiversity, agreements and laws have to be created to regulate agricultural activities, urban growth, industrialization of countries, use of natural resources, control of invasive species, the correct use of water and protection of air quality. Before making any decision for a region or country decision-makers, politicians and community have to take into account what are the potential impacts for biodiversity that any project can have.

Population growth and urbanization are the great contributors for deforestation and causing directly an impact on the health of society, development and environment. Also, population growth requires more intense agricultural areas use, which also results in necessity of new areas to be deforested. This causes habitat loss, which is one of the major threats for biodiversity and environment. Habitat loss and habitat fragmentation affects all species, because they all rely on limited resources, to feed on and to breed.[36]

To mitigate habitat loss, and consequently biodiversity loss, politicians and law-makers should be aware of the precautionary principle, which means that before approving a project or law all the pros and cons should be carefully analysed. Sometimes, the impacts are not explicit, or not even proved to exist. However, if there is any chance of an irreversible impact happens, it should be taken into consideration.[37] To promote environmental governance for biodiversity protection there has to be a clear articulation between values and interests while negotiating environmental management plans.[38] International agreements are good way to have it done right.

Environmental Scientists proposed the following steps to mitigate the risks of impact of disasters induced by human interventions on environment and global climate change:

- Increase natural photosynthesis by enhancing afforestation and plantations.
- Checking deforestation in the short term, enhancing agro-forestry and plantations in the medium term and use of advanced technology for efficient forest management in the long term for arresting GHG emissions.
- Waste Recycling.
- Reclaiming deserts.
- Dredging and cleaning of water bodies regularly.
- Conservation and preservation of forestry to ensure the carbon sinks, Regulation of exploration and exploitation activities in

the downstream and mining sectors by the Government of nations with penal charges attached to every default.

- Use of alternative sources of energy that do not promote emission of Carbon dioxide and other green-house gases or Chlorofluorocarbons.
- Use of "floating islands" for reducing the eutrophication in reservoirs. Floating islands provide habitats for fish and nesting sites for birds. Since, they can float, they will not be affected by the changing water levels in reservoirs.
- Disassemble old and outdated dams and make existing hydroelectric dams more efficient.
- Research on alternative sources of energy and efficient usage of water in agriculture and alternatives to new proposed dams.
- Use of GIS technology for mapping agro-ecological zones, vulnerable zones, rainfed irrigated/zones, soil-degradation zones, etc. at district-levels.
- Enhancing the incremental changes in the community participation for arresting climate changes by effective management of land.
- Specific case studies on impacts of climate change on ecosystems and water resources in the country should be conducted at micro-level where human dimensions can be incorporated.
- Implementation of former Indian Prime Minister, Dr. Man Mohan Singh's National Eight Missions' Climate Action Plan (2008).
- Managing wetlands.
- Limiting animal husbandry.

Conclusion

Environmental degradation increases the intensity of a natural disaster and is often the factor that transforms a natural hazard or climatic extreme into a disaster. As a matter of fact, the exploitation of natural base is highly characterised by indiscipline and inefficiency. Deforestation, global warming, overpopulation and pollution are the major causes for loss of biodiversity and increase the frequency and intensity of various disasters like soil-erosion/landslides, floods, droughts, desertification, etc. While on one hand, the deforestation lead environmental degradation has increased the intensity and frequency of natural disasters, on the other hand, it has also enhanced the people's vulnerability towards natural disasters. Industrialization, deforestation and non-sustainable overuse of other natural resources at large scale have increased population leading to global change in the environment, which cause many other adverse impacts on the ecology/ecosystems and society. The Government policies on industrialization in some designated places under the establishment and development of industrial areas programme along with the major factors such as natural increase of population in towns, migration of people from rural to urban areas, cities encroaching the surrounding villages and growing as bigger towns, have boosted the trend of urbanization in India. Dams have drastic damaging effects on the environment and on the populations that live near the dams. Reservoirs have large open surfaces that facilitate water loss by evaporation, which can affect the microclimate of the area as it reduces fluctuations in the extremes temperature and may change the nature and type of the vegetation and ecosystems of the area. At present, population growth and urbanization are the great contributors for deforestation and causing directly an impact on the health of society, development and environment. So, to promote .environmental governance for biodiversity protection there has to be a clear articulation between values and interests while negotiating environmental management plans. Environmental Scientists suggested some important steps, if adopted profoundly then they can mitigate the impact of human interventions on environment and global climate change.

Notes

1. Napoleon Wolanski, "Environmental Hazards and the Future of Man", in J.P. Singh and S.C. Tiwari, (1980), (eds.) *Man and His Environment*, pp.1-3.
2. http://www.unep.org/documents.multilingual default.asp?documentid=97&articleid=1503
3. The charter states in Article 30, http://www.un-documents.net/a29r3281.htm
4. Sixth Five-Year Plan (1980-85) p. 343, in Suresh Jain, (1985), (ed.), *Environmental Laws in India*, p.592.
5. http://planningcommission.nic.in/plans/planrel/fiveyr/7th/vol2/7v2ch18.html
6. http://envfor.nic.in/legis/env/env1.html
7. SAFnet Dictionary|Definition For [deforestation]. Dictionary of forestry.org (2008-07-29). Retrieved on 2011-05-15.
8. http://www.livescience.com/27692-deforestation.html
9. http://wrd.bih.nic.in/guidelines/awadhesh02c.pdf

10. http://www.worldwildlife.org/threats/deforestation
11. https://unfccc.int/resource/docs/convkp/conveng.pdf
12. Oliver, C.D., (1980), "Forest Development in North America following major disturbances". *For. Ecol. Management*, 3: 153-168.
13. Sahney, S., Benton, M.J. & Falcon-Lang, H.J. (2010). "Rainforest collapse triggered Pennsylvanian tetrapod diversification in Euramerica". *Geology*, 38 (12): 1079-1082.
14. Toral Patel-Weynand, (2002). Biodiversity and sustainable forestry: State of the science review. The National Commission on Science for Sustainable Forestry, Washington DC.
15. "Pan-tropical Survey of Forest Cover Changes 1980–2000". Forest Resources Assessment. Rome, Italy: Food and Agriculture Organization of the United Nations (FAO).
16. Committee on Forestry. FAO (2001-03-16). Retrieved on 2010-08-29.
17. Worldwatch: Wood Production and Deforestation Increase & Recent Content, Worldwatch Institute.
18. Jump up Chart – Tropical Deforestation by Country & Region. Mongabay.com. Retrieved on 2011-12-04.
19. Jump up Rainforest Destruction. rainforestweb.org
20. Amazon deforestation rises sharply in 2007, USATODAY.com, January 24, 2008.
21. Vidal, John (31 May, 2005). "Rainforest loss shocks Brazil". *The Guardian* (London). Retrieved April 1, 2010.
22. Vinod K. Sharma, (2008) Global Warming: Its impact on India, Theme paper for Forty seventh members Annual Conference, IIPA Publication.
23. S.R. Keshava (2013), Indian Urbanization under Globalization; Development or Delusion!, *Shiv Shakti International Journal in Multidisciplinary and Academic Research (SSIJMAR)*, Vol. 2, No. 1, January-February (ISSN 2278–5973).
24. UCSUSA.ORG. The Sources of Energy | UCSUSA. Union of Concerned Scientists. Retrieved November 23, 2013, from http://www.ucsusa.org/clean_energy/our-energy-choices/the-sources-of-energy.html.
25. WWF – Dam facts and figures. wwf.panda.org. org. Retrieved November 23, 2013, from http://wwf.panda.org/what_we_do/footprint/water/dams_initiative/quick_facts/
26. International Rivers (Organization). (2013, November 23). Dam Removal. International Rivers. Retrieved November 23, 2013, from http://www.internationalrivers.org/campaigns/dam-removal
27. WWF, Dam Solutions – Alternatives & mitigation. WWF. Retrieved November 23, 2013, from http://wwf.panda.org/what_we_do/footprint/water/dams_initiative/dams/alternatives/
28. World Commission on Dams (2000). Dams and development: A new framework for decision-making. London: Earthscan Publications Ltd. Retrieved November 27, 2013 from http://www.internationalrivers.org/files/attached- files/world_commission_on_dams_final_report.pdf

29. Lindström, Andreas; Granit, Jakob (August 2012). Large-Scale water storage in the water, energy and food nexus Perspectives on benefits, risks and best Practices. Retrieved from http://www.siwi.org/documents/Resources/Papers/Water_Storage_Paper_21.pdf.
30. Timofti, D., Doltu, C., & Trofin, M. (2013, November 23). Eutrophication Phenomena In Reservoirs. Retrieved November 23, 2013, from http://aerapa.conference.ubbcluj.ro/2011/PDF/TIMOFTI_CDOLTU_MTROFIN.pdf.
31. Wikipedia,. Reservoir. Retrieved from http://en.wikipedia.org/wiki/Reservoir, (7 November, 2013)
32. International Rivers (Organization). (2013, November 23). Earthquakes Triggered by Dams. International Rivers. Organization. Retrieved November 23, 2013, from http://www.internationalrivers.org/earthquakes-triggered-by-dams
33. IUCN, Natural Resource Governance Framework (2014) http://cmsdata.iucn.org/downloads/nrgf_2_pager_final_29oct_ceesp.pdf.
34. Pernetta, J.C. & Elder, D.L. (1992), Climate, Sea level rise and the coastal zone: management and planning of global changes, *Ocean and Coastal Management*, vol. 18, pp.13-160.
35. http://www.un.org/wcm/content/site/climatechange/pages/gateway/the-negotiations/the-un-climate-change-convention-and-the-kyoto-protocol
36. Steffan-Dewenter & Tscharntkae, 2000 "Butterfly community structure in fragmented habitats" *Ecology Letters*, vol. 3, pp. 449-456.
37. IUCN (2007), "Guidelines for applying the precautionary principle to biodiversity conservation and natural resource management", viewed 28 May, 2014, cmsdata.iucn.org/downloads/ln250507_ppguidelines.pdf
38. Sampford, C., (2002), "Environmental governance for biodiversity", *Environmental Science and Policy*, vol. 5, pp. 79-90.

References

"*Global Deforestation*". Global Change Curriculum. University of Michigan Global Change Programme. January 4, 2006.

http://www.voicesofyouth.org/en/posts/environmental-degradation—a-man-made-cataclysm

http://www.conserve-energy-future.com/causes-and-effects-of-environmental-degradation.php

http://greenliving.lovetoknow.com/What_is_Deforestation

http://www.msn.com/en-in/news/newsindia/farmers-fleeing-latur-drought-end-up-at-dumps-in-mumbai/ar-BBs1Tpv

http://learningenglish.voanews.com/a/paris-climate-summit-update/3085038.html

Loukas, A., (2003). Flood Frequency and Magnitude changes induced by Climate Change Scenarios in coastal British Columbia, *Geophysical Research Abstracts*, Vol. 5, 09574.

4
Climate Change: Promoting Sustainable Consumption

Suresh Misra and *Sapna Chadah*

Introduction

The importance of consumption is constantly growing in the modern societies where increased consumption is used as key indicator of economic growth. As a result Consumption has become a central feature of our society. Promoting sustainable consumption and production are important aspects of sustainable development, which depends on achieving long-term economic growth that is consistent with environmental and social needs. However, till recently the environmental impact has primarily been approached as an issue for producers and regulating authorities to deal with. The environmental, social and economic costs derived from consumption and production patterns are significant and mounting. All the environmental problems including water scarcity, land degradation, deforestation, loss of biodiversity and pollution are all connected with the consumption and production patterns. Without reorienting current consumption and production patterns there can be no genuine mitigation of climate change. Since, the late 1980s, we have been in "overshoot" – the Ecological Footprint has exceeded the Earth's bio-capacity – as of 2003 by about 25 per cent. According to the WWF, "effectively, the Earth's regenerative capacity can no longer keep-up with demand – people are turning resources into waste faster than nature can turn waste back into resources. Humanity is no longer living off nature's interest, but drawing down its capital. This growing pressure on ecosystems is causing habitat destruction or degradation and permanent loss of productivity, threatening both biodiversity and human well-being."[1]

The cause and effect is also connected to the advancing prosperity in many parts of the globe. More and more natural resources are needed to fuel this new demand putting both renewable and non-renewable resources under pressure. While some non-renewable resources are at risk of complete exhaustion, other renewable resources such as water, soil and forests are under extreme stress. The 12 per cent of the world living in North America and Western Europe account for 60 per cent of global private consumption spending, while the one third living in South Asia and Sub-Saharan Africa account for only 3.2 per cent.[2] If the present scenario continues, by 2050 we will need more than two planets due to unsustainable patterns of consumption and production.[3]

Traditionally, the people living in developed countries are the world's largest consumer of natural resources. The 20 per cent of the world's population living in OECD countries earn 85 per cent of the world's annual income; consume 75 per cent of global energy; and over 80 per cent of other resources annually. They also generate 75 per cent of annual global pollution.[4] However, with increasing affluence the number of consumers in the developing countries is also increasing rapidly. Besides this the peoples' spending on the common household goods is decreasing and they are spending more on the luxuries such as mobile and takeaway meals. Thus, while consumer class numbers are already large, there is still ample potential for growth. The major emerging economies' capacity to consume is enormous. As the Background Paper to the Yogyakarta meeting (2003) pointed out "If car ownership in China, India and Indonesia reached the world average, 20CM vehicles would be added to the global fleet – twice the number of cars in the United States today."[5]

Global warming and climate change is not a myth; it is something that is already here. This problem of global warming and climate change has now acquired such serious proportions that unless corrective steps are taken sooner than later, the very survival of humanity would be jeopardized. Man would become an endangered species. Our very survival and development is at stake. Fortunately, it is still within the powers of man to stop any further contamination of the atmosphere, and thereby, any increase in earth's temperatures and other changes before it is too late. Thus, the pertinent question before us is: what should we do as individuals, communities, and societies to take any concrete and time bound corrective action before it is too late? The belief that 'scientific' thinking is capable of solving all problems all the times is so deeply ingrained in our minds that we tend to overdepend on it and ignore the feedback control mechanism that keeps a system functioning smoothly.

We forget that in all living and health systems the 'scientific' thinking and the feedback control mechanism exist interdependently.[6]

To turn away from the basic human values such as truth, non-violence, love, compassion, human brotherhood, and respect for nature on which most great civilizations were built, is another trait of modernity. Nature becomes the resource for exploitation as do the fellow human beings. Want based conspicuous consumption does not produce happiness; and if it does, it is not for all. The need based consumption on the other hand leads to *Sarvodaya* (development of all). We have seen how nature is being robbed of its inherent capacity to regenerate. If we continue to tread on the path set by modern civilization, we are sure to destroy ourselves. We can either opt for higher GNH (Gross National Happiness) and usher in a new civilization or continue to pursue the mirage of higher GDP and be the dying generation of the so-called modern civilization. The Earth gives enough scope for progress provided that its culture and nurture go together and it is used with deference and within the limits of what its carrying capacities.[7]

Sustainable Consumption – Concept and Definition

Sustainable consumption has repeatedly been identified as a cornerstone for achieving sustainable development in society. Sustainable consumption is a significant element and is part of policies and strategies for sustainable development. Sustainable consumption and production is a practical implementation strategy to achieve sustainable development, which addresses economic, societal and environmental problems. Sustainable consumption gives consumers the opportunity to consume products and services that meet their needs in an efficient and effective way, while minimizing the negative environmental, social and economic impact. The ultimate goal of sustainable consumption is to improve quality of life for all consumers in our and future generations, while minimizing associated environmental impacts.

In such a scenario addressing the issue of consumption is of vital importance in reducing the impact of society on its environment. In this context, the statement of Mahatma Gandhi becomes quite significant: *"The Earth has resources for meeting man's every need, but not his every greed"*. Therefore, sustainable consumption is both a challenge and an opportunity. Ever increasing and irresponsible consumption is putting a catastrophic strain on the environment, by causing pollution and global warming induced by climate change; destroying the ecosystem, and undermining sustainable lifestyles. Promoting sustainable consumption and production are important aspects of sustainable development, which depends on achieving long-term economic growth that is consistent with environmental and social needs. A key issue in such a scenario will not be just reducing the volume of goods and services consumed, but also the extent to which improvement in environmental quality can be achieved through the substitution of more efficient and less polluting goods and services.

'Sustainable' here refers to a level and pattern of consumption which meets the needs of the present without compromising the ability of future generations to meet their own needs.[8] Sustainable consumption has been defined by the 1994 Oslo Symposium on Sustainable Consumption as ". . . . the use of services and related products which respond to basic needs and bring a better quality of life while minimising the use of natural resources and toxic materials as well as emissions of waste and pollutants over the life cycle of the service or product so as not to jeopardise the needs of future generations."[9] Sustainable consumption is an umbrella term that brings together a number of key issues, such as meeting needs, enhancing the quality of life, improving resource efficiency, increasing the use of renewable energy sources, minimising waste, taking a life cycle perspective and taking into account the equity dimension. Integrating these component parts is the central question of how to provide the same or better services to meet the basic requirements of life and the aspirations for improvement for both current and future generations, while continually reducing environmental damage and risks to human health. A key issue is, therefore, the extent to which necessary improvements in environmental quality can be achieved through the substitution of more efficient and less polluting goods and services (patterns of consumption), rather than through reductions in the volumes of goods and services consumed (levels of consumption).[10]

Sustainable consumption, lays an emphasis on satisfying basic human needs (not the desire for 'wants' and luxuries); favouring quality of life over material standards of living; minimising resource use, waste and pollution; taking a life-cycle perspective in consumer decision-making; and acting with concern for future generations. Sustainable consumption integrates a range of social, economic and political practices at the individual, household, community, business and government levels that support and encourage: reducing the direct environmental burden of producing, using and disposing goods and services; meeting basic needs for key consumption goods and services, such as food, water, health, education and shelter; maximising opportunities for sustainable livelihoods in the South; consuming goods and services that contribute positively to the health and well-being of women and children; increasing the development and adoption of energy and water efficient appliances, public transport and other demand-side measures; the production and sale of new goods and services adapted to global environmental constraints; and lifestyles that place greater value on social cohesion, local traditions and non-material values.[11]

Sustainable Consumption – Global Concerns

Sustainable Consumption and Production has been recognized in a number of International Summits as an important ingredient and integral part of the sustainable development. Principle 8 of the Rio Declaration on Environment and Development highlights the responsibility of nations to "reduce and eliminate unsustainable patterns of production and consumption". The principle clearly points out that this task is necessary "to achieve sustainable development and a higher quality of life for all people". The principle of common but differentiated responsibilities, as defined in Principle 7 of the Rio Declaration, focuses specific attention on the imbalances in global patterns of consumption and production and the need for governments to specify their role and responsibility in establishing the proper balance.

Chapter 4 of Agenda 21 explicitly identifies unsustainable production and consumption patterns, "particularly in industrialized countries", as "the major cause of the continued deterioration of the global environment".[12] The situation is described as "a matter of grave concern, aggravating poverty and imbalances". The chapter identifies two broad tasks for responding to this concern: (1) focusing on unsustainable patterns of production and consumption; and (2) national governments to develop national policies and strategies to encourage changes in unsustainable consumption patterns. Chapter 4 then points out the need for the developed countries to "take the lead" and developing countries to include sustainable consumption in their development process. The chapter further highlights the need for policies and strategies to address unsustainability ranging from the excessive demands and lifestyles of the rich to the lack of access to food, clean water, healthcare, shelter and education by the poor.

Agenda 21 asks each country to "develop a domestic policy framework that will encourage a shift to more sustainable patterns of production and consumption".[13] A national policy framework on sustainable production and consumption implies an understanding and appreciation of the linkages involved in balancing demand and supply-side approaches. Such a framework requires integrating various concepts such as product life-cycle, environmental space, ecological footprints, and environmental cost internalization into a concrete inter-departmental plan with measurable targets and timetables and indicators to monitor and report on progress.

To achieve these objectives, Agenda 21 recommends the following activities: use of new and renewable energy sources[14]; recycling by industry and consumers;[15] reducing wasteful product packaging[16]; expanding environmental labelling and other environmentally related product information programmes designed to assist consumers to make informed choices[17]; providing information on the consequences of consumption choices and behaviour[18]; making consumers aware of the health and environmental impacts of products, through such means as consumer legislation and environmental labelling[19]; reviewing and improving government procurement policies[20]; using appropriate economic instruments to influence consumer behaviour[21]; and promoting more positive attitudes towards sustainable consumption through education, public awareness programmes and other means.[22]

Since Rio a number of International conferences, seminars, workshops, programmes etc. have been organized to implement the various recommendations made in Agenda 21. Following the Earth Summit, the OECD began its exploration of the relationship between production and consumption patterns and sustainable development.[23] It was the Oslo Ministerial Roundtable (Norwegian Ministry of Environment, 1995) which established the most commonly accepted definition of sustainable consumption as: *"the use of goods and services that respond to basic needs and bring a better quality of life, while minimizing the use of natural resources, toxic materials and emissions of waste and pollutants over the life cycle, so as not to jeopardise the needs of future generations".*[24] These and other activities contributed to the mandate by the second and third sessions of the UN Commission on Sustainable Development to develop an international work programme on sustainable production and consumption,[25] the first such global framework of programmes for implementing Agenda 21 objectives. The agreed upon programme of work consisted of five tasks:[26]

1. Identifying the policy implications of projected trends in consumption and production patterns.

2. Assessing the impact on developing countries, especially the least developed countries and small island developing States, of changes in consumption and production in developed countries.
3. Evaluating the effectiveness of policy measures intended to change consumption and production patterns, such as command-and-control, economic and social instruments, government procurement policies and guidelines.
4. Eliciting time bound voluntary commitment from countries to make measurable progress on those sustainable development goals that have an especially high priority at the national level.
5. Revising the guidelines for consumer protection, with regard to sustainable consumption.

In the International Programme of Work on Sustainable Production and Consumption, the task of revising the UN Guidelines on Consumer Protection, with regard to sustainable consumption, represents an important contribution to meeting the Agenda 21 objective of developing domestic policy frameworks. The evolution of these revised guidelines – their development, adoption, and use – offers useful insights in assessing governments' progress achieving the policy framework objective, not to mention the overall goal of promoting sustainable production and consumption patterns. In January 1998, the Government of Brazil hosted the UN Inter-Regional Expert Group Meeting on Consumer Protection and Sustainable Consumption, producing recommendations for revising the Guidelines discussed at the CSD's Sixth, Seventh and Eight Sessions and finally adopted by the General Assembly in December 1999.

In 1999, the UN Guidelines for Consumer Protection were expanded to include elements on sustainable consumption. The expanded guidelines provide an important opportunity to include environmental protection and sustainable development and to strengthen the linkage between consumer interests and sustainable consumption, thereby stimulating national policymaking to promote more sustainable consumption. The guidelines recommend governments to take action in nine specific areas: 1. Environmentally sound products services and technologies; 2. Recycling programmes for waste and products; 3. Regulatory mechanism; 4. Economic instruments; 5. Public (product) information; 6. Impartial testing of products; 7. Research on consumer behaviour; 8. Sustainable practices (e.g. public green procurement); and 9. Awareness and information campaigns.

In addition to specific policy recommendations on consumer information (e.g., on the impacts of consumption patterns and benefits of changes), education, eco-labelling, product testing, research on consumer behaviour, subsidy and tax reform, the Guidelines stressed the importance of government promotion of consumer empowerment and public participation in policy-making, as well as the responsibility of developed country governments to support developing countries in promoting sustainable consumption and development. In particular, the revised Guidelines on sustainable consumption supported efforts to develop domestic policy frameworks on sustainable production and consumption shaped through informed partnership with all members of society.

While the environmental, social and economic aspects of production processes have been in the focus for various efforts to attain sustainable development for many years, it is only recently that the intricate interaction with the consumption side has come into focus. The Plan of Implementation, adopted at the World Summit for Sustainable Development in Johannesburg in 2002, notes in chapter 3 that *"fundamental changes in the way societies produce and consume are indispensable for achieving global sustainable development"*. The Plan also calls for a number of more specific actions to be taken by international organizations and governments to achieve such changes.[27]

On that occasion, sustainable consumption and production was identified as one of the three overarching objectives of, and essential requirements for, sustainable development, together with poverty eradication and the management of natural resources in order to foster economic and social development. The Johannesburg Plan of Implementation also called for all countries to promote sustainable consumption and production patterns, with the developed countries taking the lead and with all countries benefiting from the process, taking into account the Rio principles, including, *inter alia*, the principle of common but differentiated responsibilities as set out in Principle 7 of the Rio Declaration on Environment and Development. Furthermore, the Plan called for governments, relevant international organizations, the private sector and all major groups to play an active role in changing unsustainable consumption and production patterns and more specifically, through its Paragraph 15, to "*Encourage and promote the development of a 10-year framework of programmes (10 YFP) in support of regional and national initiatives to accelerate the shift towards sustainable consumption and production to promote social and economic development within the carrying capacity of ecosystems*".[28]

Marrakech Process named after the city where the First International Expert Meeting on the 10 Year Framework Programme (YFP) took place in 2003. It was a global platform that brought together all stakeholders to work jointly in the promotion and implementation of SCP patterns. The Marrakech Process has provided significant inputs for the elaboration of a "Global Framework for Action on SCP"; the so-called 10-Year Framework of Programmes on SCP. The United Nations Environment Programme (UNEP) and the United Nations Department for Economic and Social Affairs (UN-DESA) acted as the Secretariat of this global process, with an active participation of national governments, private sector, civil society, development agencies, UN Agencies and other stakeholders. The Marrakech Process involved the following four phases, which were implemented simultaneously: 1. Organizing regional consultations in all regions to promote awareness and identify priorities and needs for SCP; 2. Building regional strategies and implementation mechanisms with regional and national ownership; 3. Implementing concrete projects and programmes on the regional, national and local levels; and 4. Monitoring and evaluating progress, as well as exchanging information and experience at the international level. The Marrakech Process identified regional SCP needs and priorities, and supported the development of regional SCP strategies in most regions as well as the implementation of 33 demonstration projects worldwide. These included national SCP action plans, capacity building and SCP tool kits in the areas of sustainable procurement, tourism, buildings and construction, products, education and lifestyles, as well as various communications tools and awareness raising activities. The Marrakech Process informed the elaboration of the 10th YFP, which was one of five themes at CSD 18 and CSD 19.[29]

The United Nations Conference on Sustainable Development—or Rio+20—took place in Rio de Janeiro, Brazil on 20-22 June, 2012 also adopted ground-breaking guidelines on green economy policies. The Rio+20 Conference reaffirmed that Sustainable Consumption and Production is a cornerstone of sustainable development. The well-being of humanity, the environment, and the functioning of the economy, ultimately depend upon the responsible management of the planet's natural resources. It recognised that poverty eradication, changing unsustainable and promoting sustainable patterns of consumption and production and protecting and managing the natural resource base of economic and social development are the overarching objectives of and essential requirements for sustainable development. It reaffirmed the need to achieve sustainable development by promoting sustained, inclusive and equitable economic growth, creating greater opportunities for all, reducing inequalities, raising basic standards of living, fostering equitable social development and inclusion, and promoting integrated and sustainable management of natural resources and ecosystems that supports, *inter alia*, economic, social and human development while facilitating ecosystem conservation, regeneration and restoration and resilience in the face of new and emerging challenges. It accepted green economy in the context of sustainable development and poverty eradication as one of the important tools available for achieving sustainable development and that it could provide options for policy-making.[30]

The United Nations Conference on Sustainable Development (Rio+20) in 2012, Heads of States adopted the 10-Year Framework of Programmes on Sustainable Consumption and Production Patterns (10 YFP), reaffirming that SCP is one of the overarching objectives of, and essential requirements for, sustainable development. The '10 YFP' is a global framework for action to enhance international cooperation and advance the implementation of SCP in all countries and regions. It generates collective impact through multi-stakeholder programmes and partnerships, which develop and scale up SCP policies and initiatives at all levels, fostering knowledge and experience sharing, and facilitating access to technical and financial resources for developing countries.

Transforming the World through Sustainable Development Goals

At the United Nations Sustainable Development Summit on 25 September, 2015, countries have adopted the 2030 Agenda for Sustainable Development, and global agreement on climate change. This new development agenda applies to all countries, promotes peaceful and inclusive societies, creates better jobs and tackles the environmental challenges particularly climate change. The Agenda includes a set of 17 Sustainable Development Goals (SDGs) to end poverty, fight inequality and injustice, and tackle climate change by 2030.

The new Goals and targets which have come into effect from January 1, 2016 will guide the decisions for the next 15 years. SDGs also known as the Global Goals, are built on the Millennium Development Goals (MDGs), adopted in 2000, eight anti-poverty targets that the world committed to achieving by 2015. The MDGs aimed at an array of issues that included slashing poverty, hunger, disease, gender inequality, and access to water and sanitation. Though enormous progress was made on the MDGs; however, the indignity of poverty could not be ended for all. That's why new SDGs, and the broader sustainability agenda, that is much broader than the MDGs, has been adopted to address the root causes of poverty and the universal need for development that works for all people.[31]

The 17 Sustainable Development Goals are as follows:[32]

1. *No poverty* – End Poverty in all its forms everywhere;
2. *Zero hunger* – End hunger, achieve food security and improved nutrition and promote sustainable agriculture;
3. *Good health and well-being* – Ensure healthy lives and promote well-being for all;
4. *Quality education* – Ensure inclusive and equitable quality education and promote lifelong learning opportunities for all;
5. *Gender equality* – Achieve gender equality and empower all women and girls;
6. *Clean water and sanitation* – Ensure access to water and sanitation for all;
7. *Affordable and clean energy* – Ensure access to affordable, reliable, sustainable and modern energy for all;
8. *Decent work and economic growth* – Promote inclusive and sustainable economic growth, employment and decent work for all;
9. *Industry, innovation, infrastructure* – Build resilient infrastructure, promote sustainable industrialization and foster innovation;
10. *Reduced inequalities* – Reduce inequality within and among countries;
11. *Sustainable cities and communities* – Make cities inclusive, safe, resilient and sustainable;
12. *Responsible consumption, production* – Ensure sustainable consumption and production patterns;
13. *Climate action* – Take urgent action to combat climate change and its impacts;
14. *Life below water* – Conserve and sustainably use the oceans, seas and marine resources;
15. *Life on land* – Sustainably manage forests, combat desertification, halt and reverse land degradation, halt biodiversity loss;
16. *Peace, justice and strong institutions* – Promote just, peaceful and inclusive societies; and
17. *Partnerships for the goals* – Revitalize the global partnership for sustainable development.

Responsible production and consumption is one of the 17 Global Goals that make-up the 2030 Agenda for Sustainable Development. As achieving economic growth and sustainable development requires that we urgently reduce our ecological footprint by changing the way we produce and consume goods and resources. The efficient management of our shared natural resources, and the way we dispose of toxic waste and pollutants, are important targets to achieve this goal. Encouraging industries, businesses and consumers to recycle and reduce waste is equally important, as is supporting developing countries to move towards more sustainable patterns of consumption by 2030.[33]

Sustainable Consumption and Development Goals

It is important to recognize sustainable consumption as a strategy to meet other development goals such as access to basic services, economic development and poverty eradication. There is need for "sustainable economic development". *"Sustainable economic development"* denotes a situation where the national economy is able to ensure that the basic needs are fulfilled for all. In a sense it is more ambitious than the traditional ambition of "economic growth" as it also implies that the economic growth of a country should not be allowed to infringe on the access to basic needs and services of its population.[34] If successfully adopted sustainable consumption should ultimately result in a better quality of life. The main goal for sustainable consumption is to achieve a better quality of life for all. To achieve the goal of better quality of life through sustainable consumption there is need for governments to take action in nine specific areas as recognized by the UN Guidelines on Consumer Protection *viz.* Environmentally sound products services and technologies; Recycling programmes for waste and products; Regulatory mechanism; Economic instruments; Public (product) information; Impartial testing of products; Research on consumer behaviour; Sustainable practices (e.g. public green procurement) and Awareness and information campaigns.

Due to the wide disparities between countries and even more within countries, sustainable consumption would imply that consumption would have to increase for those without access to basic needs, whereas the more affluent consumers would have to change their patterns and levels of consumption. In the developing world at least two billion people need to increase their consumption in a sustainable manner to escape poverty. In contrast, millions of new consumers in developing countries, like their counterparts in the developed regions, need to reorient their consumption patterns toward sustainability. So for the developing world it can mean both more and less (or more sustainable) consumption. The developing world has the opportunity to meet its increasing consumption and production needs in a more sustainable manner than the developed countries have done so in the past.[35]

This dual complexity has made the consumption issue difficult for many countries to deal with. Sustainable consumption should, therefore, be understood as a situation where consumer needs and demands are fulfilled in an efficient and resource lean way as possible, resulting in a minimized negative environmental, social and economic impact. The ultimate goal of sustainable consumption is improved quality of life for all consumers. Sustainable consumption is directly linked with many other development priorities, such as poverty alleviation, economic growth, health and education, and environmental protection, all of them contributing to an improved quality of life. Sustainable consumption is not a prescription for how to consume less, but for how to meet the consumers' needs in a smart way. The need is for adoption of more efficient, less resource consuming and less polluting technologies like hybrid cars.[36]

The awareness on sustainable consumption is in general quite low and the concept is often misunderstood by both governments as well as civil society stakeholders. Sustainable consumption merely appears on the political agenda in countries as part of policies and strategies for sustainable development. Higher priority and relevance is usually accorded to in national development goals to sustainable production instead of sustainable consumption. Still most of the sustainable consumption activities are identified and carried out as part of environment projects rather than sustainable consumption projects. The consumer movement on the other hand basically focuses on consumer rights and consumer protection issues for getting redressal for substandard products as the means to seek compensation for such goods are limited. Sustainable consumption is generally a lower priority area for most consumer groups.

Sustainable Consumption and Production (SCP) needs an active involvement of all stakeholders and a wide range of locally-adapted policy responses. A key element of the SCP approach is the use of a range of public policies, private sector actions and investments which influence both the supply of and demand for goods and services, thus reducing the negative impacts of both their production and consumption in an integrated manner.

Role of Various Stakeholders in Sustainable Consumption

UN Guidelines for Consumer Protection, 1985 mandates that the Governments, in partnership with business and relevant organizations of civil society, should develop and implement strategies that promote sustainable consumption through a mix of policies that could include regulations; economic and social instruments; sectoral policies in such areas as land-use, transport, energy and housing; information programmes to raise awareness of the impact of consumption patterns; removal of subsidies that promote unsustainable patterns of consumption and production; and promotion of sector specific environmental-management best practices.[37] It has to be realized by all the stakeholders in the society that the costs of inaction will be too high. The Governments, industry, civil society and consumers are key stakeholders whose initiatives can reduce poverty and drive sustainable economic growth in both developed and developing countries.

(i) Consumers

Green consumers can be defined as those who care sufficiently about the environment to make a conscious effort to buy products that avoid environmental damage. Criteria for defining "green" products include organic, durable, non-toxic, recyclable and using production methods that do not threaten important ecosystems. The majority of consumers pay little attention to environmental issues. Their main interest is "value for money". Since "green" products tend to be more expensive, price "resistance" is a major constraint on market demand. Either the consumer must be persuaded by better product information or encouraged by more competitive prices. The former might be achieved by a comprehensive system of eco-labelling; the latter, by a comprehensive system of environmental taxation.[38]

Consumer decisions can play an important role in countering unsustainable trends in the following three ways: Firstly by deciding what products are to be bought, e.g. conventional *vs.* energy-efficient light bulbs. Secondly, by deciding how products are to be used, e.g. by turning the light off when leaving a room or by double-sided printing. Here, consumers exert substantial influence on the ecological and social efficiency of the economy. Thirdly, by deciding how many products are to be bought, e.g. if mobile phones are used until they are out of order instead of buying new ones every year – consumers can increase economic sufficiency, another important lever of sustainability. Consumers have to initiate structural changes towards sustainability by demanding ecologically, socially and ethically produced products.[39]

However, majority of consumers are poorly informed for several reasons: (1) *Ignorance of Environmental and social issues*, such as climate change and consumers tend to perceive all products as reasonably "sound" in terms of their environmental and social implications. (2) *Complexity*: Some issues such as climate change and the concept of sustainable development are very complex and diffuse, making them difficult for consumers to grasp from their perspective. This makes it hard to make the "right" purchasing decisions or to adopt sustainable use or disposal behaviour. (3) *Short product life cycles*: Particularly in the market of fast-moving electronic consumer goods (PCs, cameras etc.), life cycles are so short that product information becomes obsolete very quickly. In addition to testing of products on certain environmental and social criteria, sustainability labels (eco-labels, fair trade labels etc.) provide guidance to consumers and are thus an effective means of building credibility and brands. However, having too many labels tends to confuse consumers, which necessitates consolidation of labelling schemes in some product categories through government initiatives. Consumer behaviour is not only highly fragmented, varying across different categories (e.g. energy use, waste, housing, tourism and leisure), but it is also often subject to habits. These habits, which may be associated with certain societal norms, are particularly difficult to change if they are deeply engrained. It may be possible to convince some consumers to buy more fuel-efficient cars, but it is considerably more difficult to "make" them cycle short distances or to use public transport more.[40]

(ii) Government

The governments have a leading role to play in promoting the culture of sustainable consumption. Government needs to develop the right policy framework and legislation that provide incentives to producers to reduce the generation of waste at the source. This includes changing the regulations on packaging and implementing an eco-tax on packaging and/or disposable products which would encourage producers to reduce the packaging or utilize returnable or biodegradable packaging. Producers can very much influence waste minimization/generation by for example reducing unnecessary packaging, and by avoiding the inclusion of substances/components that are difficult to recycle. Likewise, some of the responsibility for waste minimization lies on consumers. For example, consumers could be motivated to repair faulty products rather than replacing them, reuse products/materials (e.g. exchange of clothes), avoid disposable products such as disposable razors, chopsticks etc. Also, based on the availability and competitive cost, consumers could engage in product substitution to use those products that offer lower resource use (e.g. energy efficient light bulbs) or produce less waste.

Also, governments could intervene on the demand side by providing the right information to consumers about products with less packaging and more environment friendly products. As regards the waste minimization is concerned production merely focusing on the production aspects alone is insufficient there is need to take into consideration consumption phase also. To prevent environment degradation, recycling of waste also needs to be encouraged. For this the principles like producer "take back" responsibility are important. Consumers must also take the responsibility for ensuring that the used products are returned to recovery system. Communities have an important role to play in ensuring that community-generated organics (food waste, yard trimmings) are composted and returned safely back into the environment.

Governments as both consumers and policy setters have an instrumental role to play in SCP. Decision-makers directly and indirectly influence consumer behaviour and the sustainability of production. Information and education campaigns, economic instruments (taxes and rebate schemes) or regulation (standard-setting) can influence consumption and production patterns. Government is also one of the biggest consumers of products and services. It can leverage its support for sustainable procurement to promote change. Further, there is a need to establish incentives for the creation and improvement of markets for sustainable goods and services, to reduce the barriers to trade, improve access to markets and promote fair trade. This is key to ensuring the competitiveness of sustainable goods and services.

However, the policies and instruments used in this respect should take into account local context, cultural values and religions. This would make it possible to recognize a region-specific approach for sustainable consumption and to develop solutions adapted to local circumstances, rather than copying Western models. For countries like India energy, waste, food and agriculture, transport and health are key action areas to implement sustainable consumption policies.[41]

(iii) Business Initiatives

Free market economics dictates that companies seek to minimize costs in order to maximize profits regardless of any environmental damage that might be caused. Unless compelled by law, companies have a strong incentive to externalize some costs by exploiting the "free" services of the natural environment. Competitive markets compel companies to cut costs to stay in business even when this damages the environment, e.g. pollution. Indeed, there is an incentive to pollute because it is cheaper to discharge waste materials in the local environment than to invest in pollution abatement. As market prices reflect private (costs and benefits), business decisions are based on faulty and inadequate assessments. By ignoring environmental costs, market prices provide the wrong signals for resource management, leading to an overuse of the environment. Short-term profitability rather than long-term sustainability is the motivating force behind private enterprise. The ethos of economic growth has created a materialistic culture and a society preoccupied with "economic progress". Business has a vested interest in promoting this "culture", thus commercializing more and more of our everyday life. As market "values" reflect society's preferences, the general public will have to campaign, both in their role as consumers and citizens, for a "greener" economy. Further, the push from government in the form of higher environmental standards is forcing more companies to invest in new products and technologies to satisfy stricter environmental regulations on better pollution control, waste management and new product design. While legislation forces companies to change, few companies go beyond satisfying the minimum requirements because of the costs involved. This is when the pull of the market can become a decisive factor and help to reinforce new laws on environmental protection.[42]

A precondition of "greenness" is a corporate philosophy which explicitly incorporates environmental criteria in management decision-making. The corporate strategy will include environmental as well as financial objectives, and indicate how these objectives will be monitored and achieved. The following criteria can be used to determine how "green" a company has become:

- ***Product criterion***: A company making products which are environmentally friendly, e.g. durable, non-polluting, made from recycled materials.
- ***Technology criterion***: A company using production/assembly

methods that minimize environmental damage, e.g. minimizing waste and pollution, conserving energy.

- ***Business ethics criterion***: A corporate philosophy that embraces environmental values, made effective by an environmental policy with specific objectives, e.g. procurement policy to buy components/services from other "green" companies.

Although all three criteria are important, the essential characteristic of a "green" company is the last one. Corporate values must change so that environmental protection becomes an integral part of the corporate strategy.[43]

The transformation imperative is clearly an opportunity for business; if more businesses adopt the principles of sustainable consumption, we have the potential to increase global prosperity while avoiding the depletion of our natural resources and still preserving the ecosystems that underpin our lives. It is equally clear that this transformation can be beneficial for business. Sustainability can and should be thought of as a way to create opportunities and become a substantial source of competitive advantage, not solely as a way to mitigate risk. An economy transformed by sustainable consumption principles will allow companies to explore new business models and design strategies that can open up new market opportunities by promoting radical innovative solutions.[44]

The WBCSD (World Business Council for Sustainable Development) has proposed a seven-point blueprint for corporations: 1. Develop technological and social innovations to improve quality of life and tackle depletion of resources; 2. Practice eco-efficiency to create more value with less impact, growing qualitatively, not quantitatively; 3. Build alliances and move towards partnerships for progress based on common goals, empathy, open feedback, flexibility, ability to compromise and share rewards; 4. Provide and inform consumer choice; 5. Improve market conditions; 6. Establish the worth of the Earth; and 7. Make the market work for everyone.[45]

Design choices about things like material weight and packaging have direct impacts on transportation costs and fuel use, while choices about energy efficiency directly impact energy consumption in a product's use phase. Good design is generally judged based on its ability to meet a need. The challenge is to develop frameworks that allow people to design with the needs of sustainability in mind. For consumer electronics in particular, most business efforts have focused on lowering the energy consumption of products through renewable energy sources and increasing energy efficiency with technological solutions. More than 80 per cent of a product's environmental impact is determined during its design phase. Products should be designed using material that could be easily reused or repaired when they have outlived their usefulness. In some cases, a focus on sustainable consumption may result in the radical redesign of familiar products, and in other cases, there may be an opportunity to deliver the same value through services (such as car-sharing) rather than products (such as car sales).[46]

Conclusion

It is amply clear that the world cannot achieve sustainable economic growth with old fashioned consumption and production patterns. Modern civilization now constitutes a dense network of sub-units which has become huge and highly complex and is unable to form a well-functioning system. Unless it conforms to the law of the nature and evolves a feedback mechanism to get over the systemic problems as and when they arise, it is sure to crash, sooner or later. Decoupling environmental impact from economic growth is an essential prerequisite for sustainable development. For this all the stakeholders need to join hand and take steps in maintaining the environmental balance and promote sustainable lifestyles. Government must clarify the objectives for consumer action, reinforce existing policies and laws, and support the initiatives of private sector and civic actors to develop sustainable lifestyles. Companies have to accelerate the trends of polluting less and of designing, producing and marketing better products and services. Consumers have to get used to the fact that environmental considerations are as important in their daily choices as considerations of price, convenience and quality. Governments and civil society have a key role to play in. There is thus need for innovative, concerted efforts to decouple economic growth from natural resource extraction and environmental degradation inspiring such a process.

Notes

1. WWF, (2006), *Living Planet Report 2006*, Geneva, WWF.
2. Worldwatch Institute (2004), *State of the World,* Washington DC, Norton.
3. Addis Ababa Meeting of the Marrakech Process, June 2006.
4. UNDP (1998). *Human Development Report*, New York: UNDP.
5. UNEP (2003). "*Forging New Paths to Sustainable Development*", UNEP Background Paper, Asia Pacific Expert Meeting on Promoting Sustainable Consumption and Production Patterns, *Yogyakarta*, Indonesia, 21-23 May.
6. R.P. Misra, (2009), "Facing Environmental Challenges: The Gandhian Way", *Anasakti Darshan*, Vol. 5, No. 2, July–December 2009, pp. 1-47 at pp. 10, 26-27.

7. R.P. Misra, (2009), "Facing Environmental Challenges: The Gandhian Way", *Anasakti Darshan*, Vol. 5, No. 2, July–December 2009, pp.1-47, at p. 9, 19-20.
8. World Commission on Environment and Development, 1987.
9. Norwegian Ministry of the Environment, Oslo Roundtable on Sustainable Production and Consumption (1994).
10. *Oslo Roundtable on Sustainable Production and Consumption, http://www.iisd.ca/consume/oslo004.html accessed on November 13, 2015*
11. "*What is Sustainable Consumption?*", www.unesco.org/education/tlfs/TLFS/theme
12. UN, 1992: para 4.3.
13. UN, 1992: para 4.17.
14. *Ibid.*, para 4.18d.
15. *Ibid.*, para 4.19b.
16. *Ibid.*, para 4.19b.
17. *Ibid.*, para 4.21.
18. *Ibid.*, para 4.22a.
19. *Ibid.*, para 4.22b
20. *Ibid.*, para 4.23
21. *Ibid.*, para 4.25
22. *Ibid.*, para 4.26
23. OECD-Organisation for Economic Cooperation and Development, *Sustainable Consumption and Production: Clarifying the Concepts*, Organisation for Economic Cooperation and Development, Paris (1997).
24. Norwegian Ministry of Environment, *Oslo Ministerial Roundtable: Conference on Sustainable Production and Consumption*, Government of Norway, Oslo (1995).
25. UNCSD-United Nations Commission on Sustainable Development, *Report of the Commission on Sustainable Development on its Second Session, 16-27 May, 1994*, United Nations, New York (1994); and UNCSD-United Nations Commission on Sustainable Development, *Changing Consumption and Production Patterns: Report of the Secretary General, Commission on Sustainable Development, Third Session, 11-28 April, 1995*, United Nations, New York (1995).
26. UNCSD-United Nations Commission on Sustainable Development (1995b) *Report on the Third Session, 11-28 April, 1995*, United Nations Commission on Sustainable Development, United Nations, New York.
27. *Introduction to Sustainable Consumption in Europe and Asia–Background paper for SC. Asia cross-learning seminar*, p. 4, http://www.unep.fr/scp/nap/pdf/BackgroundSC.pdf
28. Sustainable consumption and production, https://sustainabledevelopment.un.org/topics/sustainableconsumptionand production accessed on November 13, 2015.
29. UNEP, (2008), *Planning for Change – Guidelines for National Programme on Sustainable Consumption and Production*, United Nations Environment

Programme, pp. 10, 20-21 and Sustainable consumption and production, https://sustainabledevelopment.un.org/topics/sustainable consumptionandproduction accessed on November 13, 2015.

30. Report of the United Nations Conference on Sustainable Development Rio de Janeiro, Brazil 20-22 June, 2012, United Nations • New York, 2012,http://www.uncsd2012.org/content/documents/814UNCSD% 20REPORT%20 final%20revs.pdf
31. Sustainable Development Goals (SDGs), http://www.undp.org/content/undp/en/home/sdgoverview/post-2015-development-agenda.html
32. http://www.undp.org/content/undp/en/home/sdgoverview/post-2015-development-agenda.html
33. http://www.undp.org/content/undp/en/home/sdgoverview/post-2015-development-agenda/goal-12.html
34. Introduction to Sustainable Consumption in Europe and Asia – Background paper for SC. Asia cross-learning seminar, p. 13, http://www.unep.fr/scp/nap/pdf/BackgroundSC.pdf
35. UNEP (2008), "*Planning for Change – Guidelines for National Programme on Sustainable Consumption and Production*", United Nations Environment Programme, p. 20.
36. Introduction to Sustainable Consumption in Europe and Asia – Background paper for SC. Asia cross-learning seminar, pp. 2-3, http://www.unep.fr/scp/nap/pdf/BackgroundSC.pdf
37. UN Guidelines for Consumer Protection, Section G SC.
38. Roarty, Michael; (1997), Greening business in a market economy, *European Business Review*, Bradford, Vol. 97, Iss. 5, p. 244.
39. Regina Schwegler, Burcu Tuncer, Daniel Peter; (2008), CSCP Background Paper -Sustainable Consumption Consumers as Trendsetters for Sustainability? INRATE, Zurich, March, 2008, p. 5. http://www.inrate.com/Inrate/media/Documents/Studies/2008-03-Study_Sustainable-Consumption_EN.pdf
40. *Ibid.*
41. For Sustainable Consumption Tools see UNEP, (2005), *Advancing Sustainable Consumption in Asia – A Guidance Manual*, Division of Technology Industry and Economics, UNEP, pp. 15-19.
42. Roarty, Michael (1997), Greening business in a market economy, *European Business Review*; Bradford, Vol. 97, Iss. 5; p. 244.
43. *Ibid.*
44. *The New Frontier in Sustainability – the Business Opportunity in Tackling Sustainable Consumption*, BER, July 2010, www.bsr.org
45. UNEP, (2005), *Advancing Sustainable Consumption in Asia – A Guidance Manual*, UNEP Division of Technology, Industry and Economics, p. 47.
46. *The New Frontier in Sustainability – the Business Opportunity in Tackling Sustainable Consumption*, BER, July 2010, www.bsr.org

5

Opportunities and Challenges Facing Training and Higher Education to Promote Sustainable Disaster Risk Reduction – 1973-2016

Ian Davis

"Education costs money, but then so does ignorance"?

–**Claus Moser**

Introduction

This chapter focuses on the development of sustainable training and education for disaster risk reduction, through training courses and higher education. The priority of education, as a unique long-term investment into the future is emphasized, however, as explained the reality is one of official neglect by governments, UN agencies and NGOs. The chapter relates the theme of education to certain aspirational statements made within the 2015 *Sendai Framework for Disaster Risk Reduction*, but questions whether they are followed up with actions on the ground. A number of the author's experiences are documented, as examples of good initial intentions to develop effective learning, that ultimately was un-sustained and some reasons for their collapse are suggested. One example concerns a UN agency office in Geneva, and ambitious international NGO programme and an abortive attempt to train UN and Government staff.

The chapter also considers ways to develop sustainable university programmes. A number of suggestions are set out that relate to requirements in leadership, finance and the links between education and related academic tasks. This section also notes some of the positive and negative experiences in supervising and examining Ph.D. research.

The final discussion makes a plea for 'downward accountability'. This concerns the need for trainers and lecturers to become more accountable to those they seek to train or teach. At the conclusion summarizes the text by noting the changes needed by various stakeholders if sustainable education is to occur. An appendix lists some detailed requirements for sustainable training and education.

Sustainable Education

Therefore, the chapter is primarily concerned with sustainability, a vital yet ubiquitous term that through over-familiarity has lost much of its power. However, the basic concept remains of central importance in an age of rapid change, environmental crisis, changing fashions, short memories, and the fluctuating whims of officialdom. For the first time in the past writing I am grasping the opportunity to apply the notion of sustainability to just one neglected topic: training and higher education. This subject has been a personal preoccupation throughout decades of rapid change within the disaster risk reduction field in architecture, education, writing, research, consultancy, advocacy and NGO management. Therefore, with this background in this chapter, unapologetic in recalling personal experiences that highlight negative and positive attitudes.

The common element in each organization *viz.* humanitarian, NGOs, universities, governmental and international agencies has been the aim to reduce disaster risks or adapt to climate change. In these environments, there were occasional examples of agencies that were diligent in their respect for learning and staff development. But more often it was the opposite. Apologies from staff, along the broad lines of *"do not expect too much from us, we re-invent the wheel twice daily in this department"*, were common. Reasons were rarely offered for their frustrations, but answers seemed to lie in a lack of staff that are adequately educated or trained for their tasks, high levels of staff turnover, changes in leadership and an absence of 'learning culture' within their organizations (Davis, 2015:16-17).[1]

The need for education and training is highlighted repeatedly in the

---

1. Throughout this chapter I have drawn on my earlier writing about training and education in pages 18-20 in the introduction to the book I edited in 2015: *Disaster Risk Management in Asia and the Pacific,* Abingdon: Routledge Publications.

Sendai Framework (UNISDR, 2016) but ignored in the unedited 'Chair's Summary' of the World Humanitarian Summit held in Istanbul in May 2016 (United Nations, 2016).

The Educational Priority

The famous Chinese saying "*give a man a fish and you feed him for a day; teach a man to fish and you feed him for a lifetime*", should be placed in a prominent place on the office walls of all managers of disaster risk management. The reality is inescapable: any disaster risk reduction measure, whether it be a flood protection barrier, or a curriculum to train school children earthquake safety is limited to the state of knowledge at the time that flood protection was designed, or the curriculum devised. The developments have certainly occurred in all structural and non-structural risk reduction measures with consequent changes, since knowledge is never static.

However, if someone is trained in an effective training course, or well educated in a fine Masters course, or educated to an even further level through undertaking Ph.D. research, the situation is totally different. Clearly, the work of all trainers and educators is also determined by the current state of knowledge, but the difference is that a well-educated person will be able to function more effectively in twenty or forty years time, in radically different contexts *as a direct consequence of their original training or education.* Thus, education, unlike other projects, can be regarded as a long-term investment deep into the future, and that is what makes it unique. This reality was expressed powerfully by the poet T.S. Elliot:

> "*It is in fact a part of the function of education to help us escape, not from our own time – for we are bound by that – but from the intellectual and emotional limitations of our time.*"

So, why do visible risk reduction measures tend to be the preferred options of authorities to 'hidden' training or educational initiatives? Probably, the explanation can be found in a media led political context, where leaders and dignitaries can perform opening ceremonies in highly visible, highly photographed and highly publicised events.

UN Declarations Concerning Training and Education

You would expect the reality of the priority of the power of education to have been long recognised and applied throughout the disaster management field, but alas that is certainly not the case. The following pair of examples of "declarations of intent" emerging from UN Conferences state the importance of education, but stop short of making any reference to its strategic long-term value or radical difference from other measures to reduce risks. Further, such statements amount to brave words with a certain hollow ring about them. Aside from specialised training initiatives in emergency management, health, engineering etc. are there any current initiatives being taken by UN agencies or donor organizations to actively promote, support, initiate, coordinate, stimulate training or higher education, if so where?

> "*The Chair's summary of the Fourth Session of the Global Platform for Disaster Risk Reduction in 2013 cites that globally there is 'an unmet demand for data, tools, methods and guidance on implementing risk reduction and a shortage of specialists educated and trained for the task,', and 'integrating disaster risk management into education at all levels including higher education should be priority'.*"
>
> (Jeggle, 2015 : 261 : quoting UNISDR, 2013)

The Sendai Framework for Disaster Risk Reduction of 2016 included the following Priority for Action:

> "*To promote the incorporation of disaster risk knowledge, including disaster prevention, mitigation, preparedness, response, recovery and rehabilitation, in formal and non-formal education, as well as in civic education at all levels, as well as in professional education and training*" [UNISDR, 2015 : 15, item (l)].

An important omission from such statements as the Sendai framework, is any reference to the need for UN and aid officials within other UN agencies and International Finance institutions, such as the World Bank to be *trained themselves*. It is as if the need for training in DRR is always on behalf of others, with the obvious complacent inference that internal competency in knowledge, experience and skills is assumed to be in place in their staff at headquarters and field levels. However, as anyone who has worked closely with international officials will be well aware, this is very far from the reality.

One particularly important gap in the non-formal training field concerns the need, following disasters, to provide direct, on-the-ground training to assist local families to repair or rebuild their homes safely. In the age of cell-phone technology and the ability of families to secure immediate remittances from overseas relatives, surviving families are increasingly seeking to self-manage their recovery. But without training being readily available at this critical time they will inevitably reconstruct their dwellings as well as vulnerability.

Apathy towards Learning

The first issue is the low regard for training, education and learning within governments and agencies. In the mid-1990s, an international training course in disaster management in Oxford, UK was conducted. On the first day we introduced each other and in one early session it was asked to each participant to say why they had come to the course. One provided an unusual answer, announcing that he was attending the course as a '*punishment*' for his poor performance in his government department! He further elaborated by informing us that in his country training had exceedingly low status, with trainers being on the lowest rung of the status ladder, often being relegated to this role due to their poor work performance.

On a further occasion in the late 1980s, the CEO of one of the UK's leading Christian NGOs wanted to discuss staff training. NGO was aware that there had been a series of courses in Disaster Management within the organization, where courses had been co-led in partnership with one of his senior staff. The reasons for enthusiasm were asked which led to develop staff training programmes within his organization as well as with their partner bodies. The reply was that it was immensely rewarding experience to note the way staff changed during the progress of even short training courses from passive observers to deeply committed participants. It was also observed that meeting past trainees was an utter joy as they held senior positions within humanitarian bodies and to hear them describe how earlier training had first ignited their interest and built their careers.

At this point there was a pause in our conversation, and I sensed he did not share my enthusiasm for training, so I asked him about his experience of training as CEO. He then recounted a number of reasons for his skepticism of the value of training. He described staff returning from training requesting opportunities to attend further courses to further develop their skills. Others would ask for promotion in order to redirect their careers in the light of the training experience, whilst others might leave the NGO having gained new knowledge and skills at the expense of their organization. He said that he particularly resented staff, who on returning from training would make suggestions on changes needed within the organization. He obviously felt uneasy in using the gift income that the agency received from its supporters in what he regarded as a luxury in training his staff.

It struck me that the objections he vividly recorded were all positive and healthy signs that training was having a significant impact and I recall responding rather impertinently by asking the director why was CEO? He replied that he had been appointed on the basis of his qualifications and past management experiences. I then suggested that he was in his director's chair because people had invested in him and had given him numerous opportunities over very many years that resulted in his career developments. All that was being asked of him was to similarly invest in his own staff by offering them training to enable them to acquire knowledge and skills to advance their careers as well as benefit the organization. Our rather illuminating conversation ended when I expressed my view that leading a development agency could have a double impact in not just providing support in development projects around the world, but also in offering rich opportunities for all his staff within their headquarters building.

As I left the building I recall pondering about the rather depressing conversation and why the humanitarian sector, with its neglect of the pursuit of knowledge was so often radically different from the priorities of the corporate giants in the commercial world that seem to need no encouragement to devote massive financial and human resources to staff development to ensure that they remain at the cutting edge of knowledge.

Failures to Institutionalize Learning

That encounter occurred in the early 1990s and since then there has been a growing recognition in the development and management sectors regarding the critical need for organizations to 'learn' in order to function effectively and develop. This *collective* requirement is closely related to *individual* staff members being well educated and trained to apply the results of that training within their work. In 'best practice' both concerns are based on the need to focus on 'learning outcomes' from education, rather than 'teaching inputs' (Davis, 2015 : 20).

This organizational need is particularly vital in any agency concerned with DRM and CCA for three rather obvious reasons: high levels of staff turnover, a fluctuating policy environment and the dynamic nature of DRM and CCA, which are inevitably subject to rapid change. Organizational learning has been described as "the intentional use of learning processes at the individual, group and system level to continuously transform the organization in a direction that is increasingly satisfying to its stakeholders" (Dixon, 1994 : 77).

The Sendai Framework for Disaster Risk Reduction contains an important clause concerning the need for learning:

> "*To build the knowledge of government officials at all levels, civil society, communities and volunteers, as well as the private sector, through sharing experiences, lessons learned, good practices and training and education in disaster risk reduction, including the use of existing training and education mechanisms and peer learning*". [UNISDR, 2015 : 15 item (g)]

The following examples are of training and learning that started well, but failed to be sustained.

First Failure: A UN Agency in Geneva

First, an example of the precise opposite of the above aspiration of UNISDR that demonstrates apathy in high places to knowledge being developed and shared. This occurred in Geneva within a UN HQ office that had better remain nameless. Some years ago a colleague worked under a director who had a strong passion to enable the organization to develop a learning culture, where knowledge was developed, shared and stored for easy retrieval and application. Therefore, on returning from field missions or conference attendance, staff would be encouraged to present their experiences to their colleagues in 'brown-bag lunch' seminars, where staff experiences and reports were carefully documented and filed in a well organised office library/resource room.

My friend retired from the organization, but returned to the office in relation to a writing assignment he was undertaking. He went to the library, only to find that it had changed into an office. On asking where the library had been moved to, one of his ex-colleagues took him to the window and pointed his eyes in the direction of a large waste skip in the car park, which now contained the entire office library. As a sad example of official vandalism in the form of a failure to institutionalise learning within that agency, a new boss, with Philistine tendencies had been appointed. He had no interest whatsoever in the 'learning culture' idea, and in his quest for additional office space he had dispensed with the seminars and the books and reports.

Second Failure: An International NGO Training Programme

The second tragic example was of a failure to institutionalise a healthy NGO training initiative that had been in place for about eight years. I was asked to work with a UK based NGO that had a member of staff with an enlightened approach to building the capacity of their own staff as well as staff within their partner organizations. Therefore, in partnership with the organization's training advisor, I had the privilege in organizing and leading training courses, and training of trainers courses in London, Angola, Burkina Faso, Zimbabwe, Nicaragua, Mozambique, Bangladesh, India and the Philippines. To support the work we developed guidelines for workshop participants as well as for trainers (Davis, I. and Wall, M. 1992) (Davis, I. and Wall, M. n.d.).

When this ambitious programme was at its height, my colleague within the organization was promoted to lead an important project in Sudan and I wrongly assumed that this well established training initiative would continue to operate and flourish under a new manager. This seemed to be particularly important since at that time in the mid-1990s there was an escalating number of emergency situations requiring the services of trained staff in partner organizations. However, since that time disaster management training has not continued in that organization, and the only explanation for this two decade gap would appear to be that subsequent directors, or the overseeing management board do not regard training as important part of their mission. Thus, this valuable training initiative was just one person deep within the organization, leading to another failure to institutionalize training as a core function.

Third Failure: Training UN and Government Officials

The final example concerned an ambitious programme of training officials within the UN and in governments. The first international training course in Disaster Management was directed at governmental staff was undertaken by the Office of Foreign Disaster Assistance (OFDA) as far back as the late 1970s, and there have been many disaster risk management staff training courses since then. In Oxford I led a rather rudimentary course in Disaster Risk Management (DRM) in 1982, the first to occur in the UK. But, as with the lack of higher education collaboration, UN initiatives have failed to materialize and be sustained in a sufficiently ambitious form to meet the widespread training need.

The clear requirement is for a comprehensive training strategy, coordination of courses and development of the training capacities for UN officials and national leaders. The last time this happened was in 1990 when the progressive Disaster Management Training Programme (DMTP), led by INTERWORKS and the University of Wisconsin for the United Nations Development Programme (UNDP) and the Department for Humanitarian Affairs (DHA), was established for about five years. The programme included staff training within the UN system as well as for governmental officials. During this time 3,600 staff members from 55 countries received this training. A vital element was the development of an extensive range of training materials for trainers as well as trainees. They became the definitive course material both within the DMTP programme and for those running courses for NGOs and governments (University of Wisconsin, n.d.).

However, DMTP was prematurely cancelled by UNDP for reasons unknown, perhaps a result of bureaucratic ignorance of the strategic valuc and potential of the programme. I regard this cancellation as one of the most serious set-backs to international DRM during my entire career.

The only equivalent has been a UN initiative called Capacity Development for Disaster Reduction Initiative (CADRI), formed in 2007 as an inter-agency initiative of UNDP/BCPR (Bureau for Crisis Prevention and Recovery), the Office for the Coordination of Humanitarian Affairs (OCHA) and the UNISDR. Its mission was to advance knowledge and strengthen sustainable capacity development for disaster risk reduction worldwide (CADRI, n.d.).

However, the laudable intention behind the mandate of CADRI has never produced the excellent body of DRR training materials that flowed from DMTP, which formed the international benchmark for staff training in DRR in the late 1980s and early 1990s, nor has it run an extensive international training programme along the lines of DMTP. One reason may relate to CADRI not succeeding in attracting inter-agency funding in recent years. Therefore, it has yet to fulfil its potential as a global resource for training government and UN staff in DRM, and donors hold the key to CADRI's mission being eventually fulfilled, meeting a pressing need (Davis, 2015 :18-19). Thus, DMTP was a further valuable training initiative that lasted about five years, another failure to institutionalize training, in this case for the entire UN system and the governments they serve.

The common thread in these examples comes down to enlightened people with a vision for training creating something worthwhile on behalf of others, that were deliberately destroyed by people who lacked that vision, but of course there were additional factors, that I am unaware of that contributed to these losses. The clear lesson concerns the need for those with a training vision to seek for secure and sustainable funding support as well as building strong coalitions and alliances with like-minded colleagues to support the learning process, so that, there is always a *collective* desire to maintain programmes.

Sustainable University Programmes in Risk Reduction

I have taught in several UK universities, including Oxford Brookes University where a Disaster Risk and Recovery Management post-graduate Masters Courses well as short training courses continue to flourish in the Centre for Emergencies and Development Practice (CENDEP) since the programme started in the late 1980s.

I also developed a Masters Course in Disaster Management in Cranfield University, but this only survived for about five years in the Cranfield Disaster Management Centre (CDMC) In addition Cranfield had maintained a strong tradition of running Disaster Management training courses in the UK and internationally for over 15 years.

The reasons why CENDEP survives in Oxford Brookes and CDMC disappeared in Cranfield University are complex and relate to university power and politics and if fully explained would probably place me in the dock of a law court, so I will resist the temptation to pursue that subject! Suffice it to say that university institutions are fragile and precious assets and it can only take a mere hour to demolish something that could have taken twelve years to carefully construct.

However, certain general issues can be noted in creating sustainable higher education:

Leadership

- Inspired leadership is an essential commodity;
- Strong advocates are needed in senior university directors to maintain confidence in this work, and its staff, particularly during times of crisis.

Financial stability

- The commitment of donor governments and international agencies to training and education can be highly fickle and inconsistent depending on changing budgets, fluctuating fashions in aid allocations, personnel preferences etc.
- Secure finance will always be a basic requirement in creating sustainable programmes, but this can be highly problematic given fluctuating student admissions, variable exchange rates and the development of international competition etc.

Links between training, education and research

- In an ideal world academic centres of disaster risk management will be composed of well integrated research, advocacy, consultancy, training courses and academic programmes since each can support and balance the other elements. However, this is rarely achieved and one reason may be the reality that good researchers may not make good trainers or lecturers or *vice-versa*. While there are international centres that confine their activities to training and consultancy, without the sustaining life-blood from applied research and higher education they will always be incomplete. And the knowledge they seek to share with others can become second-hand, dependent on the work of others, and this lack of direct experience is clearly visible.
- Disaster risk management centres suffer from isolation. Their natural bed-fellow is in the field of development studies, and a healthy centre of research and learning will have close links with related fields in a host of fields such as public health/social studies/ environmental concerns/planning/architecture/human and physical geography/anthropology/engineering/management/ economics etc.
- Such links are not easy to balance and maintain, but where they can co-exist, they can all feed off each other to good effect.

Supervising and Examining Ph.D. Research

It is abundantly clear in 2016 that there is an expanding demand from students, spread right across the world, to undertake doctoral research in DRR, Disaster Recovery and CCA. Along with my colleagues working in

UK, Scandinavian and Japanese academia I have had a number of positive as well as negative lessons in supervising research students and in examining dissertations. My experiences include the following positive lessons:

- My own career was built on my Ph.D. research, and I have observed the same process in strengthening the career paths of a number of successful students I supervised;
- While undertaking a Ph.D. in University College, London (UCL), being taught well be a highly experienced supervisor: Professor Otto Koenigsberger, I was also teaching and training disaster related themes. This taught me the great value of being taught, while teaching. From this experience I would advise anyone who aspires to train or teach to undertake higher education to sharpen their skills through a Master's degree or where possible Ph.D. research in a reputable university; and
- A positive and long overdue development in the present decade-2010-2020, is that the balance is shifting away from the past dominance of education and training being based in wealthy industrialized countries to the rapidly emerging economies in India, China, Brazil, Indonesia, South Africa etc.

My experiences include the following negative lessons:

- Numerous aspects of disaster related subjects still require research. The result is that policies are often constructed on superficial assumptions rather than accurate research findings.
- Large numbers of opportunistic universities, seeking to build their doctoral research programmes, and capitalize on the popularity of humanitarian subjects are currently accepting students for Ph.D. research without having adequate internal expertise to supervise these students in DRM, recovery management or CCA. This has double negative consequences: the devaluation of high quality research that fails to advance knowledge as well as failed submissions. About 60 per cent of all the examinations I have undertaken from 1987-2011 as an external examiner in disaster related subjects in the UK, Sweden, Netherlands and Japan were significantly below a passing standard, thus, students need to make quality checks on their prospective institutions before making their applications (Alexander and Davis, 2014).

- Many cross-cultural issues surface when students from one country travel to undertake Ph.D. research in another. One issue I repeatedly experienced was the difficulty faced by students who came from countries with conservative or authoritarian governments, in undertaking creative analysis. Some would express their difficulty in adopting a creative ability to assess the factual date they had collected, since their entire previous education had been based on accepting facts at face value, without critical challenge.
- Certain universities retain the final decision to award a Ph.D. thus over-riding objective assessments by external examiners. This practice seriously devalues the quality standard of research.

Sustainability and Accountability

The Sendai Framework for Disaster Risk Reduction contains a guiding principle concerning the need for accountability:

> "Disaster risk reduction and management depends on coordination mechanisms within and across sectors and with relevant stakeholders at all levels, and it requires the full engagement of all State institutions of an executive and legislative nature at national and local levels and a clear articulation of responsibilities across public and private stakeholders, including business and academia, to ensure mutual outreach, partnership, complementarity in roles and accountability and follow-up."
>
> [UNISDR, 2015 : 13 item 19 (e)]

For there to be significant progress in establishing sustainable education and training, progress is needed in creating improved patterns of accountability, to give account to the beneficiaries of teaching and training. In the four decades that I have been associated in leading courses in Disaster Risk Management, I have seen a gradual growth in accountability between the teacher and student. In the 1970s and early 1980s there was minimal accountability between a trainer, lecturer or supervisor and the person(s) they taught. If the training or education was sub-standard there was minimal opportunity for the person being taught to express their concern, or "hold the teacher to account". But gradually that pattern began to change. Evaluations became the norm and courses were monitored. Organisors of courses, as well as participants began to write detailed, confidential appraisals of the quality of courses to the funding agencies. I recall that we lost the support of a key donor following some negative feedback on one of our courses, and that appraisal put all those of us teaching future courses on our toes.

One day I arrived at work to lead a training course and noticed a large packing case being unpacked after it had been taken from a truck that had collected it from the airport. The packing case contained a delicate piece of scientific equipment for one of our research laboratories. The case resembled the diagram in Fig. 5.1. Strong elastic cords were attached to each corner of the equipment so that it could bounce freely when in transit without causing any damage.

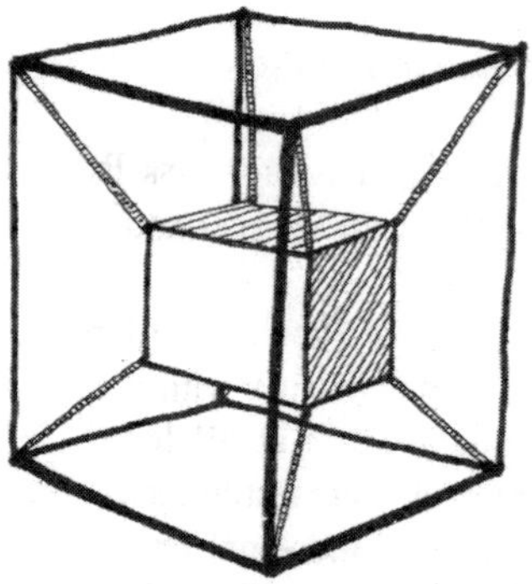

Fig. 5.1: A box suspended within a box as a picture of multiple accountability.

As I looked at the box, within a box I realised that this was a good picture of how teachers and trainers should behave with upward and downward cords constraining their actions. I was continually made aware that I was accountable upwards to my university authorities and to the funding bodies who had sponsored the course. In addition I was also accountable to my colleagues with whom I was working. The downward accountability was to course participants and my university students, who were at that time just beginning to exercise their power to ensure that the teaching met their needs. Although we initially found it irritating and difficult to accept being accountable to those we taught as well as having to give account to our lords and masters, we gradually realised that courses were significantly improving in response to the ability of participants and students to express their criticisms and demands. As accountability grew, trainees and students changed into active partners in learning.

If this model was to be applied to the universities noted above who enrol students for advanced research in Ph.D. studies without the necessary expertise, the cords for downward accountability would not exist, since any academic body without the essential credentials to supervise would be unaccountable to their potential student.

Summary

To create, and maintain sustainable training and education, certain developments are needed by the various stakeholders.

Training Directors, Trainers, Education Directors, Lecturers and Supervisors

To give priority concern for training, teaching and learning as the foundation block of effective risk management. To become more accountable to those they train and teach. The content of their training needs to reflect advances in the subjects being taught as well as the needs of those they train and teach in response to continual monitoring of their requirements in a fast changing environment. There is a need for teaching and training centres to collaborate, sharing resources with parallel organizations rather than competing with them for resources and students.

To regard their work as a vocation, a vital public service to build a safe and sustainable future. To encourage all being trained or taught to share their knowledge and experience with colleagues, since this form of sub-conscious 'horizontal learning' has massive potential.

University Authorities

To support their staff and create an environment where they, and their students can flourish. To develop quality assurance to ensure that their expertise matches the demands of excellent and relevant education.

Directors of UN Agencies, (such as UNISDR), Donor Bodies, such as the International Finance Institutions (IFIs), donor countries and NGOs who advocate and sponsor education and training

To practice what they preach by developing learning cultures within their organizations with staff development opportunities for their own staff.

UN Agencies, NGOs, IFIs, Governments, the Private Sector etc. who employ graduates and trained officials

To develop mentoring schemes, internships, and ways to employ trained and educated staff and apply their knowledge and skills.

Students seeking training and Students seeking post-graduate Masters Courses

To devise means where they are able to make informed choices concerning which course is best suited for their needs.

I hope that these thoughts will encourage those who train and teach, those who facilitate the process and those being taught to recognize the strategic importance of their work. Together these groups can produce improved and sustainable education and training as foundation blocks of improved safety.

This chapter is dedicated with warm affection to my good friend and esteemed colleague Vinod Sharma with thanks for his magnificent contribution to education for sustained risk reduction and adaptation to climate change.

Appendix

What are the Requirements of Sustainable Training and Education?

Sustainable Training requires:

- Recognition by donors and decision-makers that this requires priority attention.
- Awareness by authorities that training is needed at every level and sector if risks are to be reduced.
- Detailed training needs assessments to be carried out on a regular basis.
- Evaluations of agency performance to include a description of training requirements to rectify any gaps.
- Training, retraining, and continual staff development that is built into job descriptions, to enable all staff within a given organization to operate at high levels of competency.
- The development of innovative approaches to training: internet based, 'on-the-job training', mentoring relationships etc.

Sustainable Higher Education requires

- Recognition by donors and decision-makers that support for higher education requires priority attention.
- Awareness by authorities that if risks are to be reduced it is essential to employ well educated and well qualified staff in all senior positions.
- The creation of active partnerships, involving student and staff exchanges, joint research, knowledge exchange between university institutes or centres within wealthy countries and with those with more limited resources that focus on disaster studies.
- Recognising that there are many students now wanting to undertake Ph.D. Research in this subject, work is needed to provide guidance on specific research needs.

References

Alexander, D. and Davis, I., (2014), Fit to supervise? How can it happen that substandard work is submitted for doctoral examination? *Times Higher Education,* 20 February, 2014, pp. 35-38.

CADRE n.d. About us Retrieved from UNDP/BCPR, OCHA and UNISDR website, www.cadri.net/about-us/cadri-core-organizations/unisdr

Davis, I., (2015) (ed.) *Disaster Risk Management in Asia and the Pacific.* Abingdon: Routledge.

Davis, I. and Wall, M. (1992), *Christian Perspectives on Disaster Management,* Teddington: Interchurch Relief and Development Alliance (IRDA), Training Unit Tearfund.

Davis, I. and Wall, M. undated *Christian Perspectives on Disaster Management. A Trainers Guide,* Teddington: Interchurch Relief and Development Alliance (IRDA), Training Unit Tearfund.

Davis, I. and Alexander, D., (2015), *Recovery from Disaster.* Abingdon: Routledge.

Dixon, N., (1994), *Organizational learning cycle: how we can learn collectively.* Abingdon: Gower Publishing.

GFDRR & INEE, (2009) *Guidance notes on Safer School Construction.* Global Facility for Disaster Reduction and Recovery (GFDRR) and Inter-Agency Network for Education in Emergencies (INEE), Washington, DC:GFDRR, the World Bank.

Jeggle, T. (2015) "Disaster risk management at the regional level", Chapter 9, p. 261 in Davis, I. (ed.) (2015) *Disaster Risk Management in Asia and the Pacific.* Abingdon: Routledge.

UNISDR, (2013) *Chair's Summary of the Fourth Session of the Global Platform for Disaster Reduction: Resilient People, Resilient Planet.* Geneva 21-23 May, 2013. Geneva: UNISDR.

UNISDR, (2015) *Sendai Framework for Disaster Risk Reduction 2015-2030* Geneva: United Nations International Strategy for Disaster Risk Reduction UNISDR.

United Nations, *Chair's Summary. Standing up for Humanity: Committing to Action,* World Humanitarian Summit, Istanbul, 23-24 May, 2016.

University of Wisconsin. n.d. Report on the work of the Disaster Management Centre in Developing the DMTP (DMC) Madison: University of Wisconsin-Madison.

6
Towards Science Policy Action Linkages in Asia

Rajib Shaw

Introduction

Science and Technology for disaster risk reduction has always been there in some form in different countries. Through the advancement of scientific research, disaster risk reduction has been benefited, especially in terms of early warning system, to identify risk in both spatial and temporal scale, strengthening of buildings and infrastructures for different types of hazards etc. There have also been significant achievements in recognizing higher education in disaster risk reduction, either as a specialized subject and/or integration of the disaster studies into other higher education curriculum. In recent years, apart from hard science, which is more on innovations and engineering, soft science or social sciences have also got prominence and importance. Through different major disasters, it has been realized that there needs to be a good balance between the hard and soft technology, and engineering solutions and social solutions.

Science, Technology and Academia Role and Engagement during the International Decade for Natural Disaster Reduction (IDNDR)

The relation of science and technology in a formal way in inter-governmental issues dates back in 1980s, when Frank Press, then President of International Association of Earthquake Engineering [IAEE] perceived the idea of an international decade of disaster reduction. The basic idea behind this proclamation of the Decade (1990-1999) was and still remains to be the unacceptable and rising levels of losses, which disasters continue to incur on the one hand, and the existence, on the other hand, of a wealth of scientific and engineering know-how which could be effectively used to reduce losses resulting from disasters. The 1987 UN General Assembly Declaration (UN, 1987):

> "...calls upon all Governments to participate during the decade for concerted international action for the reduction of natural disasters and, as appropriate, to establish national committees, in co-operation with the relevant scientific and technological communities, with a view to surveying available mechanisms and facilities for the reduction of natural hazards, assessing the particular requirements of their respective countries or regions in order to add to, improve or update existing mechanisms and facilities and develop a strategy to attain the desired goals."

During the IDNDR, Science and Technical Advisors [STA] group was formed to support: "*Application of scientific knowledge and technology for disaster prevention, preparedness and mitigation, including the transfer of experience and greater access to relevant data.*" In the concluding year of the IDNDR, the Geneva Programme Forum has identified the progress of Science and Technology research as (UN, 1999):

> "Substantial progress has been achieved in understanding the cause and effects of natural hazards. Nevertheless, further efforts are needed, especially with respect to risk assessment and warnings. Multidisciplinary efforts are needed for many problems, especially to better integrate physical and social sciences."

IDNDR had been able to enhance and raise the awareness of disaster issues of the national and local governments, highlighted the need of pre-disaster preparedness, and emphasized roles of different stakeholders, including the science, technology and academia sector.

Hyogo Framework for Action and Role of Science, Technology and Academia in Asia

Following the establishment of the ISDR (International Strategy for Disaster Reduction) in year 2000, there has been more focus on regional level collaboration and networking, while keeping the global agenda in perspective. The key change from IDNDR to ISDR was to develop a comprehensive framework of disaster risk reduction [focusing on "*risk reduction*" issues], to identify priorities, and to measure the periodic progress. The Hyogo Framework for Action [2005-2015] had five key priorities. A quick look at the priorities of HFA document (UNISDR, 2005) revels a strong role of science and technology in Priority 2 (Identify, assess and monitor disaster risks and enhance early warning), as mentioned below:

> "Support the improvement of scientific and technical methods and capacities for risk assessment, monitoring and early warning, through research, partnerships, training and technical capacity-building. Promote the application of *in situ* and space-based earth observations, space technologies, remote sensing, geographic information systems, hazard modelling and prediction, weather and climate modelling and forecasting, communication tools and studies of the costs and benefits of risk assessment and early warning."

During the HFA implementation, science and technology sectors have observed increasing demands in the disaster risk reduction both at the global and regional levels. However, its national prominence was missing, except a few selected countries. Thus, the upcoming years need to focus on:

- To bring science into national and local government decision-making in the Asian countries.
- To encourage innovative research and education linked to field practices.

Related Global and Regional Initiatives

The IDRC (International Disaster Risk Conference) Davos meeting of 2014 has analyzed and presented some key issues on the current status of Science and Technology [S-T] in disaster risk reduction (IDRC, 2014). It emphasized the need of shift to "science of how" from "science of what", so that necessary skills and knowledge bases are properly utilized, and meet the "last mile" challenge of risk reduction.

The "Tokyo Conference on International Study for Disaster Risk Reduction and Resilience" called on policy-makers to empower their national DRR platforms through greater engagement with science and technology. The "Tokyo Statement" outcome document specifies that Governments need to empower national platforms so that they can practice evidence-based disaster risk reduction for sustainable development (Tokyo Statement, 2015).

In a recent report of Science and Technology Advisory Group [STAG] of UNISDR (STAG, 2015), it is mentioned that:

> "While political leadership and community partnerships are required for the successful implementation of effective, science-informed initiatives, the research community has a responsibility to formulate applicable methodologies and tools that respond to real-world challenges".

STAG proposed the following six areas as highlights of the post-HFA framework:

"(1) Assessment of the current state of data, scientific knowledge and technical availability on disaster risks and resilience (what is known, what is needed, what are the uncertainties etc.);
(2) Synthesis of scientific evidence in a timely, accessible and policy-relevant manner;
(3) Scientific advice to decision-makers through close collaboration and dialogue to identify knowledge needs including at national and local levels, and review policy options based on scientific evidence;
(4) Monitoring and review to ensure that new and up-to-date scientific information is used in data collection and monitoring progress towards disaster risk reduction and resilience building.
(5) Communication and engagement among policy-makers, stakeholders in all sectors and in the science and technology domains themselves to ensure useful knowledge is identified and needs are met, and scientists are better equipped to provide evidence and advice; and
(6) Capacity development to ensure that all countries can produce, have access to and effectively use scientific information."

Sendai Framework for Disaster Risk Reduction

The Sendai Framework for Disaster Risk Reduction (SFDRR, 2015) has seven specific goals:

1. Reduce global disaster mortality.
2. Reduce number of affected people.
3. Reduce direct disaster economic loss.
4. Reduce disaster damage to critical infrastructures.
5. Increase number of countries with DRR strategies.
6. Enhance international cooperation.
7. Increase access to multi-hazard EWS, risk information and assessment.

To achieve these goals, there are four key targets:

1. Understanding disaster risk.
2. Strengthening disaster risk governance.
3. Investing in risk reduction.
4. Enhancing disaster preparedness for collective response, and to "build back better" in recovery, rehabilitation and reconstruction.

Fig. 6.1 shows a schematic diagram of relative roles of stakeholder engagements. A quick analysis shows that the Priority 1 has a strong role of S-T community in the following areas:

- *National and local levels*: Data generation and management, Baseline survey to measure progress, Hazard, risk and vulnerability maps, GIS data bases, Good practices, training and education, Dialogue and cooperation of ST communities and policy-makers, science-policy interface, Strengthen technical and scientific capacity, Promote investment in innovations and technology development, and Incorporate disaster risk knowledge in formal and non-formal education.
- *International and regional levels*: Development and dissemination of science based methodologies and tools, ST and academia partnership, Enhancing ST work on DRR through existing networks and research institutions with support of ISDR STAG.

In contrast, in Priority 2 area, roles of S-T are limited to:

- Promote the development of quality standards, such as certification and awards for DRM with private sectors, civil societies, professional association and scientific organization and UN [national and local levels]; and
- Promote mutual learning and exchange of good practices and information through *inter-alia*, voluntary, self-initiated peer review among interested states [international and regional levels].

For Priority 3, S-T roles are:

- Promote disaster risk resilience of work place through structural and non-structural measures, and Encourage the revision of existing or new standards, codes, rehabilitation or reconstruction practice [at national and local levels]; and
- Promote academic, scientific and research entities and networks and private sectors to develop new products and services to help reduce disaster risk [international and regional levels].

In case of Priority 4, S-T roles are:

- Develop guidance for preparedness and reconstruction [land-use planning, structural standards improvements and learning from recovery] [at national and local levels]; and
- Promote further development and dissemination of instruments as standards, codes, operational guides and other guiding instruments [international and regional levels].

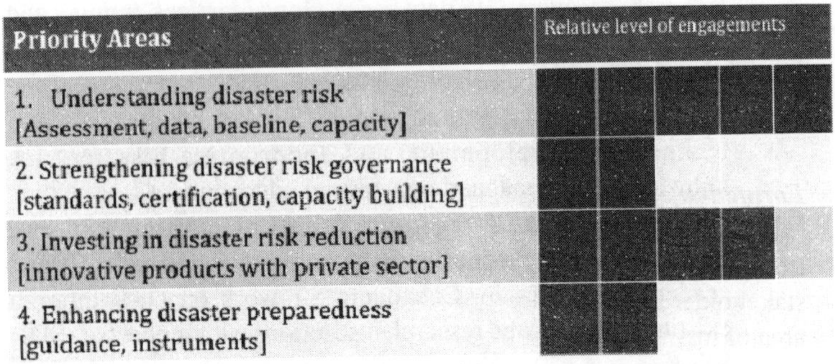

Fig. 6.1: Relative level of engagement of S-T in SFDRR priority areas.

Science and Technology Road Map for Implementation of SFDRR

Given the call in the Sendai Framework for science and technology-based DRR, in addition to a number of commitments made by the scientific and technology community at the Third UN World Conference on Disaster Risk Reduction, there is a need for a stronger partnership with a clearer direction and strategy for implementation as a mechanism to foster collaboration across global and regional mechanisms and institutions for the implementation and coherence of instruments and tools relevant to disaster risk reduction around common goals and actions identified in the road map. The science and technology community, as well as other stakeholders, came together at the UN Office for Disaster Risk Reduction (UNISDR) Science and Technology Conference held 27-29 January, 2016 in Geneva. The "Science and Technology Roadmap to Support the Implementation of the Sendai Framework for Disaster Risk Reduction 2015-2030" and accompanying partnerships are the main outcomes of the conference.

The "Science and Technology Roadmap (Fig. 6.2) to Support the Implementation of the Sendai Framework for Disaster Risk Reduction 2015-2030" includes expected outcomes, actions, and deliverables under each of the four priority of actions of the Sendai Framework (UNISDR, 2016). The science and technology community can then link to and plan around the implementation of the Roadmap. Work plans for several of the deliverables (with responsibilities, outputs and a timeline) in the Roadmap can then be developed as appropriate. These can be developed on a needs basis with identified partners with the support of the UNISDR Science and Technology Advisory Group. The partnerships that have been developed both for the Third UN World Conference on Disaster Risk Reduction in March 2015 and the UNISDR Science and Technology Conference in January 2016 are a core part of implementation of the Roadmap. The science and technology partnerships and initiatives help to complement and strengthen collaboration among the partners, within their respective mandates and expertise.

Formation of Science Technology Academia Stakeholder Group in Asia

In regional level in Asia, the Science Technology and Academia [STA] stakeholder group has been part of the ISDR Asia Partnership. The core area of interest and work of the group is to increase support for research and academia related to DRR to be encouraged, supported and

Sendai Framework Priority for Action	*Science and Technology Expected Outcomes*
1. Understanding Disaster Risk	1.1 Assess and update the current state of data, scientific and local and indigenous knowledge and technical expertise availability on disaster risks reduction and fill the gaps with new knowledge. 1.2 Synthesize, produce and disseminate scientific evidence in a timely and accessible manner that responds to the knowledge needs of policy-makers and practitioners. 1.3 Ensure that scientific data and information support are used in monitoring and reviewing progress towards disaster risk reduction and resilience building. 1.4 Build capacity to ensure that all sectors and countries have access to, understand and can use scientific information for better informed decision-making.
2. Strengthening Disaster Risk Governance to Manage Disaster Risk	2.1 Support a stronger involvement and use of science to inform policy- and decision-making within and across all sectors at all levels.
3. Investing in Disaster Risk Reduction for Resilience	3.1 Provide scientific evidence to enable decision-making of policy options for investment and development planning.
4. Enhancing Disaster Preparedness for Effective Response, and to "Build Back Better" in Recovery, Rehabilitation and Reconstruction	4.1 Identify and respond to the needs of policy- and decision-makers at all levels for scientific data and information to strengthen preparedness, response and to "Build Back Better" in Recovery, Rehabilitation and Reconstruction to reduce losses and impact on the most vulnerable communities and locations.

Fig. 6.2 : Science Technology Road Map for implementation of SFDRR.

implemented across all geographic levels. This should be done in an integrated fashion to support sustainable development, augment existing activities and mechanisms as well as support new activities that adopt a trans-disciplinary approach.

The 6th AMCDRR [Asian Ministerial Conference on Disaster Risk Reduction] in Bangkok, the voluntary commitment of the STA stakeholder group has identified following key objectives where STA can play important roles (AMCDRR, 2014):

- *Research*: Promote, prioritize and advance research on natural, social, engineering and technology aspects of disaster risk in an integrated environment; enhance team efforts in hazard and disaster monitoring and research, building on existing networks, universities and initiatives; and integrating various stakeholder needs on all levels.
- *Higher education*: Strongly promote multi disciplinary disaster risk reduction in university education as well as professional training. This will ensure human resource development in the DRR field.
- *Integration*: Ensure that disaster research programmes, policies, and applications are integrated across disciplines, and contribute to enhancing policy-making and capacity building for the effective DRR and sustainability.
- *Global Standards*: Develop and coordinate globally standardized open source information and data, event documentation and analysis procedures, guidelines and frameworks for integrated and effective disaster risk management and sustainable development.
- *Awareness*: Raise awareness of decision-makers and the public by promoting effective, integrated, demand-driven, evidence-based disaster risk initiatives and increased advocacy.
- *Increase Funding*: Motivate funding sources (public, private, humanitarian, development, scientific etc.) to allocate priority funding to address the urgent need for applied and basic integrated research on disaster risks.

The statement [AMCDRR, 2014] has also identified short, medium and long term priorities on number of universities providing higher education in the region, attempt to increase research funding from the countries, enhance the effectiveness of early warning system to reach the most needy people.

While there has been increasing interest among the science technology academia communities to be part of the national and/or regional process of disaster risk reduction [as evidenced from the HFA implementation], still there are remaining challenges to bring science into decision-making or policy-making at the national level, and implementation in the local level. Therefore, an advisory group, named "*Asia Science Technology Academia Advisory Group (ASTAAG)*" was formed in May 2015, and was approved in the ISDR Asia Partnership meeting in Bangkok in June 2015. The advisory group have eight members: *Peijung Shi (China: Chair), Rajib Shaw (Japan, Co-Chair), Vinod Sharma (India), Takako Izumi (Japan), Joy Pereira (Malaysia), Antonia Loyzaga (Philippines), Sugeng Triutomo (Indonesia),* and *Jamilur Choudhury (Bangladesh).* The key purpose was to bridge the gap between regional discussion to national and local policy-making, decision-making and implementation.

Principles

Technology does not necessarily means high-tech issues including the IT (information technology). It is required to recognize the local knowledge and traditional knowledge as well as local processes (*Process Technology*) to enhance local skills and actions. Technology has different meaning to definition. Kameda (2009) defines technology as "a set of rational means and knowledge pertinent to realizing specific objectives that have solid logical bases and stability". In a conventional recognition, technology meant just engineering products. But when we consider implementation strategies, technologies should involve not only products, but processes as well. This requires innovation of research community to reform from "product focused research" to "process oriented research", or "product-process linked research".

The basic principles in S-T involvements lie in: Innovations, Customization, Implementation, and Transparency.

- **Innovation** is the key of science and technology, for developing new tools, and methods of disaster risk reduction.
- **Customization** is another principle, which is required, keeping in mind the diversity of the Asia-Pacific region. The diverse socio-economic-cultural and disaster risk context need to be kept in mind while applying the S-T tools in different location and customize it.
- **Implementation:** There needs to be clear implementation focus of S-T tools, which links "the last mile" of knowledge to practice.
- **Transparency:** There needs to clear mandate of scientists and technical community to stick to the code of conduct of scientific research and will act with honesty, integrity, and transparency.

Strategy

The three key overlaying strategies of the advisory group would be:

- To enhance and strengthen capacities of the science technology academic communities in terms of disaster risk reduction.
- To assist the governments for science based decision-making to implement SFDRR.
- To enhance the networking for better utilization of scientific innovations and higher education.

In doing so, the following sub-strategies are formulated (Fig. 6.3).

1. Promote innovative research in DRR through new and multi disciplinary approaches: One of the key challenges lies in the capacity of innovation and research in different countries. The advisory group will try to promote and enhance the capacities of research and innovations on DRR in different Asian countries.

2. Promote university programmes of higher education to link and integrate DRR, and developed trained practitioners and researchers: To ensure proper education and training as well as quality control, the universities and research institutions have strong roles to play to generate qualified professionals in DRR by providing higher education and research facilities. Through development of the certificate courses and customized higher education courses, young professional development will be ensured, which is linked to the sustainability of the disaster preparedness activities in the targeted countries and communities. The advisory group will promote synergy and linkages of DRR in higher education in different countries.

3. Link STA institutions and networks internally and to the relevant governments and regional intergovernmental organizations: STA institutions need to be linked through networks to facilitate mutual exchange and sharing of research results, and academic collaboration, which will strengthen the implementation of SFDRR. This is required for sharing good practices, principles and methods beyond the national boundaries, and will serve the regional needs in the S-T role in DRR. Existing networks need to be strengthened in the region, and a synergy among different higher education and research networks is required.

4. Support countries implementing SFDRR through research outputs by providing science based sectoral and thematic guidance: The key of the SFDRR needs to be link of S-T into national government

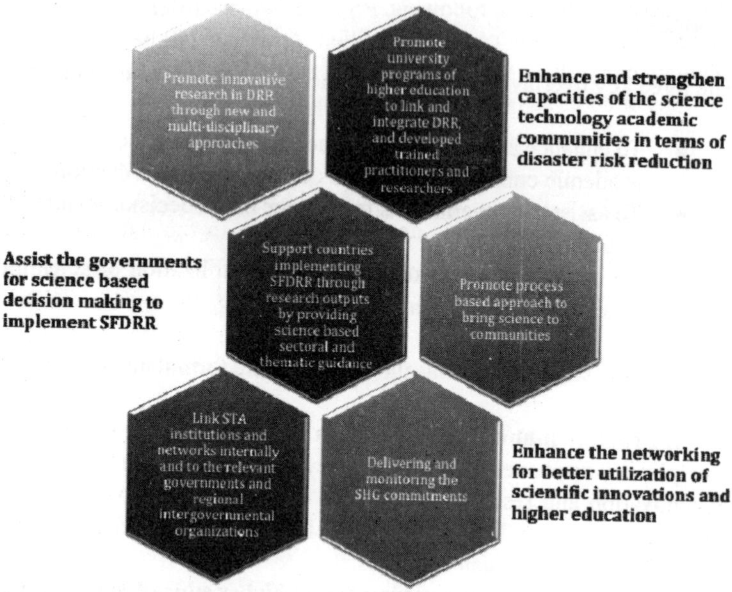

Fig. 6.3: Strategy of Science Technology Academia Advisory Group for Asia.

decision-making. This can be done through promoting scientific bodies/ academy/associations/institutions/individuals to the NDMO. This is required for all four priority areas, and level of interventions will vary depending on the status of governance and advancement of risk reduction approaches. The advisory group will encourage the national STA institutions and networks to provide science based advices to the respective countries.

5. Promote process based approach to bring science to communities: Similar to the national level, the needs are also to link science into policy in the local and community levels. The local government-local institutions linkage needs to be strengthened under the basic framework of the national disaster risk reduction strategy. This will ensure sustainability of the resources in the local level.

6. Delivering and monitoring the SHG commitments: The advisory group will also work closely with the STA stakeholder group for the delivery and monitoring of the commitments made in the AMCDRR.

Actions

Several potential actions, which the S-T Advisory Group for Asia Pacific will undertake, are as the following. Priorities will be different in different countries based on the country condition. A review will be made to the voluntary commitments of the 6th AMCDRR S-T stakeholder group, and revisions or additions will be made on the course of actions :

1. *Establish/Promote Science Technology National Focal Group*: Several countries have already S-T advisory groups, which needs to be re-focused or needs promotion in the national DRR priorities. Promotion will also ensure the focal group has enough resources both in terms of financial as well as technical. Policy advocacy and informed decision-making would be the key target of this group.
2. *Science Technology Advancement Index*: A composite indicator would be developed to measure the S-T progress in the Asia Pacific region, in terms of an index system. This will be linked to periodic monitoring, possibly coinciding with the SFA monitoring system.
3. *Science Technology Databases*: Disaster Reduction Hyper-base [DRH] is an existing database of different types of technologies in the field of disaster risk reduction. This database can be enhanced, updated and enlarged for wider usage.
4. *Professional development and higher education*: Several universities in Asian regions are promoting higher education as well as professional development programmes in DRR. Efforts will be made to link these initiatives and to ensure certain levels of quality control.
5. *Using social media to link S-T to actions*: Role of social media becomes important to disseminate knowledge and information of S-T and to break the digital divide. Proactive use of social media and/or SNS [Social Networking System] would be done to share knowledge and information.

Science Technology Indicators

To measure the impacts and progress of science and technology in disaster risk reduction, the ASTAAG has come out with 21 preliminary indicators (Fig. 6.4).

The measurement is based on three pillars of science policy action interactions: (1) science and technology in decision-making; (2) investment in science and technology; and (3) link of science and technology to people.

1. Science and Technology in decision making (8)	2. Investment in Science and Technology (6)	3. Link of Science and Technology to people (7)
1.1 Presence of Science and Technology advisory group to Disaster Risk Reduction (DRR) nodal ministry and/or related ministries. 1.2 Presence of Science and Technology group in DRR national platform. 1.3 Existence of inter-ministerial discussion/ dialogue on science related issues. 1.4 Implementation of risk, needs and damage assessment with involvement of Science and Technology group. 1.5 Existence of Early Warning system and mechanism with Science and Technology knowledge and tools. 1.6 Availability of disaster data/statistics on damage and impacts and its data collection mechanism. 1.7 Involvement of Science and Technology group in infrastructure design. 1.8 Scientific revision/updating of regulations, policies and guideline for DRR including building code, disaster response and preparedness plan etc.	2.1 Existence of grant support by the national government to researchers in disaster related topics that focus on Science and Technology. 2.2 Establishment of disaster related courses in higher-education. 2.3 Presence of national research institute and organization for disasters. 2.4 Investment/support by the national government in national/ international conferences and events on disasters for knowledge sharing. 2.5 Support to collaboration with academia and the private sector for developing innovative technical solutions. 2.6 Support to collaboration with academia and civil society for developing innovative social solutions.	3.1 Availability of a hazard map to people, developed based on scientific knowledge. 3.2 Scientific validation of indigenous knowledge. 3.3 Involvement of Science and Technology group in developing programme for evacuation drills. 3.4 Availability and participation of Science and Technology group in community discussion as facilitator or advisor/commentator. 3.5 Dissemination of science based early warning and forecast to people. 3.6 Involvement of Science and Technology group in developing disaster related education curriculum. 3.7 Existence of facilities such as museum and events such as expo to disseminate disaster knowledge and deepen. understanding on disasters among citizens.

Fig. 6.4 : Science Technology impact indicators (*Source*: ASTAAG).

	Attributes of Science and Technology to DRR	1	2	3	4	5
1	**Science and Technology in decision Making**					
1.1	Presence of Science and Technology advisory group to Disaster Risk Reduction (DRR) Nodal Ministry and/or related Ministries				■	
1.2	Presence of Science and Technology group in DRR national platform			■		
1.3	Existence of inter-ministerial discussion/dialogue on science related issues		■			
1.4	1.4 Implementation of risk, needs and damage assessment with involvement of Science and Technology group				■	
1.5	Existence of Early Warning system and mechanism with Science Technology knowledge and tools					■
1.6	Availability of disaster data/statistics on damage and impacts and its data collection mechanism			■		
1.7	Involvement of science and Technology group in infrastructure design			■		
1.8	1.8 Scientific revision/updating of regulations, policies and guideline for DRR including building code, disaster response and preparedness plan etc.				■	
2	**Investment in Science and Technology**					
2.1	Existence of grant support by the national government to research in disaster related topics that focus on Science and Technology			■		
2.2	Establishment of disaster related courses in higher-education			■		
2.3	Presence of national research institute and organization for disasters					
2.4	Investment/support by the national government in national/international conferences and events on disasters for knowledge sharing			■		
2.5	Support collaboration with academia and the private sector for developing innovative technical solutions		■			
2.6	Support to collaboration with academia and civil society for developing innovative social solutions		■			
3	**Link of Science and Technology to people**					
3.1	Availability of a hazard map to people, developed based on scientific knowledge			■		
3.2	Scientific validation of indigenous knowledge	■				
3.3	Involvement of Science and Technology group in developing programme for evacuation drills		■			
3.4	Availability and participation of Science and Technology group in community discussion as tacilitator or advisor/commentator			■		
3.5	Dissemination of science based early warning and forecast to people					■
3.6	Involvement of Science and Technology group in developing disaster related education curriculum				■	
3.7	Existence of facilities such as museum and events such as expo to disseminate disaster knowledge and deepen understanding on disaster among citizens		■			

Fig. 6.5: Science Technology preliminary evaluation for India (*Source*: ASTAAG).

	Attributes of Science and Technology to DRR	1	2	3	4	5
1	**Science and Technology in decision making**					
1.1	Presence of Science and Technology advisory group to Disaster Risk Reduction (DRR) Nodal Ministry and/or related ministries		■			
1.2	Presence of Science and Technology group in DRR national platform		■			
1.3	Existence of inter-ministerial discussion/dialogue on science related issues			■		
1.4	1.4 Implementation of risk, needs and damage assessment with involvement of Science and Technology group	■				
1.5	Existence of Early Warning system and mechanism with Science Technology knowledge and tools				■	
1.6	Availability of disaster data/statistics on damage and impacts and its data collection mechanism		■			
1.7	Involvement of science and Technology group in infrastructure design			■		
1.8	1.8 Scientific revision/updating of regulations, policies and guideline for DRR including building code, disaster response and preparedness plan etc.		■			
2	**Investment in Science and Technology**					
2.1	Existence of grant support by the national government to research in disaster related topics that focus on Science and Technology	■				
2.2	Establishment of disaster related courses in higher-education		■			
2.3	Presence of national research institute and organization for disasters		■			
2.4	Investment/support by the national government in national/international conferences and events on disasters for knowledge sharing			■		
2.5	Support collaboration with academia and the private sector for developing innovative technical solutions	■				
2.6	Support to collaboration with academia and civil society for developing innovative social solutions			■		
3	**Link of Science and Technology to people**					
3.1	Availability of a hazard map to people, developed based on scientific knowledge	■				
3.2	Scientific validation of indigenous knowledge	■				
3.3	Involvement of Science and Technology group in developing programme for evacuation drills		■			
3.4	Availability and participation of Science and Technology group in community discussion as tacilitator or advisor/commentator		■			
3.5	Dissemination of science based early warning and forecast to people			■		
3.6	Involvement of Science and Technology group in developing disaster related education curriculum		■			
3.7	Existence of facilities such as museum and events such as expo to disseminate disaster knowledge and deepen understanding on disaster among citizens			■		

Fig. 6.6: Science Technology preliminary evaluation Myanmar (*Source*: ASTAAG).

The indicators are evaluated in a qualitative scale of 1 to 5, 1 being the lowest, and 5 being the highest. A periodic evaluation will be made in different Asian countries using these indicators, and will be compiled as Science Technology Status Report of Asia. Fig. 6.5 shows the evaluation for India, while Fig. 6.6 shows the evaluation for Myanmar.

As exemplified in case of India, science technology in decision-making indicators have relatively higher scores while, there needs improvements in investment in science and technology, especially in private sector investment. For link of science and technology, the indicator shows mixed results. While science has been used for brining early warning system to people, the validation of local or indigenous knowledge needs more emphasis in future. In contrast to Indian case, the evaluation status of Myanmar shows relatively lower scores in most of the indicators, except the availability of science-based early warning system. Similar analysis is being made for other Asian countries, and it is hoped that these benchmarks would be used for future usage of science and technology for implementation of Sendai Framework for Disaster Risk Reduction.

Finally, as mentioned at the beginning, science has always been there for providing innovative solutions to disaster risk reduction. With the evolution of the field of disaster risk reduction, science needs have changed. With the new global frameworks in place for development, disaster risk reduction and climate change adaptation, more synergistic approach is required. The initiative mentioned above is the first step to make systematic efforts of bringing science into decision-making and bridging science policy people gap. This would need support from different stakeholders, including national, local governments, civil society, private sectors, media etc.

Acknowledgements

The author acknowledges the support of UNISDR Asia Pacific office and fellow ASTAAG members for the development and implementation of indicator system.

References

AMCDRR (2014): Statement of Voluntary Commitments of Asia Science, Technology and Academia Stakeholder Group for the 6th Asian Ministerial Conference for Disaster Risk Reduction, Annex. 10, Bangkok.

IDRC, (2014), Integrative disaster risk management: role of science technology and practice, *IDRC Davos Summary Report*, 16 pages.

Kameda, H. (2009), Implementation technology for disaster reduction, in Disaster Management: Global Challenges and Local Solutions, Shaw, R. and Krishnamurthy R., (eds.) 206-219, Hyderabad, India.

SFDRR, (2015), Sendai Framework for Disaster Risk Reduction, 2015-2030, 25 pages.

STAG (2015), Science is sued for disaster risk reduction: UN ISDR Science and Technology Advisory Group Report, 50 pages.

ST Statement (2015) Statement by the Scientific and Technological Community Major Group, Third World Conference on Disaster Risk Reduction, 14-18 March, 2015, Sendai.

Tokyo Statement, (2015), Tokyo Statement: Towards a new science and technology to consolidate disaster risk reduction and sustainable development, Science Council of Japan, UNISDR, IRDR and University of Tokyo.

UN, (1987), United Nations General Assembly Resolution A/RES/42/169.

UN, (1999), United Nations General Assembly 44th Session, Report of the Secretary General, A/54/132 - E/1999/80.

UNISDR, (2005), Hyogo Framework for Action 2005-2015: Building the resilience of nations and communities to disasters, 22 pages.

UNISDR, (2016), The Science and Technology Roadmap to Support the Implementation of the Sendai Framework for Disaster Risk Reduction 2015-2030.

7
Excellence and Partnerships in Disaster Research and Education

Anshu Sharma

Introduction

The concept of Centres of Excellence (CoE) is the current benchmark for excellence in imparting education and training, backed with research, in any discipline. The subject of disaster management is so inherently multi disciplinary that the concept needs to be further advanced to a network of such centres for delivery of quality education and training in the subject to be enabled. The quality of such an approach is characterised by the scope of its operations, mandates, funding, executive sponsorship, commitment, responsibilities and powers. It is an organization committed to be at the forefront of research, innovation and technical skills irrespective of its field of expertise. At present, different organizations have their own definition. However, in general, a Centre of Excellence is an institution that possesses special knowledge or expertise in a particular area "of concern and incorporated into collaborative environment to facilitate development of the products supporting (key) functions and operations". It is with this approach that this chapter discusses the operational systems of such centres and networks, towards building a network of this kind of India, the region and even globally.

A Centre of Excellence refers to a team, a shared facility or an entity that provides leadership, best practices, research, support or training for a focus area. The focus area can vary from a specific skill to a broad area of study. In academic institutions, a centre of excellence often refers to a team with a clear focus on a particular area of research. This may bring together faculty members from different disciplines and provide shared facilities.

A Centre of Excellence can also refer to a network of institutes and research/training centres/organizations that collaborate with each other in order to enrich the capacities of the officials and other functionaries of the state and district administration (in specific areas). It can also engage in capacity building for the enhancement of research and training/ education. Most Centres of Excellence run various kinds of graduate and post-graduate courses to impart knowledge and skills in a specific subject to practitioners in that area in order to improve their competence and to enhance the level of professionalism in that area of work in general.

In the case of CoEs for disaster management, excellence in service delivery would be achieved only when there is rigorous adherence to standards for quality research, training and education. In order to ensure excellence, qualified faculty, adequate equipment, infrastructure and updated course materials would be required. Close collaborations with national and international expertise and institutions are needed for teaching, research and resources.

***Vision and Objective*:** Different CoEs have their specific vision. The vision for CoE for DM is to advance the quality of knowledge, expertise and services in DM which makes a difference at the ground level in terms of ongoing DM practices, research and education.

The objective of establishing Centres of Excellence is to augment and strengthen qualitative capacities for disaster management through resource development. Research and Development activities at such centres enable the development of disaster mitigation and management strategies; the development of databases for rapid dissemination of information and knowledge experience sharing; and efficient deployment of quality training modules and trainers.

Types of CoEs

A CoE can be purely academic, technical, advanced technological group or a mix of these that delves deeper into teaching, training and research.

***Academic CoE*:** The scope of the academic CoE is narrow in some cases. A CoE though provides guidelines on how projects should be approached, not necessarily conducts all research activities by itself, such as modelling, development of a new technology or its deployment. There can be individual teams within the organization that can carry out such activities. The CoE looks at design and other aspects from a quality assurance perspective and might have enforcement powers in this regard. The CoE may also supervise the training and certification. Such a CoE develops over time. It may start with an informal group of experienced faculty and then gain its power with its long-term committed contribution in a specified field. The status gained over time also helps to get additional funding, which helps to expand its scope of operations.

***Technical** CoE:* A technical CoE has a broader scope than an academic CoE. This type of CoE has more funding and powers and is staffed as a full-time operation with dedicated resources. It has knowledgeable and experienced members from other parts of the organization including both the business and technical side of operations which also participate in the CoE activities. A CoE can be asked to select, deploy, and run the infrastructure for a certain period of time. This type of CoE is vested with wider powers of enforcement with regard to design decisions, best practices, quality control and testing approaches. In the field of DM, technical CoEs are close to national and state DM institutions which conduct research and training for specific disasters or emergency situations.

Advanced Technical CoE: The advanced technical CoE incorporates the activities and salient features characterised by the academic and technical CoE. What sets it apart is further responsibility to conduct research into new and moving technological trends for the growth of the institute. This type of CoE, apart from having wider scope, powers and funding, might play an influential role in funding decisions for new projects. In the field of DM, an advanced technical CoE would be one which is engaged in all aspects of disaster management.

There are some common characteristics which apply to all three types of CoEs identified above. A few specific characteristics particularly with reference to DM are as follows.

Expertise: The Centres of Excellence stand not just at the forefront of the knowledge domain, but also have high competency win other areas. With its core experts, highly specialised technicians, advanced equipment and resources, it drives innovation on an ongoing process at the national and international scale. It hires and trains professionals who are known for their work and gives them the opportunity to reach their potential through quality performance. CoEs for DM must either have hazard-specific, theme-specific or function-specific expertise. In the workshop, it was also noted that CoEs can also be built around individuals who are known for their work along a specific disaster or function, who could then play a key role in integrating knowledge around the specific task. This is the idea of 'transformational leadership' which led to the formation of ISRO in India.

Infrastructure: CoEs are also associated with quality infrastructure as expertise and people from diverse background and nations visit them to learn and collaborate. As CoEs conduct research on the forefront of knowledge, they need to have advanced labs (both physical and virtual) that bring the best minds together and ignite new ideas and innovative solutions. Overall, the CoEs are not just meant to serve as isolated units but need to work together to create a niche of excellence in any specific theme or function. This needs both fixed and flexible infrastructure to promote movement of people, ideas and functions over space and time.

Location: The location of a Centre of Excellence is an important characteristic as CoEs play an integrative role. Apart from CoEs at the national and state-level, the experts in the workshop were also of the view that there should be zonal and function-specific CoEs. Besides that, enthusiastic institutes should be encouraged and nominated to be CoEs, rather than imposing performance standards on unwilling and underperforming institutions.

Funding: The cost involved in establishing Centre of Excellence is likely to be enormous given the state of the existing institutions. As these institutions are committed to engage in quality and innovation, they require constant funding sources. In such cases, some funding has to essentially come from the government to promote their role and their existence in the future. Aside from this, a public-private partnership approach can be explored. Consultancies and other service delivery can invite performance based funding for these institutions.

Outreach: The outreach of a Centre of Excellence is another characteristic feature of such institutions. Unlike any other research, training and educational institutions, both the collaborative and impact area of a CoE is likely to go beyond a particular state, region or nation for its services.

Duration of operations: Another consideration is the CoEs duration of operations. A Centre of Excellence can be established with either a short-term tactical role spanning the duration of the main transformation effort with an evaluation of further roles thereafter. Or it can be established as a permanent body. The choice depends on the long-term view of the organization, funding outlook and cultural and political considerations. The CoE leaders might have to overcome obstacles such as scepticism and resistance to change among various team members. Usually, such institutions gain more powers and prominence depending on successful outcomes over time.

Functions

CoEs perform various characterising functions that may range from horizontal to vertical integration of knowledge and flow of information to achieve quality output in the domain of expertise. In the field of disaster management, a Centre of Excellence can play varied roles. Some of the key areas of their contribution may include, but are not limited to the following aspects:

1. Advance knowledge and expertise on different aspects of DM such as mitigation, preparedness, emergency response and recovery.
2. Enhance communications for effective DM on the ground across vertical and horizontal scales.
3. Transfer knowledge across local, state, national and global contexts to create new solutions.
4. Create of databases and expertise to be readily used.
5. Identify and document of best practices; and develop of local resources for their implementation.
6. Develop training modules for all levels and train master trainers.
7. Conduct research that is at the forefront of DM in India and create new pathways for further research and applications of the findings.
8. Play the role of an incubator – identifying and nurturing institutions that have the ability to be CoEs in long-term.
9. Serve as a platform for public policy consultation.
10. Maintain the standards in training and education by providing certificates for quality performance. They can also be turned into 'deemed universities'.

Needs and Priorities

India faces disasters almost every year and is ranked among one of the most vulnerable countries in the world. Even though investment in disaster management has grown significantly over time, it is found to be insufficient to reduce disasters on the ground and gaps have been noted on various fronts. These need to be identified, precisely measured and the gaps filled in the domain of knowledge, training and services to create actual impact. The need for Centres of Excellence can be broadly summed up in the following categories.

Capacity Building with Area and Hazard Specific Expertise

The National Disaster Management Plan 2016 identifies the need for capacity building. Resources for training are however limited in terms of faculty and training material, with particular reference to local context and situations. There is also an absence of coordinated response for the advancement of knowledge, skills and quality assurance of current trainings and education. Further research is needed to identify key gap areas and the strategies needed to fill these. In addition to many institutions which are providing capacity building, Centre of Excellences are also required to provide an overarching vision and goals for the advancement of training, knowledge and expertise in specialised areas. Apart from trainings, CoE can also help to enhance local awareness and to build human resources in terms of educators, researchers and professionals which can contribute to the disaster management at the local level.

While there are many institutions dealing with earthquakes, the same cannot be claimed for all hazards. India is exposed various hydrological, meteorological, geological and climate change hazards, which need to be assessed individually as well as collectively. Creating hazard-specific CoEs is an important requirement. Similarly, there is also a need to create area-specific CoEs, as adjoining areas are frequently exposed to similar hazards. Integrated research on different bio-climatic regions can help to build cost-effective and local solutions. They are also required to bring multiple stakeholders on to one platform for knowledge and capacity building.

Identification and Assessment of Local and Global Risks

While many research organizations are looking into local and global risks, the research is found to be fragmented in space and time. In view of expanding disaster risks in many Asian countries, there is a growing need to profile hazards and the associated exposure, vulnerability and risks to populations. Centres of Excellence could not only identify critical gap areas in research, but also place emphasis on the regular assessment of local and global risks; which could result in integrated solutions to create a low-risk environment. CoEs could offer services ranging from conducting risk assessments at various levels to building capacities of national agencies and universities to undertake such risk assessment. This could involve a multi disciplinary team of specialists and GIS/RS capacity for data presentation and analysis.

Documentation and Developing Research Agenda

Disaster management research in India has grown significantly. However, much of this is still uncoordinated and also not adequately documented. This has caused repetitive research in various domains of disaster management. There is thus a need for systematic cataloguing of research and identification of areas that can guide future research agendas. Centres of Excellence can fulfil this gap by documenting and creating an inventory of ongoing research and thus guide new knowledge based on the direction facilitated by the existing studies. For integrated disaster management research and comprehensive knowledge management at the national level, CoEs are required to encourage and define key priority areas. These centres may also be responsible for a National database for all disasters and DM related data.

Developing Advanced Methodology and Leading Innovations in Technical and Social Domains

In a developing country like India, which is facing several technical and social issues relating to development, innovation is a critical need to meet the demands and identify solutions to local problems. Centres of Excellence are seen as the key drivers of innovation in the field of research and training enhancing both knowledge and their practical implications. Due to an overarching view of research in a particular field of disaster management, CoEs are also able to develop new and advanced methodologies for application at the local level. This can lead to innovative solutions, which are both cost-effective and readily applicable in areas of urgent need. Apart from identifying such solutions, CoEs also can conduct research on their applicability, viability, any particular bias, as well as their impact and effectiveness in addressing local issues. CoEs are also able to integrate best practices not just across different subject fields, but also across different cultural contexts. They can provide a platform to integrate both indigenous and scientific knowledge. CoEs can contribute to the understanding of the impact of disaster management solutions in societal and environmental contexts and demonstrate the need for sustainable development. In the face of rapid urbanization and deforestation, such knowledge is essential.

Project and Process Management

Centres of Excellence can keep a track of ongoing projects along with studying the process of knowledge building. The engagement of a CoE in disaster management projects adds not just to the project's efficiency, but also to broader understanding of disaster management processes which is frequently ignored. Poor quality of research and training makes quality assurance a key priority for disaster management in India. As one of the main purposes of a CoE is the pursuit of excellence, it can help ensure quality in disaster management. A CoE can also play a key role in developing and applying ethical principles in the research and practice of disaster management. The disaster space is noted as one of the most abusive spaces in terms of violation of ethics. CoEs can develop risk management compliance rules and capability to monitor and manage these over time. In India many such risk compliances are either not developed or not maintained over time. CoEs can help to develop and scrutinise standards and facilitate understanding for various stakeholders.

Expert Guidance and Specialised Training for Disaster Management

The expertise available with the Centres of Excellence can offer both support and guidance for on-going research, innovation and training programmes in the field of DM. Each year, a large number of students and faculty pursue such research and education in disaster management. However, most of the time, this research is either repetitive or fails to meet international criteria due to lack of adequate supervision. Centres of Excellence could coordinate and set research agendas in which such university researchers could participate, learn, gain degrees and contribute to the gap in research in the real world. While there are many research centres, often researchers face challenges around data, technology and expertise on different disaster management issues. CoEs can facilitate all kinds of support for researchers which will help in fulfilling a two-way research agenda and goals.

International and National collaborations, Strategic Partnerships and Networks

Centres of Excellence are also required to build international and national collaborations particularly to promote quality research. This not just enhances the research participation, which is found to be low in the international context for India, but also enhances visibility and learning across cross-cultural contexts. CoEs provide a platform to interlink multiple stakeholders from different backgrounds. They can also invite other already available network or form new networks to facilitate knowledge exchange as well as collaborative activities for research and capacity building.

Efficient use of Funding for Research and Training

Centres of Excellence can also act as a centre for research and field-work relating to areas of particular significance in disaster management. At present, even though funding for disaster research is available, students or researchers needing funding are not fully aware of their access. CoEs could provide grants, scholarships and fellowships for disaster research which will promote action research in disaster management as well as engaging more students and researchers in the field. Similarly, funding for training can also be used efficiently with identified needs and specialised training for different stakeholders.

Knowledge Sharing and Communication

Communication across different levels of government, various stakeholders and the general public is an important need for efficient disaster management. A CoE can provide a common platform for both producer and consumer of research and training, which can bring awareness of disaster management to the ground level. On the one hand, these Centres of Excellence can act as facilitators of the advanced knowledge, providing a platform for regional or national conferences where various stakeholders can come and share their ideas. On the other hand, they can be a hub to translate, simplify and communicate actionable disaster management knowledge to the general public.

Policy Research, Formulation and Accomplishing Strategic Goals

Frequently in India, there is an inadequate research base to guide policy in different aspects of disaster management. This results in ineffectiveness of the policy at the ground level. Centres of Excellence could offer a platform to bring scientists and policy-makers onto one platform where decision-making is supported by the advanced knowledge available at the centre and networks of other institutions and expertise working in the field. They are also likely to have regional and local data sufficient to inform policy decisions. Further, these centres can also monitor and assess the impact of disaster management policies across states and their implications.

The Disaster Management Act (2005) and Disaster Management Policy specify many key strategic actions, which not just need in-depth research for implementation, but also for their relevance in the changing times. CoEs can help to accomplish strategic goals for research, education and response for disaster management.

Step-wise Approach to Establishing a CoE

There are numerous factors that need to be considered in the development of a Centre of Excellence. A step-wise approach may including evaluation of different criteria that characterises the Centre of Excellence and make it different from any other institute of disaster management engaged in training, research and education. It begins with defining the goal and strategy design to environment to set-up, organization design and so on. These steps are discussed below:

1. ***Goal design***: Two fundamental goals for an organization are efficiency and effectiveness. *Efficiency* is a primary focus on inputs, resource use and costs. *Effectiveness* is a focus on outputs, products, services and revenues. CoEs must ideally aim for both high efficiency and effectiveness. While this is more costly as compared to aiming for one, a balance between the two goals is necessary to help govern its sustainability. While a highly specialised expertise, state-of-art infrastructure and intricate national and international collaborations add to the efficiency of the CoE, the innovation and application of disaster management practices bringing national and local shift in disaster management and reducing vulnerability would mark their effectiveness.

2. ***Strategy design***: Strategy is the operation of organizational goals of efficiency and effectiveness, which again separate it from the rest of the organizations in the field. This must include exploration and exploitation. *Exploration* is the process of seeking new technologies or new ways of doing things and includes search, variation, risk-taking and innovation. *Exploitation*, on the other hand, is taking advantage of current or known technologies to do things in a new and novel way. It includes refinement, efficiency, selection and implementation. CoEs need to stand high on both, as they are committed to excellence and standing at the forefront of new research, technology and training. It is a dual strategy combining aspects of both a defender and a prospector. CoE in disaster

management has to take a balance approach in innovating new methodologies, solutions and services, and at the same time optimising the use of current resources and market positions. The analyser with innovation is both efficient and effective.

3. ***Environment***: Environment is everything outside the boundary of organization which can influence its performance including customers, competitors, suppliers, financial markets and the political systems. It plays an important role in organizational design as it creates both opportunities and limits. The environment of an organization can be classified based on the influencing factors of complexity and uncertainty.

In an environment of high *complexity*, more elements have to be monitored and the effects of change need to be estimated. In the case of high *uncertainty*, more plans have to be established and a higher degree of flexibility may be needed.

The four environmental conditions across the uncertainty and complexity dimension include calm, varied, locally stormy and turbulent. CoEs for disaster management and DRR fall into the turbulent environment category with high complexity and high unpredictability. There are many interdependent factors which are not predictable. It requires organizations to have a large and fast information-processing capacity so that they can choose alternate actions and make adjustments quickly. While their regular activity is to bring excellence to various DRR aspects, they are also required to take immediate action and make adjustments in case of sudden and new disasters. Uncertainty, which has always been an important component of disasters, is now being further enhanced by climate change. Additionally, there are multiple agencies involved in local development and actively engaged in increasing and decreasing vulnerability, it is very important for CoEs to make sense of this high level of complexity and uncertainty and design their solutions accordingly.

4. ***Organizational Design***: Organizational design for centre for excellence is likely to differ depending on the functional area. However, an important aspect of all organizational design is managing work across distances. Therefore, locating the organization in relation to optimal sourcing and local restiveness is important. *Optimal sourcing* refers to the decision to locate operations in a place that brings the greatest advantage in terms of customer contact, cost efficiency, human resource skill need or other objectives. *Local responsiveness* refers to the decision to distribute work in many locales *versus* consolidating work in one or a few centralized locations.

CoEs for disaster management and DRR are likely to be multi-domestic with a few being transnational such as SDMC. Multi-domestic CoEs take a decentralised approach to organise these centres. In context of India, these centres can be organised according to various criteria. This includes functional areas, geographic areas, geographic zones, thematic areas, hazards and ownership.

5. ***Task Design***: Task design is decomposing work into subtasks while considering the coordination among the subtasks to meet organizational goals. This can be categorised into the two important dimensions of repetitiveness and divisibility.

If a task is well defined and repeated again and again, then it has higher *repetitiveness*. This brings about greater standardization in execution and results in low uncertainty. On the other hand, when a bigger task is broken down into subtasks which require little coordination (i.e. the subtasks are independent), it has high *divisibility*.

The tasks design for CoEs are likely to range widely in this category.

6. ***People***: People or human resources is the basic determinant of the nature of any organization. This includes number of people and professionalization. The *number of people* is simply a count of all individuals in the organization. *Professionalization* is the collective skill level of the individuals and a measure of their capability for the work tasks at hand. Professionalization depends upon employees' education, training and experience (whether accumulated prior to or on the job).

CoEs would need a high level of professionalization, while the number of people would depend on the type of activity and location.

7. ***Leadership***: Leadership is one of the essential characteristics of a CoE. Leadership style is the predominant mode used by the top management of the organization to manage employees. Two dimensions used to analyse leadership style include preference for delegation and uncertainty avoidance.

Preference for delegation is the degree to which the top management encourages lower-level managers or other employees to make decisions about what and how work is to be done. This means the level of autonomy among lower-level managers and employees is high and decisions can be made without top-management approval.

Uncertainty avoidance is the degree to which the top management shuns taking actions or making choices that involve major risks. It is low if top management tend to be risk taking and high where top management is risk averse.

CoEs depend on innovation and stand at the forefront of new technology and research areas. Therefore, there needs to be more risk-taking and delegation of work.

8. ***Coordination***: Coordination systems support flexibility and adaptiveness within and across departmental and divisional boundaries. This includes formalization and centralization. *Formalization* is the degree to which the organization specifies a set of rules or codes to govern how work is done, who is to do it and under what circumstances or constraints. Formalisation is high if these rules are very detailed and consistently communicated to organizational members. It is low if there is not a set of strongly written or accepted rules or code of conduct. *Centralization* is the degree to which coordination and control are managed by a core person or level of the organization. Decentralization is the degree to which responsibility for coordination and control lies in the subunits of the firm and individual managers, rather than corporate headquarters or one specific level of hierarchy. Decentralized systems better accommodate diverse needs and allow more local responsibility.

The lack of coordination is one of the major criteria that brought forth the need for CoEs which can coordinate and direct ongoing DRR activities. Coordination is required not only within the centre, but also across the centres of excellence and other institutes actively engaged in similar fields. Therefore, the mosaic model can be seen as optimum for CoEs. Here, there is a greater tendency for heterogeneity rather than similarity of systems and the rules are not identical throughout the organization. However, there is a high degree of formalization.

9. ***Information Systems***: As compared to any other organization, information systems play a central role for CoE and therefore, it has been addressed separately. The term information systems is used in a broad sense that includes all systems that collect, store, and process information within the organization. The supplier of information may be located outside of the organization. The type of information system can be categorised along the two broad dimensions of amount of information and tacit nature of information.

Amount of information is the overall volume of data that an organization must collect, process, and store on a regular basis. To some extent it is a function of the size and domain of the organization. The second dimension is the *tacit nature of information* which is exchanged within the organization. Tacit knowledge is characterised by causal ambiguity and difficulty of codification. It is not readily articulated as a set of facts or rules and so is difficult to transfer. It is in contrast to explicit knowledge which can be expressed formally as a system of symbols and facts and therefore more readily communicated.

Event driven models presume low amount of information and low level of tacit information. They are designed to process information associated with specific occasions or results as they occur. They are reactive to needs as they arise.

Data driven systems are designed as the amount of information to be processed increases and system can no longer be based on reactive model and rather needs ongoing capture, analysis and transfer of vital information. It is appropriate for organizations that must process high volume of information and do so in systematic and intelligent manner.

People driven model is used by organizations that process highly tacit information that is relatively low in volume. It emphasises capture, processing and transfer of data that is embedded in the minds and action of people. It presumes that the vital information of the organization is difficult to codify in a routine way and therefore, the priority of systems should be either to bring people together face to face so that they can share tacit knowledge or to use computer or telecommunication based systems that readily support subtle, rich knowledge transfer. Meeting, conferences are also part of this knowledge transfer.

The most complex design is that of relationship driven model which has the greatest potential for promoting firm efficiency and effectiveness. It emphasises capture, processing and transfer of data that is embedded in the links or relationships, between people and data. This is an appropriate design if the overall amount of information to be processed is high and the tacit nature of information is high. It integrates hard (codified) data with soft (interpretational data) to yield rich results for organizational decision-making.

The information systems for CoE may range from data-driven to relationship driven depending on the focus of a particular centre on disaster management.

10. ***Incentives***: Incentives are the means or instruments designed to encourage certain actions or behaviour from employees. Apart from monetary rewards in the form of salaries, wages, and benefits, incentives also include praise, acceptance, belongingness, recognition or award for their services. These incentives can be strategically designed to bring new local solutions which help to promote a culture of disaster safety and awareness at different levels.

Incentives can be given to individual, centre or research cluster-based on their performance. Personal pay relates to the individual behaviour in the organization, which does not emphasise on results or outcomes, but depends on individual compliance with rules or directives. This includes conditions of the contract, maintaining integrity around time of work and holidays etc. Skill pay include pay differentials as per the skills or position-based and is most widely used in organizations which are often measured on the basis of formal education and seniority. Bonus-based incentive changes the focus from behaviour to results, i.e. from process to outcomes. For this organizational results can be mapped for accountability and bonus is paid on top of skill pay. On the other hand, profit-based sharing is group-based. It can be given to the outstanding results achieved by a particular group. People are rewarded on the basis of effective collaborations with others to yield high performance. For CoEs, the incentives can be both skill based and profit-sharing depending on the project creation and management over time.

11. ***Institutional set-up and Programme Design:*** CoEs can also be classified and established as per their prime purpose. This is likely to influence the number of faculty and nature of infrastructural resources along with programme details. In most administrative training institutes, curricular content is usually *ad hoc* and driven by limited faculty and resource persons, while universities dealing with disaster management need to have a full-fledged resources for theoretical and practical research along with faculty. The five broad classifications of CoEs for institutional set-up and programme design include research, training, education, data collection and monitoring and communication.

12. ***Certification***: At present certification is *ad hoc*, with some organizations giving certification-based on quality of performance in the trainings, some having no element of examination of quality of performance and some providing no certification for DM. Except for a few international case studies, there is no evidence of upward linkages, credit systems or cross-linkages in credit accrual, particularly in India. CoEs can play an important role in defining the criteria and standardizing the process of certification.

13. ***Quality Assurance and Accreditation***: Quality assurance and accreditation vary across the institutions engaged in disaster management training, research and education. Institutions providing short term training in non-educational institutions are mostly not accredited for their training courses. Universities have umbrella accreditations from their respective core sectors, and these by default apply to the disaster management courses and trainings. The accreditation of CoEs for DRR and disaster management, therefore, needs to be planned at different levels starting

with those with highly specialised services at the national level to ATIs, State Universities and Colleges providing education at the state-level; and skill based, vocational and polytechnic institutions offering applied DRR education to local people, masons and other first order workers at the district-level.

Partnership Structure for Collaborative Excellence

The CoEs are envisioned at National and State level to have an optimised use of local information, data and infrastructural resources. An important criterion to design CoEs is their ownership. This has been considered in order to introduce diversity in their maintenance and source of information. It will also increase partnership across various stakeholders, which can play an important role in exposing different areas of research and needs. It is suggested that the CoEs at various levels include government, private organizations, CoEs and civil society and academic institutions.

The factors for choosing a CoE include functional, geographic zones/ area, hazard and thematic expertise. This approach has been taken in order to best address the identified gaps and priority areas in disaster management. It also helps ensure that detailed subject-specific research can be consolidated into broader areas for cross-linkages, better sharing and usage at a policy level; as well as translated into actionable material for widespread dissemination to concerned stakeholders and communities. This outline is further detailed and suggestions of possible institutions are provided in the sections in Table 7.1.

Functional Areas

At the national level, CoEs are envisaged across the five core functional areas where gaps lie. These are expected to also help consolidate thematic, hazard and area based inputs from a more functional perspective. Such CoEs may help promote consistency and fulfilment of the core purpose.

Research and Education: One of the most important facets of CoEs is the conducting of research and academic information.

Training: As mentioned in earlier parts of this report, training at all levels is often *ad hoc* and insufficient. A CoE devoted primarily to coordinating training initiatives is necessary.

Policy and Advocacy: Though rarely seen as a separate functional area for CoEs, the policy and advocacy perspective will play a key role

Table 7.1: Design Criteria of CoE

<table>
<tr><td colspan="12">NATIONAL INSTITUTE OF DISASTER MANAGEMENT (NIDM) – Overall Coordinator</td></tr>
<tr><td colspan="12">NATIONAL LEVEL CoEs</td></tr>
<tr><td>Functional</td><td colspan="3">Education and Research</td><td colspan="2">Training</td><td colspan="2">Policy and advocacy</td><td colspan="2">Media</td><td colspan="2">Public Awareness</td></tr>
<tr><td colspan="12">STATE LEVEL CoEs</td></tr>
<tr><td>Zone / area</td><td>Arid</td><td>NE Hills</td><td>NW Hills</td><td>Coastal</td><td>Island</td><td>Urban</td><td>North</td><td>South</td><td>East</td><td>West</td><td>Central</td></tr>
<tr><td>Hazard</td><td colspan="2">Cyclone</td><td>Flood</td><td colspan="2">Drought</td><td colspan="2">Landslide</td><td colspan="2">Earthquake</td><td colspan="2">Tsunami</td></tr>
<tr><td rowspan="2">Thematic</td><td rowspan="2" colspan="2">Early warning and last mile connectivity</td><td rowspan="2">First response</td><td rowspan="2" colspan="2">Mainstreaming DRR into policy development</td><td rowspan="2" colspan="2">Public awareness and media</td><td colspan="4">Sector specific DRR plans and policies</td></tr>
<tr><td colspan="4">Health, Housing. Water and sanitation, Education, Rural Development, Public works, Telecommunication, Human settlements and Social welfare and inclusion</td></tr>
<tr><td colspan="12">STATE LEVEL CDMs (Providing basic research and serving as dissemination points)</td></tr>
<tr><td colspan="12">DISTRICT LEVEL EoCs (Providing ground inputs and documentation during peace time)</td></tr>
</table>

in the DRR sector in the years to come, especially as the impacts of climate stresses on day-to-day life intensify.

Public Awareness: The knowledge, ability and will of the general public to take action on DRR and during emergencies is one of the strongest determinants of the safety of the communities in question. Public awareness needs to be anchored in a civil society organization which is both respected and has significant reach across the country.

Media: The media plays a critical role in informing the public during disasters and in promoting risk reduction behaviour during non-disaster times. There is a critical need for future research on the roles of the media and for journalist training.

Hazards

India is exposed to a range of natural hazards and disasters. However, a few of them cause recurrent and mega disasters. It has thus become important to identify CoEs specific to different hazards, so that, the research can be directed to specific areas that need focused attention. The following categories have been noted to locate CoEs at the state-level:

- Cyclones
- Floods
- Landslides
- Earthquake
- Tsunami
- Drought

Geographic Areas and Zones

India is divided into various physiographic regions, the number of which varies on the basis of the criteria identified. The location of CoEs in different parts of India will ensure identification of local as well as national problems; along with solutions across administrative boundaries which often limit the free flow of information and resources. The geographical zones and areas to consider for CoEs include the following:

- Arid
- NE Hills
- NW Hills

- Coastal
- Island
- Urban
- North
- South
- East
- West
- Central

Thematic Areas

There are certain processes and issues which are closely linked with disaster occurrence, mitigation and response. While there are many institutions dealing with these processes, they do not necessarily focus on disasters. Locating CoEs for these specific areas can also help to bring new knowledge and expertise which can contribute to disaster mitigation and management. The following thematic areas are suitable around which to build CoEs in India:

- Early warning and last mile connectivity
- First response
- Mainstreaming DRR into policy development
- Public awareness and media
- Sector specific DRR plans and policies
  - Health
  - Housing
  - Water and sanitation
  - Education
  - Rural Development
  - Public works
  - Telecommunication
  - Human settlements
- Social welfare and inclusion
  - Other issues will need to be taken into consideration under this thematic focus that may form CoEs in themselves, but will need to be integrated into the thinking process. This includes issues such as fire and the training of fire servicemen.

Implementing Institutions

Centres of Disaster Management (CDMs) at the state-level and Emergency Operation Centres (EOCs) at the district-level can serve as supporting and implementing institutions. They can help both to document at the local level and present specific needs; as well as serve as dissemination points for information to the general public. In order to enable this, every district must have a functioning Emergency Operation Centre at all times.

Apart from individual research centres as centres of excellence for research in disaster management, research clusters should also be identified and developed based on location, ownership, focus on specific hazards and so on. Development of research clusters will help to generate quality infrastructure and may attract both national and international visitors and collaborators interested in particular area of research.

Partnership Model: Decentralised but Networked

One of the major roadblocks in the functioning of current CoEs is the lack of autonomy in decision-making. In order for innovation to thrive and fast decisions to be made, it is proposed that power be decentralised and CoEs be given freedom to run (within the established boundaries of the accreditation process). However, it is important that this decentralization does not translate into working in silos. Therefore, networking is an important component of the way the CoEs will function. Rather than a vertical hierarchy, these need to function more as horizontal partnerships, supporting and helping strengthen each other's work. In order to ensure that this is actually implemented, collaboration is a core component of the accreditation process.

Aside from the actual CoEs, there will be need to have resource institutions which form a part of this network to provide advice and expertise.

Public-private Partnerships (PPP)

A PPP approach should be adopted for the running and long-term development of CoEs. Not only is this important for long-term sustainability in terms of funding, but it can also help bring products and ideas into the mainstream market. In terms of broader change and adoption of innovative ideas on a large scale, involvement of private institutions will be necessary.

Outcome-based Approach

The fundamental research, training, policy advocacy, public awareness and media activities should not be judged on the basis of what has been carried out alone. Rather the impact or outcomes need to be monitored and evaluated to actually determine the value of the work. This is another component that must be built into re-accreditation schemes.

Action Research and Links to Academic Networks

The interface between science and governance requires research that is multidisciplinary, interdisciplinary and trans-disciplinary in approach (Pereira, *et al.,* 2010). Multidisciplinary approaches refer to the study of an issue from the perspective of several disciplines; with minor changes in methodology of individual disciplines (goal-oriented). Interdisciplinary approach involves the transfer of methodology from one discipline to another; at advanced levels leads to changes in epistemology. In trans-disciplinary approaches, there is simultaneous integration of knowledge from various disciplines and perspectives, involving various stakeholders. Researchers and practitioners create synergies, drawing on explicit, tacit and indigenous knowledge as well as inputs from stakeholders to develop various policy (regulatory, economic, voluntary etc.) communication and assessment tools. The goal is knowledge that is policy relevant, which facilitates informed decision-making at various levels (i.e. international, regional institutions, federal, state and local, organizational). Stakeholders include government, industry, investors, non-government organizations, community-based organizations, scientific organizations and professional bodies, among others. Peers in academia are also a stakeholder and they play a critical role in quality assurance for the research through the production of reviewed journals.

The Asian University Network of Environment and Disaster Risk Management (AUEDM) is a great example of this kind of collaboration. It brings together prominent Asian universities to share knowledge resources related to environment and disaster risk management; both amongst themselves and with the larger group of stakeholders working on these issues. AUEDM members work in close collaboration to conduct education and research, share findings and find ways forward in a region that is increasingly at threat due to climate change impacts. AUEDM also works closely with governments, international agencies and corporate and civil society organizations to establish collaborations that eventually lead to resilient communities. AUEDM reflects each member's commitment to implementation-oriented education and research in the field of environment and disaster risk reduction.

It has three main imperatives:

- ***Educational imperative***: To discuss the status and scope of environment and/or disaster management curriculum in the higher studies in each university. Each country has its own perspective. Some countries have full two years DRR master programme. Some universities have some modules of DRR in the post-graduate programmes. Therefore, the attempt is not to standardise the programme, but to learn and understand the process in DRR. The challenge is how effective the process can be customised into each context.
- ***Research imperative***: To discuss the possibility of climate change adaptation as the key entry point of collaborative research. Each country has a high prevalence of impacts of climate change being borne by the most vulnerable communities. Impacts are most visible on coastal, mountain, urban poor and migrant communities. Since adaptation is a relatively new subject, heavy investments need to be made in research on effective local adaptation as a means for coping with imminent climate change impacts and linked disasters.
- ***Network imperative***: To discuss the establishment of the Asian Universities network. While there are integral commonalities in the vulnerability context and the nature of impacts, the local setting and contextual nuances are highly varied across Asian countries. Networking is the only way to share knowledge and experiences, and to draw lessons based on principles derived from practices. The network is thus expected to go a long way in the development of a regional knowledge base, making it accessible for practitioners, and using it to influence the policy environment.

Conclusion

India is poised to make advances in all fields with its upward economic growth curve. This also places it in a position of vulnerability as its evolving assets get exposed to increasing risks. A big capacity gap that needs to be addressed is in the area of disaster management knowledge, skills and support systems. Establishment of appropriate thematic and geographic Centres of Excellence covering the multidisciplinary aspects of disaster management is an urgent requirement. These need to cover all anticipated hazards, all geo-climatic regions, and all stakeholders adequately to ensure a safe future for all.

The mainstreaming of disaster risk reduction approach, which has been talked about for quite some time, is possible only if there is capacity across all sectors to be able to understand, formulate programmes, and implement and manage them towards effective disaster management. Establishment of a network of Centres of Excellence in Disaster Risk Reduction that will operate in a coordinated and collaborative manner is the only way to deliver the capacity in the country to achieve this goal.

8
India's Quest for Freedom from Landslide Disasters

R.K. Bhandari

Introduction

Landslides are among the major hydro-geological hazards that affect large parts of India, especially the Himalayas, the north-eastern hill ranges, the Western Ghats, the Nilgiris, the Eastern Ghats and the Vindhyas, in that order. India's north-eastern region, the Darjeeling district of West Bengal, Sikkim, Tripura, Meghalaya, Assam, Nagaland and Arunachal Pradesh are all landslide-prone. Its landmass, which supports one-sixth of the world population, is badly bruised by landslide disasters.

Once upon a time, the Himalaya, which is now a home of landslides, touched the skies of our imagination with the scintillating charm of its natural dynamics. For centuries, its peaks lay unscaled and its hinterland remained locked in mystery. At that time, in the forbidding and awesome terrain of the Himalaya, a robust people did embellish their frugal lives with rich endowment of faith and respect for Nature. The Himalaya, and the other Indian mountain ranges, evoked wonder, praise and veneration. The precipices, the mountain peaks and fierce torrents gushing down to the deep valleys, though geologically active, seemed permanent and enduring.

Then came a time when human intervention started as adventure. Even whipping winds, fury of avalanches, bullet like fragments of shooting rocks, death traps of crevasses, not even the face of death could deter man from providing a thrilling display of skill and indomitable courage to match the mountains.

What started as adventure, however, eventually turned into greed, exploitation and violence galore. Today, the beauty of our mountains is charred with landslide scars as we remain busy building dams, roads, railways, tunnels, bridges and hydro-power plants, turning the blind eye to the bleeding wounds, environmental plundering and the fate of the generations still unborn. Yesterday's small slope failures are today's big landslides and many of them have the potential to hit us hard as major disasters.

In those golden days, landslide disasters in India were few and far between, and the people rarely talked about them. Even the professionals learned about them either by the word of mouth or through books. The subject was not taught in the colleges and universities in those years. Look at any catalogue of the Indian landslides including the scores of recent publications and you will invariably find less than one dozen major landslide events listed in the whole of the nineteenth century.[1] The NDMA publication of June 2009 mentions just about two or three major landslide events of 1867, 1880 and 1893 from Uttarakhand. Gohra landslide of October 1893 and those resulting from the floods in Birehi Ganga of the same year appear in most of the lists.

The landslide scenario, however, did change substantially in the twentieth century. The landslides have not only increased in frequency, magnitude and their devastating power but they have also become more complex to investigate, map and analyse, and far more difficult to control.

In fact, in the twenty-first century[2], the landslide scenarios have turned truly scary. Very often, within a single monsoon month, more than a dozen major landslide disasters get reported by the vigilant media from the different parts of the country. The irony is that even before the affected people recover, these very locations get hit again during the next monsoon season, making recovery even more difficult.

Today, the landslide problems we face are of a bewildering variety and of all types and description, spread across the country. We have a large stock of old landslides, growing in size and devastating power, faster than ever before because of the unprecedented levels of human interventions and shocking neglect of slopes. Landslides which had remained dormant for centuries and were nearly forgotten are now getting reactivated because of the abuse of lands, urbanization and construction. Monsoonal rains and extreme weather events are also adding to the stock of landslides. As the development plans get implemented with the business as usual, the landslide scenarios will be far more dreadful. Many fresh slides will get added, and the existing ones will get bigger.

Currently, India has no national mission for fighting war for freedom from landslide disasters. It is all a *pep talk!*

The Writing on the Wall

The writing on the wall is an idiomatic expression that points to a sure doom or misfortune in the offing. As India's development plans get rolled out, it will have more and more of townships, smart cities, roads, railway lines, tunnels, bridges, water resources projects and the associated multi-purpose infrastructure in disaster prone areas. If the past experience is any indicator, unless landslide risk mitigation measures are integrated with development planning, Indian landslide scenarios will look even more dreadful. This is the writing on the wall for all of us to read, and do something about.

Take for example, India's hill roads on its sensitive international borders. Although so critical for the country's defence, they remain highly vulnerable to landslides even in the normal times. Imagine our plight, especially during the periods of crisis on our borders, if landslides were to block the march of our army in league with extreme weather events and earthquakes. Some of our strategic roads become impassable when landslides get activated because of an earthquake trigger. In fact more damage was done by landslides during the Kashmir earthquake of 2005 as the earthquake-induced landslides hampered the rescue and relief operations. Similar was the experience during the Sikkim earthquake of 18 September, 2011. Major communication routes like the North Sikkim highway and the connecting roads, already known for their landslide history, were the hardest hit by the Sikkim earthquake, making disaster management there a daunting task.

India has plans to build about 28,000 km of road length by 2030 at a cost of over Rs. 500 billion along its borders with China and Pakistan and we cannot afford these to be blocked by landslides. Presently, CPWD and MoRTH have been entrusted with responsibilities of constructing roads in frontier areas. Are we sure on the strength of an independent peer-review, that enough care is being taken to ensure safe and environment friendly road alignments and constructions?

Many of our original pilgrim routes have been destroyed by landslides. Are we sure that the new routes will not meet with the same fate. In June 2013, the pilgrims to Kedarnath saw the ruins of the road *via* Gaurikund because of floods and landslides. The new route to Kailash Mansarovar *via* NathuLa is now open. The question as to how safe it is, given that the history of landslides in the area is older than the road itself. Even in recent years, NathuLa Changu road was hit by landslides because of the known landslide hotspots at 15th and the 17th mile. At the same location, in September 2012, a major landslide killed 4 people. Again, on 23 July, 2014, 130 people were evacuated by the Indian Army when two dozen vehicles got stranded on the road due to a landslide.

There are several landslides more than half a century old. For example, the Kaliasaur landslide at km 350.6 on the Rishikesh-Joshimath-Mana Road in Uttarakhand, has hit us more than 40 times since its inception in 1952. By neglect it is getting bigger by every monsoon season. Like Kaliasaur, the Sonapur landslide on NH44 in the Jaintia Hill district of Meghalaya was also a nightmare, but with its control, the problem is more or less behind us and the pace of development has quickened in the North-Eastern States, thanks to the Border Roads Organization.

India has a poor track record of finding science and technology-based solutions to its landslide problems despite its great experience of construction in difficult terrains. To counter future disasters, the question to be answered is whether we have any plans for introducing sound engineering practices to make construction safer, economical, speedier, durable, and more eco-friendly? We built Leh-Manali Highway, which ranks among the highest in the world, for development and defence needs, but not without taking away a part of safety back by creating the associated landslide problems and threats. The Chenab Bridge under construction (across deep Chenab, between Bakkal and Kauri in Jammu & Kashmir), ranks among the tallest rail bridges in the world, and would enhance mobility within the State and across, but only time will tell, whether the landslide risk reduction measures are integrated with its construction efficiently.

There are numerous scary mountain roads like: Kollmalai Ghat Road (46.7 km) on the eastern coast of Tamil Nadu with nearly 70 continuous hairpin bends; Keylong-Kishtwar road (233 km) in Himachal Pradesh and the road to ZoziLa in the Western Himalayan mountain range. Unless pro-actively and timely attended, the threats of landslide disasters will not only persist but grow bigger.

Let us not forget that while we are still grappling with the existing problems, the ongoing and proposed development projects are rapidly adding to their numbers. Landslides associated with our existing infrastructure, including railway routes such as the Kangra Valley Railway (1925); Darjeeling Himalayan Railway (1881) and Kalka-Shimla Railway (1898) will also be more problematic in the years to come.

By building the 8.8 km long Rohtang tunnel, ranked amongst the world's highest, we have created a lasting advantage by reducing the distance between Leh and Manali by as much as 46 km. On the negative side, we have affected the fragile ecology of the eastern Pir Panjal range and accentuated the threat of landslides. In many areas, existing infrastructure falls hugely short of need, calling for widening of the existing roads. In dealing with such problems of expansion, we need care of detail far above the standards of routine practice.

In the good old days, Disaster Management in India captured national imagination only because of famines[3] and threats of landslides were completely out of its Radar. What to speak of landslides, even the subject of disaster management did not find mention in any of the three lists in the 7th Schedule of the Constitution of India. The practice was to provide financial assistance to the State Governments for meeting expenditure on calamity relief. Every State had a calamity relief fund into which the annual assistance was credited and funds were utilized as per the guidelines issued by Union Finance Ministry. The approach to disaster management was fragmented inasmuch as the controls rested with individual ministries. For instance, the Ministry of Railways attended to the problems of landslides on its rail routes.

Thanks to the 73rd and 74th Constitutional Amendment Acts (1992 & 1993) which asked all States to promulgate their own new Acts or amend old ones by April 1994. The 73rd Amendment covered *inter alia*, land improvement, land reforms and soil conservation. The 12th Schedule of the 74th Constitutional Amendment Act of India defined 18 new tasks in the functional domain of local urban bodies which included urban planning and regulations of land-use. Subsequently, a chapter on Disaster Management got added into the Tenth Five Year Plan prepared by the Planning Commission of India. The successive Five Year Plans succeeded in capturing the national priorities in disaster mitigation and management.

The Malpa landslide tragedy of August 1998 proved to be a game changer. Management of Landslides was placed on the National agenda. Geological Survey of India was identified as the National Nodal Agency by the Home Ministry and a High Powered Committee on Disaster Management set-up in August 1999. Its scope was enlarged in April 2000 to cover man-made disasters. The HPC in its October 2001 report suggested that a separate ministry of disaster management may be created in a phased manner with appropriate instrumentalities. The HPC further recommended a Cabinet Committee on Disaster Management; an all party

National Council on Disaster Management, assisted by a Working Group. A National Institute of Disaster Management and a National Centre for Calamity Management were also recommended to assist in the operalization of the plans and procedures of the higher level bodies. A Cabinet Committee was envisioned to effectively manage cataclysmic events in the hour of a national crisis. There was no special focus on landslide disasters. The committee submitted its report in October 2000 with significant recommendations on landslide disaster mitigation. Unfortunately, the HPC report steadily got erased from our minds by the time the National Disaster Management Act was signed on the 23 December, 2005.

The National Disaster Management Authority (NDMA) took in hand the task of writing a fresh set of Guidelines on Mitigation of Landslides and Avalanches. It took 10 core group experts, 26 extended group experts, and 50 contributors almost three years and scores of meetings to write the Guidelines on Landslides which were finally released in June 2009 with an impressive set of recommendations. Seven years down the lane of memory, these Guidelines too have been forgotten in the sense that most of the projected work-plan in the NDMA Guidelines has remained either a non-starter or a part of work-in-progress, without committed deadlines to watch. Let us not forget that even "The finest of the plans are always ruined by the littleness of those who ought to carry them out, for the Emperors can actually do nothing".[4]

Geological Survey of India – the National Nodal Agency on Landslides

The Geological Survey of India (GSI) is the declared National Nodal Agency for landslides. The GSI has been involved in landslide and slope stability related studies since 1884. It started investigating landslides since 1950. Its mapping work which started in 1980 mainly on the basic and regional scale (1:50,000), got some stimulus with the declaration of the GSI as the national nodal agency for landslides since 2004.[5] A good part of the national effort has been made in developing regional and macro-scale landslide susceptibility zonation maps. By 2013, the GSI had already produced LSZ maps covering about 60,000 sq km of the landslide prone landmass, but these can rarely be updated.[6] These maps will be useful in macro-level planning only, provided (1) an approach is found to update the maps from time-to-time, despite the handicap of their being in the analog format; and (2) they are packaged to serve the felt needs of the end-users, and reliability check on these maps is exercised through peer-reviews.[7]

India has entered the digital world of mapping with the GSI's launching of National Landslide Susceptibility Mapping (NLSM) programme in 2014-15, and setting the landslide susceptibility mapping target of 4,20,000 sq km of area on 1:50,000 scale by 2020. Presently 70 GSI officials are engaged in this programme throughout India.[8] In Uttarakhand, by 2014, GSI has completed NLSM in 18,000 sq km of areas. Surprising the GSI does not have even a single Geotechnical engineer on its roll. The situation is akin to a team of doctors performing a surgery without a physician in the team.

A legitimate question that must be asked is why so much of continued thrust on the LSZ mapping for macro-level planning at a time when the country feels totally starved of the landslide hazard maps at scales of 1:10,000 and larger, and for site specific studies at scales on the order of 1:500 -1:1000? If our work stops at macro-scale Susceptibility Zonation mapping as the trend appears to be at this time, it will be an exercise of a limited value.

For meso-scale mapping, the GSI has recommended scales of 1:5,000 or 1:10,000[9] which are reasonable and deserve to be endorsed for adoption throughout India. Large scale landslide hazard mapping ought to be our national priority because we need such maps for meaningful local-specific landslide hazard assessment, risk analysis, mitigation and management. One highly visible example of the felt need is the safety of pilgrim routes which get frequently destroyed by landslide disasters.

The GSI attempted to address this need by the mapping of the landslide hazards on the Yamunotri, Gangotri, Badrinath, Kedarnath and Kailash Mansarovar pilgrimage routes. But the maps produced are at 1:50,000 scale, unsuitable for responding to the location-specific studies and problems.

Contributions of other Indian Institutions

Building Materials Technology Council of the Ministry of Urban Development was the first to produce an Atlas of Landslide Hazard Maps of India on a small scale. Similarly, the National Remote Sensing Centre (NRSC) of the Department of Space has published the Atlas of Landslide Hazard Zonation maps in two volumes as far back as 2001. It too includes pilgrim routes of Uttarakhand mapped at 1:25,000 scale which are limited utility in disaster management. Twelve years after the publication of the Atlas, in 2013, when the spate of landslides during the Kedarnath tragedy struck the pilgrim routes, the disaster managers were seemingly unaware of these maps.[10]

The macro-scale landslide susceptibility zonation maps of the pilgrim routes, completed years ago have not benefited their end-users so far. They remain isolated from the pool of new knowledge and experience gained from the studies of actual landslide events. The time has come to ensure that instead of continuing monotonically with macro-scale mapping of limited use, the attention would turn to the meso-scale and site specific hazard maps of limitless value. Our attention must also turn to making use of hazard mapping initially done for the restricted use only and ask the question why the restriction now when most of the information is already in the public domain? The Remote Sensing Application Centre of UP in 2003, upon completion of the LISMAP project (Landslide Information System and the techniques for Monitoring and Prediction of Landslides in the Sikkim Himalayas) published an Atlas on Terrain Information and Landslides of the Part of Sikkim. It is not known whether, in the last 12 years, this Atlas was ever updated and declassified.

Currently, many institutions in India are engaged on diverse aspects of landslide mitigation and management related studies, but there is no binding force, coordinated effort, and accountability to the nation. Under the National Disaster Management Act of 2005, we created National Institute of Disaster Management, *inter alia*, with the training mandate. It runs training programmes on landslide management but these are yet to be taken to the state-of-the-art level. There are a large number of institutions other than GSI who are also contributing in the area of landslide studies and mitigation. The CSIR laboratories like CRRI, CBRI, CMRI, SERC all work on landslides according to their own agenda, but there are hardly any joint initiatives at display. Like GSI, the institutions such as ISRO, NRSA, CSRE, WIHG, CBRI and CRRI are also engaged in hazard zonation mapping but country has yet to witness a unified approach to hazard mapping and the release of user-friendly time-tested hazard maps.

Universities, IITs, IISc and other educational institutions too occasionally get funded for landslide related research but the impact of their work is limited to project specific consultancies and advancement of knowledge.

Border Roads Organization battles hard against landslides and fixes them on their own initiative without much of a support from knowledge institutions.

The Proof of the Pudding is in the Eating

It is for the Government of India to examine, on the basis of its over 18 years of experience since the Malpa landslide tragedy, whether its plans to mitigate landslide disasters have made any difference on the ground. The performance of the nodal agency (GSI) over the period of years is out in the open and it needs to tell to the nation by self-assessment whether it has delivered? Does it have the vision, necessary plans and programmes, multi-disciplinary expertise, institutional capacity, resources and the operational freedom to be able to make a dent on the ground?

Just as the test of pudding is in the eating, the nation will judge the performance of the nodal agency by the number of disasters prevented, landslides fixed, lives saved, best practice examples established, human resource trained and sound engineering practices introduced. Before the disaster-torn nation begins to inquire about the fate of the promises previously made and the investigation reports filed without action, it will be wise to learn from the past experiences and use those very lessons in forward planning, capacity building and proof-testing of the institutional mechanisms. In any case, with the present levels of engagement of the GSI, the need for an autonomous centre is not diminished because the existing institutional mechanisms have fallen short of delivering, all these years, and their mere cosmetic reorganization or strengthening will not suffice. The need for an apex national institution for landslide management, accountable to the nation, can never be over-emphasized.

The Perils of the Status Quoist Approach

Despite the felt national need for a dedicated institution to manage landslides, and unimpressive performance levels of existing institutions over the period of many years, some of the existing institutions continue to believe that their mere strengthening with a national level centre of excellence established in one of these institutions may meet national needs and aspirations. The essentiality of multi disciplinary expertise in landslide studies and the destructive effects of urbanization, extreme weather events and the fragile eco-system have failed to capture the imagination of these institutions, chiefly working in their respective comfort zones.

The resistance to the proposal of creating a dedicated institution has often come with the argument that in a country of India's size and diversity with multi-institutional framework comprising a number of government and private organizations and academic institutes, the idea of a single dedicated agency will not work.

This status-quoist view has been countered by the recent national level round table meetings of experts organized by the Indian National Academy of Engineering in May and November 2015. It has been pointed out that, over the period of last two decades, despite the repeated national calls for synergistic action by our knowledge institutions, the team work, coordinated effort and accountability is rarely to be seen in the implementation of projects and programmes. The different institutions have their different mandates and priorities and there is already more than enough evidence on the ground to conclude that, merely repeating the same call for priming and refueling the existing institutions time and again will not bring about the much awaited transformational change in the work culture. Moreover, since, the work of different institutions is not governed by one holistic vision and identical end objectives, relying on merely strengthening of existing institutions seems to be an emphasis misplaced.

The Positive Fall Out of the Long Drawn Struggle

Although India's struggle for freedom from landslide disasters is both uneventful and unremarkable, it has repeatedly taught us many priceless lessons. It has taught us that landslide hazards may be natural but most of the landslide disasters are man-made and therefore, in a sense, our wounds are self-inflicted. These days, it has become a matter of routine to blame Nature for disasters. However, it is neither scientifically true nor morally right to call landslide disasters as natural calamities, and that too, even before an investigation starts. That the causative factors like extreme weather events, urban-sproll, non-engineered construction, illegal quarrying and mining, deforestation and such other non-natural factors have emerged as game changers, is a fact which can no longer be ignored. It is therefore unfortunate that, instead of investing our efforts in protecting slopes and predicting landslide disasters for stitch in time, we spend time in mastering the art of deflecting accountability, explaining away the events as natural calamities, and dousing the fire of the ensuing pain and suffering, by shedding crocodile tears. Let us not forget that "The most perfidious way of harming a cause consists of defending it deliberately with faulty arguments."[11]

And if we too are responsible in one-way or the other, why not we candidly admit so and mend our ways? In theory and speeches, we talk of zero tolerance against any careless wrong doings but in reality, do we have even the right kind of techno-legal environment in place to hold people accountable for their acts of omission and commission, and the political will to punish the guilty, strengthen dysfunctional institutional mechanisms and put our house in order?

It is in fact a sad story more of *forgetting* rather than *facing* landslides and *embracing* rather than *eliminating* landslide disasters. *"I shall revenge myself in the cruellest way you can imagine. I shall forget it"* is what John Steinbeck wrote in his novel *The Winter of Discontent.* We too have been doing exactly the same thing, despite the prolonged pain and suffering. Our silence between the two landslide tragedies is so deafening that, one wonders whether we have lost the faculty to remember.

With the business as usual, the future landslide scenarios will therefore be far more dreadful. In his novel, Steinbeck further writes that "*To be alive at all is to have scars*". We already have plenty of scars and can bear no more. Our struggle for *survival* must therefore become our struggle for *freedom* from landslide disasters. Rather than frittering away the limited resources on tinkering with the isolated landslide problems, we should strive hard to promote the culture of safety.

Our struggle against landslide disasters has been long drawn also because we have consistently failed to walk the talk. While we continue to speak of prediction and prevention, in practice, we attend to the landslides only after they occur. While we continue to map landslide hazards and print Atlases, in practice, our planners, architects, engineers, builders and disaster managers do not make use of the hazard maps because they are neither user-friendly nor field validated. For solving location-specific problems we need large scale hazard maps. In practice, most of our hazards mapping projects produce hazard maps at small scale not suitable for anticipating hazards and estimating risks. And imagine, if we cannot reliably anticipate the hazards before they strike, how can we ever prevent them from happening?

In the real world, we can be only as successful as our ability to foresee hazard scenarios and assess the corresponding levels of vulnerability and risk. Production of large scale, user-friendly and field validated landslide hazard maps for reliable risk assessment ought to be our highest priority. Such maps ought to be based on a nationally accepted common terminology, classification system and mapping methodology.

The landslide mismanagement in India is also because the professionals and decision-makers have failed to insist on scientifically tenable, intellectually uncompromising and morally satisfying DPRs, investigation reports and technical opinions. The career prospects of upcoming young professionals in India generally depend on the frequency of monographs, papers and reports they write and this is certainly one of the reasons that most literature on landslide studies read more like newspaper reports rather than in-depth scientific documentation. Similarly, professionals in departments and ministries also succumb to such temptations. In the process, the search for truth gets aborted prematurely, quantity over rides quality, culture of peer-review fades, trash gets published, intelligentsia gets marginalized and the wheels of progress keeps turning without any significant forward movement. Going by how the things have unfolded over the period of the last three decades, the score-card of the path-breaking contributions of professionals has been disappointing to dismal. Their contributions in policy formulation, national capacity building, raising standards of engineering interventions, giving fillip to multi disciplinary culture and building multi-institutional team work, leave much to be desired.

The experience has further taught us that the sloppiness in landslide management can largely be overcome by ensuring that there is no hiatus between our scientific and operating tempers. In the classroom, we preach that landslides can be prevented, predicted and controlled. Why then, we have not yet demonstrated by examples that by taking recourse to a systematic programme of geological and hydro-geological mapping, geotechnical investigation, instrumentation, monitoring and real time data analysis, a great majority of landslides can be predicted, prevented and controlled. India is still without best practice examples of landslide investigation, prediction, early warning, prevention and control.

If the modern science and technology has given us the power of permanently fixing major landslides in any situation, why hundreds of the well-known landslides keep killing people and yet they remain unattended for decades and we remain silent spectators?

Recipe for freedom from landslide disasters

For putting the house to order, all of us – the politicians, the bureaucrats, the scientists, the technocrats and the people at large will have to act as an organized *Team India* to wage a full scale war against landslide disasters. The primary responsibility in fighting this war is that of the government which must give to the nation, a strong political will, national vision, a sense of direction, functional and empowered institutions, and adequate funding.

India can boast of an impressive pool of highly qualified human resource, but that perception is illusory in this case because the great majority of the current pools of professionals have merely switched gears to also deal with landslides without science-based experience and specialized training. The expertise in different sub-disciplines related to landslide studies is scattered across numerous institutions which virtually act as islands of sporadic activity of their own choosing. India badly needs a cohesive binding force strong enough to galvanize *Team India* to lead the war against landslide disasters from the front.

The Indian National Academy of Engineering (INAE) took *suo moto* cognizance of the current ground realities and organized a round table meeting of landslide experts on 11 May, 2015 in New Delhi to address a variety of landslide related issues. The meeting concluded with a highly positive note that a pro-active-strategic and determined-approach, powered by a strong *political and administrative will,* we can put India back on the track to safety because, unlike earthquakes and tsunamis, most landslides are predictable, preventable, and controllable, if managed with appropriate interventions of S & T.

Of the various recommendations made at the round table, the most significant is the one seeking the establishment of an autonomous and empowered National Centre for Landslide Management for focused, coordinated and holistic attention to landslide management. Currently, many institutions in India are engaged in pursuing diverse aspects of the subject, but there is no visible excitement, binding force, coordinated effort, and accountability to the nation. Under the National Disaster Management Act of 2005, we created National Institute of Disaster Management. It, *inter alia*, runs training programmes on landslide management, way below the state-of-the-art level. It being the disaster mitigation face of India, now is the time for a SWOT analysis to know how much it has delivered, what difference it has made on the ground, and how it could be strengthened to measure up to its responsibilities?

There are large parts of our country in which hazards due to landslides co-exist with other hazards, like floods and earthquakes. In these multi-hazard areas, the landslide risk reduction plans will necessarily have to be subordinated to the multi-hazard risk reduction plans. Currently no such plans and strategy exists. If they do, they are insensitive to the multi-hazard reality. It is in this background that the round table has laid emphasis on preparation of short- (0-3 years), medium- (3-10 years) and long-term

(10-20 years) landslide management plans at the national, state and district-levels in the multi-hazard context, through multi disciplinary teams, within one year. Besides frontally addressing the present and the emerging challenges, providing strategies for coordinated action, and promoting sound engineering practices, the round table saw the need for a standing order to ensure regular updating, reaffirmation and re-notification of the various plans, in keeping with their dynamic nature.

One wonders why India, with such a rich pool of human resource, has resigned to the option of living with landslides, relying for so long on palliative and quick-fix approaches to landslide remediation. Paucity of funds, absence of delivery capacity, and urgency to deal with immediate landslide danger are generally being cited as the reasons. The capital intensive nature of permanent measures and unaffordability are the arguments often advanced to justify inaction. However, the truth is that the benefits of permanently fixing landslides far overweigh capital investments. It is with this thinking that a time-bound national programme for controlling all major landslides has been recommended with one-time funding by the Central Government. There is the need to ensure that the solution finally picked for adoption out of a plethora of technological possibilities, must necessarily pass through the process of comparative evaluation of all options, with the eco-friendly bias.

No matter what we do, the success will continue to elude us if we do not fortify landslide management by introducing innovative techno-legal and techno-financial practices. For all on-going and new development projects involving landslide risk management, the project construction and the corrective action for countering the construction-related, visible or anticipated slope failures and environmental damage before, during or after the construction stage, ought to be considered in design as its inseparable parts. This could be achieved by discontinuing the conventional practice of reflecting the costs of corrective actions as separate budget items, and by creating innovative techno-legal and techno-financial enabling environment. Adequate budget for the above purpose, including the maintenance costs, must be sanctioned as a package and all major landslide projects should pass through a mandatory peer-review by independent panels of experts.

The INAE round table, *inter alia*, unmasked the contentious link between the poor quality of Detailed Project Reports (DPRs) and the contractual disputes, and cost and time overruns. Ensuring eco-friendly and techno-economically sound DPRs was therefore considered critical to efficient project implementation. The need for accreditation of consultancy firms, capacity building of technical agencies within the Government, strengthening of the institutional arrangements for vetting and approvals of DPRs, a Third Party Inspection and audit, Disaster Impact Assessment of all major projects, and permitting mid-course modification of ongoing sanctioned works (to account for the new information exposed during investigation) was underscored.

The INAE round table meeting also recognized the need to establish strong communication between senior professionals, development planners and decision-makers for building teams and teamwork; create pace-setting best practices of community-centric early warning systems and accord the highest priority to R&D on topics such as earthquake-induced landslides, role of extreme weather events in landslide studies, approaches to landslide risk and damage assessment, development of innovative technologies for effective utilization of landslide debris and other wastes, and unfolding of fundamental mechanisms of the most problematic Indian landslides.

Credible and comprehensive documentation of landslides and landslide disasters should become part of our routine engineering practice. The emphasis stems from the fact that the universe of landslides is fascinating because *every inch of landslide exposed*, deepens our questions and further taxes our imagination. What a landslide reveals at its surface, if not explored deeper, may sometimes make us conclude at the expense of what is hidden, not-known, unseen or not-understood. Our ensuing research papers and study reports naturally reflect more of our own perceptions built on the pile of observations and past experience known for subconscious loyalty to the widely accepted trends and theories. In many cases, vital field evidences get erased even before landslide investigations begin and facts get lost until they resurface in some other landslide at some other time and location. Many landslide case-records published after due process of scholarly studies and debate go seldom challenged because *the publications appear scholarly at their face value.* The need to write credible monographs is therefore critical.

Concluding Remarks

If the *Team India* forges ahead with a visionary plan, clock, compass and a deep sense of commitment, the freedom from landslide disasters will come. Broadly speaking, our approach must shift from mere problem solving to establishing the culture of safety against landslides. The best way to sum-up the recommendations is to repeat Antoine de Saint

Exupéry's words: *"If you want to build a ship, don't drum up men to collect wood and do not assign them tasks and work, but rather teach them to long for the endless immensity of the sea."*

Anais Nin reminds us of the *"day which came when the risk to remain tight in the bud was more painful than the risk it took to blossom."* Indeed it is becoming more painful for us to remain in the discomfort zone of our inactions and it is time to wriggle out of it and let the culture of safety blossom.

Notes

1. The number will change, if unreported events also get included.
2. Which started on 1 January, 2001.
3. The Bengal famine of 1943 was perhaps the worst ever of this subcontinent in the last Century. According to one report, nearly 3 million people perished in one year.
4. Bertolt Brecht in Mother Courage, 1939.
5. MoM's letter No.11 [5]2004-M.I dated 29th January, 2004. The Gazette notification came much later.
6. E-mail from Dr. Saibal Ghosh of the GSI to INAE.
7. GSI has conveyed in its correspondence with the INAE that the methodology of their landslide hazard mapping has been internationally peer-reviewed when the papers were published in journals of repute. A distinction is however necessary between peer-review of finally delivered, validated and certified maps using a particular methodology and the peer-review of the methodology itself.
8. It will be of educational value for other knowledge institutions to get a feedback from the GSI on the progress made and the difficulties experienced in this new initiative during the current year 2015-16.
9. Draft SOP proposed by the GSI.
10. Central Building Research Institute has informed that the copies of Atlas were distributed to all the District Administrators of the Uttarakhand State. But mere distribution of maps and spreading of awareness are two different things.
11. Friedrich Nietzsche.

References

Bhandari, R.K., (2013) "Challenges of devastating Indian landslides". Guest Editorial, *Journal of Current Science*, Volume 105, No. 5, 10th September Issue.

Bhandari, R.K., (2014) *Disaster Management in India – The urgency of fresh thinking*. Published by the Vivekananda International Foundation on 28 August.

Bhandari, R.K., (2015) "Indian National Agenda for Landslide disaster mitigation– Challenges and Recommendations." *Journal of Current Science,* Volume 109, No.5, 10 October.

INAE, (2015) *Proceedings of the Round Table Meetings on Landslide Disasters*, Volumes 1 and 2.

9
Learnings from Large-Scale Housing Reconstruction Following the Sikkim Earthquake of 2011

Sandeep Tambe, Sarika Pradhan and *Pema Donka*

Introduction

In the wake of the increasing frequency and intensity of disasters in the country like the Gujarat earthquake 2001, Indian ocean tsunami 2004, Jammu & Kashmir earthquake 2005, Bihar floods 2008, cyclone Phalin 2008, cyclone Aila 2009, Leh cloud burst 2010, Sikkim earthquake 2011, Uttarakhand flood and landslides 2013, Srinagar flood 2014 and Chennai flood 2015, governments are increasingly having to relook at the effectiveness of their preparedness and post-disaster response mechanism. Over the years, the disaster management paradigm has grown beyond disaster relief to disaster preparedness, vulnerability reduction and building back better. The post-disaster restoration projects are taken up after the rescue, relief and temporary restoration works are completed, and eventually play a significant role in securing the lives of the victims. While providing emergency rescue and relief is critical, post-disaster reconstruction to improve the living conditions of the affected communities when media attention has waned, needs to be addressed effectively as well. There is a need to better understand the strategic interventions that can aid community recovery after a disaster (Jordan & Javernick-Will, 2014).

Post-earthquake reconstruction in developing countries comprises of rebuilding the community infrastructure like roads, bridges, schools, hospitals, irrigation offices etc., and reconstruction of the damaged houses.

Urban reconstruction is much more complex, since suitable relocations sites which maintain the socio-cultural and livelihood linkages are not easily available. Comparatively, rural reconstruction largely happens *in situ*, where these issues normally do not crop up. In developing countries, where victims in rural areas do not have house insurance, the onus is largely on the government to provide the houses (Hidayat & Engbu, 2010). Consequently, 30-50 per cent of the post-disaster financial allocation is on housing reconstruction (Freeman, 2004). In terms of the nature and scale of the work, reconstruction is an unchartered territory and most implementing agencies need to climb a steep learning curve (Silva, 2010).

The Indian response to post-disaster reconstruction and the outcomes achieved have been diverse (Barenstein & Iyengar, 2010). A Contractor Driven Approach (CDA) was adopted following the Latur earthquake of 1993 and resulted in serious drawbacks. Post the Gujarat earthquake of 2001, the Owner Driven Approach (ODA) was adopted with technical support from the government agencies resulting in lasting owner satisfaction and was much acclaimed. Following the Indian ocean tsunami of 2004, Tamil Nadu outsourced the construction to NGOs most of whom opted for the Contractor Driven Approach (CDA). This reconstruction did not take into account the culture of the fishing communities, resulting

Fig. 9.1: During the earthquake, the stone masonry walls laid on mud mortar collapsed, thereby compromising the house.

in significantly lower owner satisfaction levels. In the Jammu & Kashmir earthquake of 2005, Cash Transfer Approach (CTA) to the owners was adopted which is often not adequate to rebuild technically sound and safe houses. Following the floods of 2013, the Uttarakhand Government assisted by the world bank adopted an Owner Driven Approach (ODA) with facilitation by NGO. Global experiences have shown that the ODA has resulted in faster construction with higher owner satisfaction (Hidayat & Engbu, 2010; Shilderman, 2010; Ophiyandri 2013).

Sikkim Earthquake

Sikkim was hit by a 6.9 magnitude earthquake of intensity VII on 18th September, 2011 which triggered hundreds of boulder falls and landslides, causing extensive damage to public and private infrastructure (Martha, Govindharaj & Kumar, 2015). A post-earthquake assessment by Tambe, Kumar, Arrawatia and Ganeriwala (2012) found that in rural areas, the superstructure of these wooden framed houses with *ekra* walling and light iron sheet roof was mostly intact, while the stone masonry load-bearing walls laid on mud-mortar and not having reinforcement suffered maximum damage. The traditional house is typically a two-storied structure with a light *ekra* (wooden frame with bamboo infill) or wooden walling and plastered with mud or cement plaster on thick stone masonry walls. Generally, these stone masonry walls are of undressed stones laid in mud mortar with height up to 2m above the plinth. The light weight sloping roof is made of Corrugated Galvanized Iron (CGI) sheets having rafters and purlins made of wood. While the top floor is normally used for residential purposes, the ground floor is generally used to keep cattle or as a store-house. While the upper storey comprising of wooden framed structure with bamboo walling and a light iron-sheet roof was found to be mostly intact, the ground storey stone masonry walls with mud mortar performed poorly. These stone masonry walls suffered widespread damage thereby compromising the structure above. Private houses with RC-frame structure and iron-sheet roof performed well, showing only non-structural damage. However, damage to structures was disproportionate to the observed intensity of shaking, primarily due to poor compliance with seismic codes, inferior quality of raw-materials and shoddy workmanship (Rai, *et al.*, 2012). Consequently, half of the 92,000 rural houses in the state suffered various degrees of damage, but there were only a few deaths due to these houses, highlighting their inherent earthquake safe character.

Objectives

Reconstruction experiences are not well documented and this study aims to bridge this gap by focusing on the applied aspects of post-earthquake house reconstruction in rural areas. We provide a practitioner's account of how the reconstruction planning was done post the Sikkim Earthquake of 18th September, 2011 during the period 2011-2016. We took-up this study in action research mode focusing on three main questions – what are the key decisions during the planning phase, what are the main challenges faced during execution and what are the lessons learnt. While answering these questions, the options available and strategy adopted during the planning stage, common pitfalls in execution as well as the key learnings are also discussed.

Methodology

This study was undertaken as an action research on a post-earthquake reconstruction project wherein the authors had full management authority over the project. This study provides a unique insider's view on what worked and what did not and the adaptive action taken to solve the operational problems. Independence of the study and research bias was avoided by delinking the planning, implementation and evaluation functions. The authors were part of the planning and evaluation aspects, while the implementation was carried out by the sub-state teams. The evolving policy framework was documented from the various circulars, notifications and administrative orders available at www.sikkimrmdd.gov.in. Progress reports were also accessed from this online MIS and from the reports provided by the sub-state teams. This study documents the process adopted for reconstruction which will be specially relevant to mountain states. Learnings from this project will benefit other reconstruction initiatives to take informed decisions and execute and complete their projects effectively.

Findings

Key Decisions in the Planning Stage

Designing a housing reconstruction project involves taking certain key decisions related to planning the reconstruction, institutional strategy, financing strategy, beneficiary identification strategy, house design strategy and procurement strategy. These decisions along with the execution capabilities eventually determine the reconstruction outcomes.

Planning Reconstruction

In post-disaster situations, widespread public distress, media glare and impending adverse weather conditions override the value of comprehensive project planning, risk assessment and adequate resource allocation. The immense pressure to start reconstruction on the ground, results in planning steps being cut, inadequate detailing in the technical design and operational procedures not getting prescribed. Consequently, the reconstruction plan is prepared by not following standard planning procedures (Yourdon, 2004). The seeds of failure of projects are often sown during the flawed planning phase itself (Pinto, 2013). Limited experience and institutional memory of managing projects and logistics of this scale makes the reconstruction planning process even more vulnerable. Following the Sikkim earthquake, the Reconstruction of Earthquake Damaged Rural Houses (REDRH) project was conceived by the Rural Management and Development Department, Government of Sikkim (RMDD). This project was launched in March 2012 with the philosophy of *Build Back Better*. Both in terms of the number of houses to be rebuilt as well as the budget, this was the single largest project ever implemented in the state. The RMDD had earlier launched the Chief Minister's Rural Housing Mission (CMRHM), in which a grant of Rs. 4 lakh was provided to the poor residing in *katcha* houses. This experience enabled the RMDD to quickly conceive and plan the reconstruction project duly incorporating earthquake resistant features in the CMRHM house design.

Institutional strategy

The approach to post-disaster reconstruction of houses are diverse and include Instant Prefabricated Housing (IPH), Departmental Construction Approach (DCA), Contractor Driven Approach (CDA), Joint Approach of Department and Owner (JADO) which is similar to the Owner Driven Approach (ODA) and the Cash Transfer Approach (CTA) as indicated in Fig. 9.2. The institutional strategy involves deciding on the implementation approach as well as the support agency who will provide technical support to the masons and home-owners. Considering the vulnerability of the earthquake victims who had lost their houses, a policy decision was taken to take-up the reconstruction in DCA mode. No support agency was shortlisted for this purpose and the existing staff of RMDD were given this function.

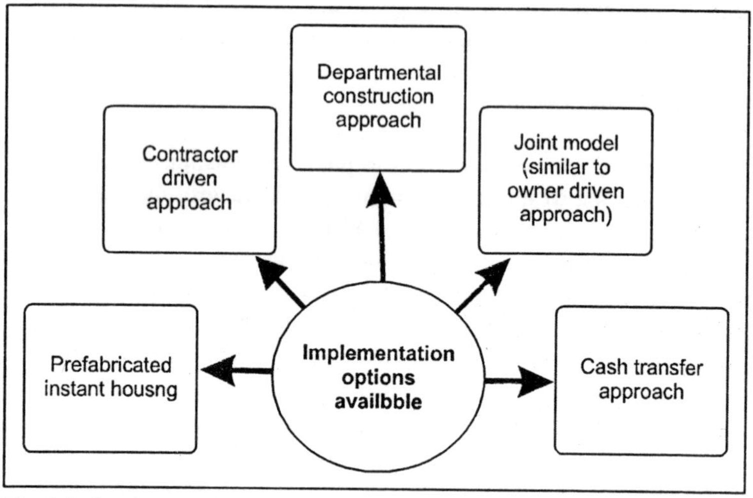

Fig. 9.2 : Implementation options available for post-disaster reconstruction.

Financing Strategy

In this project of the estimated cost of Rs. 6 lakh, the grant component was fixed at Rs. 4.89 lakh ($ 7,500) to rebuild the damaged houses. This quantum of support provided in other disasters for house reconstruction was Rs. 65,000 in Bihar (2008), Rs. 2 lakh in Ladakh (2010), Rs. 5 lakh (with assistance from the World Bank) in Uttarakhand (2013) and Rs. 1 lakh in Srinagar (2014). This sizeable grant enabled the State Government to have a larger say in integrating disaster resistant design in the reconstruction process. Had it been a smaller grant, the role of the State Government would have been limited to co-financing and providing technical advisories and trainings. Based on the unit grant of Rs. 4.89 lakh, a total budget to Rs. 389.83 crore ($ 60 million) was sanctioned, which comprised a sizeable 39 per cent of the total central allocation of Rs. 1,000 crore ($ 154 million). This project funded under the Prime Minister's National Relief Fund from the Planning Commission, Government of India is the single largest project in the history of the state.

Innovative Steps to Reduce Costs

Since, full funding support was not provided; various innovative steps were taken to reduce the cost of construction as listed below:

(a) ***Exemptions on construction material from tax, cess, commission and transport supervision*:** Exemptions of VAT (12.5% for cement and 4% for TMT bars), environment cess (1%), transport supervision charges and commission of the government procurement agencies (1%) were obtained. This resulted in a savings to the tune of Rs. 40,000 per house.

(b) ***Royalty on forest produce*** such as stone, sand and timber was exempted.

(c) ***Stock material strategy*:** The strategy of centralized material purchase directly from manufacturers with decentralized management through block-level stores was adopted. Sizeable transportation costs were saved by decentralizing material storage from the two central stores by creating 29 new block-level stores. Obtaining these exemptions was possible, due to this centralized purchase directly from the manufacturers.

(d) ***Cluster approach*:** Economy of scale was attempted by taking up house construction in clusters of ten so that supervision by master mason, reuse of shuttering material, supply of stock material could be clubbed together.

Beneficiary Identification Strategy

Ex-gratia payments were released to the house owners to take up temporary repairs immediately after the earthquake. These payments ranged from Rs. 5,000 to Rs. 30,000 depending on the type of house (*katcha* or *pucca*) and the extent of damage (minor, major, severe, full). Adequate field verification prior to releasing *ex-gratia* relief was not feasible, as rescue and relief operations were also in full swing. For the purpose of reconstructing the fully and severely damaged houses, this *ex-gratia* beneficiary list was cross-checked and a three-stage prioritization criteria was framed to prioritize the poor households. This criteria comprising of automatic exclusion, automatic inclusion and ranking was exercised in a special *gram sabha*. Households where the main house was not damaged but only the kitchen, cattle shed or toilet was damaged or where more than one adult beneficiary was linked to the same damaged house or where the household owned a *pucca* house in addition to the damaged house or where any member of the household was a regular government employee were automatically excluded. Following automatic exclusion, the landless households, or those whose main source of income is agriculture or labour work or the vulnerable or poor households were included automatically. The remaining households were prioritized based on the intensity of poverty and vulnerability.

House Design Strategy

During the initial deliberations on the project, there was a demand from the civil society organizations to promote traditional house design using locally available construction material specially bamboo. However, this idea did not meet the aspirations of people, who aspired for concrete houses and also considered traditional houses as *katcha*. Accordingly, building on the success of the CMRHM model, a four-roomed RC frame house with earthquake resistant features was designed with the following core specifications:

(a) ***Size***: Total floor area should not be less than 56.20 m^2 (605 sq. feet).
(b) ***RC frame structure***: With nine columns, plinth beam, roof beam and sill beam.
(c) ***Columns and beams*** with cross-section of 0.3m × 0.3m, with sill beam of 0.15 m × 0.15 m.
(d) ***Rings*** of 8 mm dia with the ends bent at 135 degrees and a spacing of 8 cm near the joints.
(e) ***Walls***: brick walling over RC frame or traditional ekra (wooden frame with bamboo infill) panels.
(f) ***Flooring***: cement concrete.
(g) ***Roofing***: RCC Slab 0.1m thick or CGI sheet sloping roof.
(h) ***Sanitation***: toilet along with septic tank.

This design of the house which incorporated earthquake-resistant features was communicated using a mason training handbook with comic-book style, illustrations.

Core Design Concept

Instead of the usual, top-down, one-size-fit-all model for housing reconstruction, the project provided the option to the homeowner to choose the house type appropriate to their lifestyle, family size and budget. Beyond the core house, flexible design options were permitted. Flexibility was provided to the home-owner by providing the following options:

(a) ***Toilet and kitchen was permitted outside the house***: This is as per the prevalent traditional practice, as many households use firewood for cooking; and toilets are not perceived as hygienic inside the house.

(b) ***Plinth area option in two storeys*****:** Few cases came to light where the households owned less than 56m^2 of land. In these cases, the plinth area was compensated by building rooms on the second floor. The design of this two storied house with new design was technically vetted to ensure that it was earthquake resistant and prior administrative approval of the district-level committee was also taken.

(c) ***Internal partition of ekra material*****:** The transportation and head load costs of bricks especially for houses located away from the road head was quite substantial and was not adequately accounted

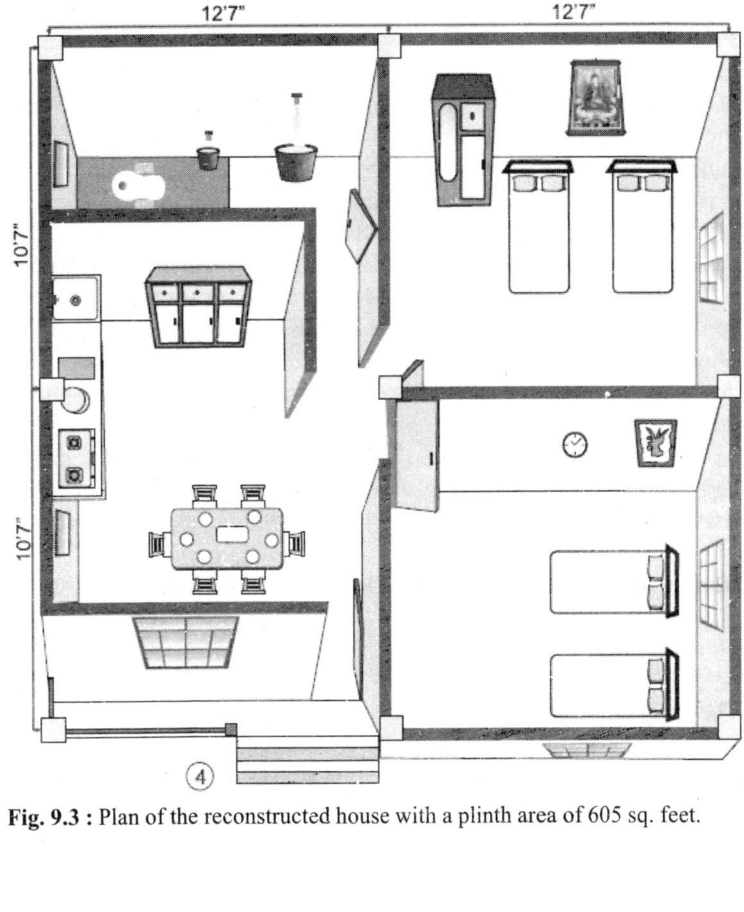

Fig. 9.3 : Plan of the reconstructed house with a plinth area of 605 sq. feet.

for in the standard unit cost estimate. Hence, the internal partition of the house was permitted to be made of *ekra* material (wooden frame with bamboo infill).

(d) ***CGI roof option in select remote areas***: Option of CGI sheet roof was permitted for beneficiaries in select remote areas in all the districts to save on transportation costs with prior approval of the district-level committee.

(e) ***Advisory to the beneficiary:*** Advisory was given to the beneficiary indicating that the foundation of the house has been designed for maximum two storeys, with the second storey having CGI sheet roof. Any modification in the design involving slab roof on the second storey or subsequent storeys would need corresponding modification in the foundation and supporting reinforcement.

Procurement Strategy

Quality construction material like cement and steel which was not available locally, was purchased by the project from the manufacturers at concessional prices and provided to the block-level stores from where it was issued directly to the beneficiaries. This resulted in significant cost savings and also provided easy access to quality construction material for the home-owners. For each house, stock material in the form of 300 bags of cement and 26 quintals of TMT Bars was provided. Funds and construction material was provided in four instalments, with checks on progress and construction quality. Providing the right material, in the desired quantity, at the right time, without any leakages was accomplished largely due to efficient public delivery systems of centralized purchase and decentralized management. The implementation steps were simplified and prescribed by preparing various guidelines available at http://www.sikkimrmdd.gov.in/pdfs/Circulars/REDRHCircularsList.aspx.

Main Challenges and Common Pitfalls in Execution

Slow Progress

The philosophy of *Build Back Better* was the guiding principle for this project. The project started in the departmental construction mode, wherein the department took the responsibility to construct the house for the beneficiary. Since, the department did not have the necessary staffing and capacity to directly implement a project of this magnitude, adopting this model resulted in a slow start. Also, there was reluctance on part of the sub-state teams to take the plunge as only partial costs for house construction was provided (Rs. 4.89 of Rs. 6 lakh). Consequently, construction of only 1,500 houses was taken up in the first year. In order to accelerate the construction, the joint model was started in the second year, wherein the stock material (cement and steel) was procured by the department, while the house construction was taken up by the owner. This mode was termed as *joint* since the core house design, building standards, construction material (cement and steel), technical supervision and co-financing capital was provided by the project, while the home-owners undertook the actual construction, procured local construction material (stone, sand, timber etc.), arranged for mason and labour and also added their own finances. This model resulted in an additional 5,000 houses taken up for construction. However, the supply of stock material could not keep pace with this rising demand, resulting in many houses getting stalled. Hence, for the remaining 1,400 houses, the self-purchase model was approved, where the total house construction including procurement of stock material was to be done by the owner. In both the joint and self-purchase models, the funds were provided directly to the owner in instalments after reaching pre-defined milestones. The shift from departmental model to joint and self-purchase resulted in a greater participation and buy-in from the owners and also accelerated the pace of construction (Table 9.1). A comparative analysis of these implementation models is shown in Table 9.2.

Stalled Houses

Since only partial cost (i.e. Rs. 4.89 lakh of the total Rs. 6 lakh) was provided, instances where the beneficiary was very poor or where the house location was remote, the house construction either did not start or was suspended after starting. In order to give a push to these stalled houses, additional funding support was provided to the 500 suspended houses from the MGNREGA Programme, Ministry of Rural Development (MoRD). Also, an in-kind grant of 30 cubic feet of timber per household from the Forest Department was provided to the 100 suspended houses. For the landless, convergence with the land-bank scheme of the State Government was initiated to provide title to 0.25 acre of land.

Table 9.1: Diverse implementation models and the resulting pace of construction

Year	*Implementation Approach*	*Plinth Completed*	*House Completed*
March 2012	Project initiated with departmental model	—	—
March 2013	Slow progress of departmental model, hence joint model also enabled	1,229	55
March 2014	Good progress of joint model, however material supplies could not keep pace, hence self-purchase model also provided	6,228	1,398
March 2015	All three models — departmental, joint and self-purchase in operation. For stalled houses, additional support in convergence mode provided	7,604	4,087
March 2016	Project nearing completion	7,875	6,200

Table 9.2: Comparative analysis of various implementation models

Parameter	*Prefabricated house*	*Contractor driven*	*Department driven*	*Joint model (similar to owner driven)*	*Cash transfer approach*
Cost incurred	Medium	Highest as includes profit motive	Moderate as no profit motive	Least as savings in bulk purchase of construction material	Low
Speed	Fastest	Fast	Slow	Medium	Medium
Design	Standard and rigid	Standard and rigid	Standard and rigid	Responsive to site conditions	Responsive to site conditions
Quality	Poor	Medium	Patchy	Best	Poor
Risks involved	Long term performance not known	Quality issues in remote locations	Slow pace due to less staff	Funds diverted by 2% households, timely supply of construction material	Diversion of funds, quality of construction
Option of owner co-financing	Disabled	Disabled	Disabled	Enabled	Enabled
Owner satisfaction	Low	Patchy	Patchy	High	Patchy

Irregular Supply of Construction Material

As the number of houses increased under the joint model, the supply of construction material (steel and cement) could not keep pace with this rising demand. Since, the construction material was to be provided by the department, the owners had no other option as they could not purchase it from the local market. Soon, the construction pace dropped, and the houses got stalled due to want of construction material. Hence, for the leftover houses, self-purchase model was approved, which helped in accelerating the pace of construction, as the home-owners procured the construction material on their own.

Capacity Building

The construction capacity of the RMDD is to the tune of 2,000 houses per year which was already saturated under the ongoing CMRHM programme. The REDRH project resulted in an additional target of 7,972 houses to be delivered in three years using the existing public service delivery mechanism which was already strained. The following steps were taken to counter these challenges:

(a) ***Trainings of technical staff***: The AE/JEs were trained in the technical aspects of house construction and management of stock material at the block-level stores in various training workshops. Also the "mason training handbook" was prepared to simplify the technical aspects of house construction. This handbook was prepared in illustrated comic-book style and also translated into the local language.

(b) ***Trainings of accounts staff and store keepers*** to maintain accounts and manage stock material was also conducted.

(c) ***Uniform record keeping***: Record keeping at district, block and block-level stores was simplified by providing pre-printed registers and trainings were also conducted.

(d) ***Trainings for the masons*** was organized in all the blocks resulting in knowledge upgradation of nearly 200 engineers and 1,000 masons. These training programmes were organized in partnership with IIT Delhi under the Rural Housing Knowledge Network (RHKN) initiative of MoRD.

Fig. 9.4 : Record keeping at the block-level in prescribed registers being verified in a record keeping training workshop.

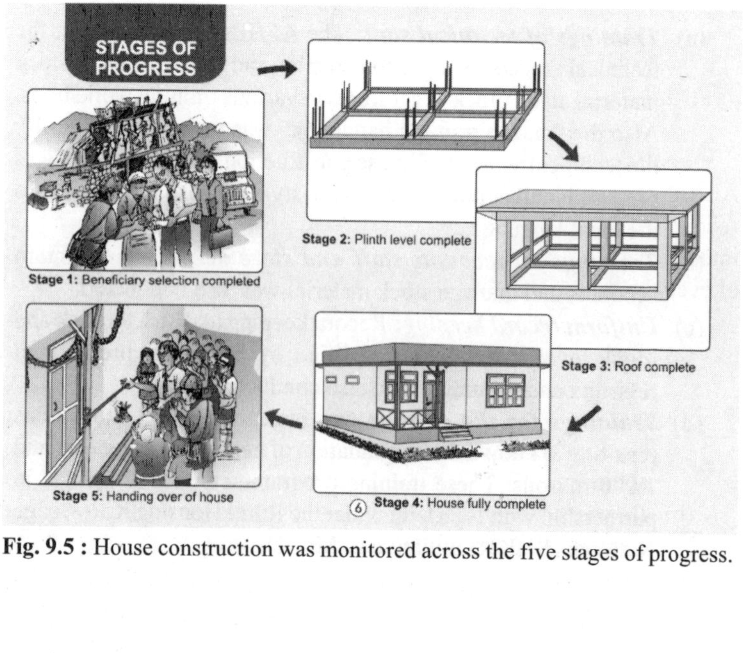

Fig. 9.5 : House construction was monitored across the five stages of progress.

Fig. 9.6: During the Planning Phase, The Procedures Need to be Prescribed and The Technical Elements Simplified and Explained in Visual Form.

Tracking Every House

Since each house is a separate entity, it had to be monitored individually. Also, the construction material passed through three stages and had to be reconciled at the manufacturer, store and beneficiary-level. Hence, intensive tracking systems were put in place to monitor the construction of every house:

(a) ***Stage-wise progress monitoring*** was done after completing the pre-determined stages of construction, i.e. plinth level, roof level and house completed. Release of financial grants and issue of stock material was made contingent on the physical progress achieved.

(b) ***District level monitoring*** was carried out by the district-level committee headed by the district collector.

(c) ***Web based MIS*:** A web based MIS - www.sikkimrmdd.gov.in was developed jointly with the Department of Information Technology with modules such as beneficiary details, drill down physical progress, e-stores, circulars and gallery.

What are the Lessons Learnt?

Managing this project over five years, resulted in several key learnings which can benefit other post-disaster reconstruction projects as listed below:

(a) ***Financing strategy***: The government assumed a larger role in project planning, execution and monitoring. Consequently, the project took-up functions related to house design, provisioning of quality construction material, record keeping, web-based MIS, mason trainings etc.

(b) ***Procurement strategy***: Centralized procurement and decentralized management through block-level stores and issuing the construction material directly to the beneficiaries resulted in several benefits. One, it speeded-up the construction as the beneficiary was saved the hassle of procuring the construction material. Secondly, bulk procurement of raw-material brought in economies of scale and various exemptions could be availed resulting in sizeable cost savings which were passed on to the beneficiaries. However, timely supply and reconciliation became an issue severely hampering the progress forcing a shift to the self-procurement mode for those houses where the construction had not yet started. In hindsight, instead of depending on the State Government mandated procurement agencies, it would have been better if the RMDD had procured the construction material directly from the manufacturers.

(c) ***House design strategy***: Ease in implementation and quick results should not be the basis for selection of the construction technology. Instead, beneficiary satisfaction, quality living standards and long term sustainability need to be the prime concern. After the earthquake, many firms offered the technology option of instant pre-fabricated houses that could be assembled in a few days. However, long term socio-cultural and environmental viability of this technology was not tried and tested in the Sikkim context, and hence was not adopted though it was easy and quick to implement. The CMRHM project had shown high levels of owner satisfaction with the RC frame houses, and the same design was adopted after adding earthquake resistant features.

(d) ***The core design concept*** with possibilities of free combinations became popular as it could meet the varied demands of the

Fig. 9.7 : Completing the houses in remote locations required higher co-funding from the owners and/or additional funding support using convergence approaches.

households. Beyond the core design, other design features such as type of in-fill material, location of kitchen and toilet, CGI sheet roofing etc. was kept flexible and this provided the home-owners with the option to choose the house type matching with their lifestyle, aspirations, family size and budget. Houses made from local materials using traditional technology, e.g. *ekra* (woven bamboo splits within wooden frame) with a light, sloping CGI sheet roof are eco-friendly and safe. However, many of these houses got damaged in the earthquake as the stone masonry load-bearing walls laid on mud mortar and not having reinforcement suffered maximum damage. Also, these traditional houses do not live up to community aspirations, who prefer RC frame houses. For remote areas, carriage of construction material like cement and steel proved prohibitively expensive. In these areas, improved "ekra" having RC foundation would have provided a more economical and feasible option.

(e) ***Implementation strategy***: In the ***joint*** approach, the construction material and the financial grants were provided directly to the beneficiary in phases and resulted in fast and quality construction with highest owner satisfaction. However, as the timely supply of construction material could not be assured, the self-purchase approach had to be resorted to where the total grant was released to the beneficiary in instalments who procured the construction material as well. With increasing frequency of extreme weather events, the preparedness of governments in managing post-disaster reconstruction is being severely tested. In this context, the Sikkim model of participatory reconstruction can be customized and used by other agencies in future. Providing construction material, financial assistance and technical support directly to the beneficiaries, coupled with good record keeping and an updated web-based MIS resulted in high transparency and intense involvement of the beneficiaries.

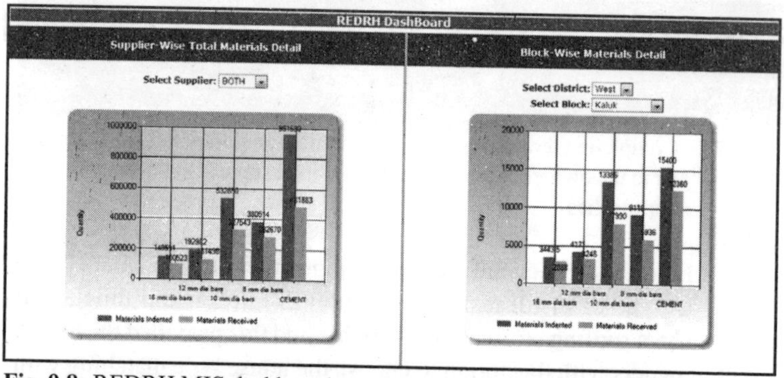

Fig. 9.8: REDRH MIS dashboard.

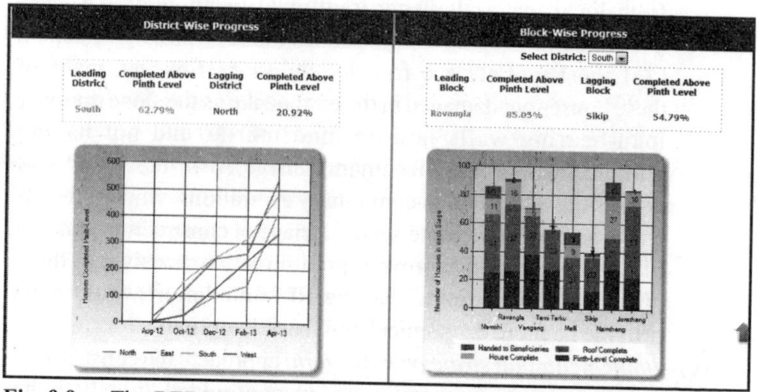

Fig. 9.9: The REDRH MIS dashboard comprising of analytical, drill down reports and visuals helped to monitor the project closely.

Fig. 9.10: A reconstructed house getting the final touches for the house-warming party.

(f) ***Beneficiary identification strategy*:** Allowing for fresh beneficiary identification with detailed field verification and community involvement brought in transparency and openness in the selection process. Various deficiencies in the earlier beneficiary list also came to light. In hindsight, photographs of the damaged house along with the beneficiary highlighting the extent of damage should have been insisted upon, as it would have served as a strong evidence on the basis of entitlement. This opportunity was lost, as the damaged house was subsequently dismantled.

(g) ***Convergence strategy for providing additional funding to the stalled houses*:** About 2 per cent of the houses remained incomplete due to diversion of the construction funds to meet other emergent needs, fresh natural calamities affecting the under-construction houses, very poor households not able to invest any money or the location of the house being very remote needing sizeable additional transportation costs. Additional financial assistance in convergence with the rural development programmes is needed to complete these stalled houses.

(h) ***Capacity building strategy*:** The project aimed to upgrade the skills in earthquake resistant construction by training the masons who are the providers of building technology at the local level. Building the capacity of masons and providing them with simple training material is vital to bring about a permanent change in the construction practices.

Conclusions

To conclude, the outcomes of a reconstruction project are usually measured in terms of the number of houses built, but following the principle of *build back better*, the outcomes can be better quantified using a four pronged criteria quantified by Build Change (2013) of safer houses built, better builders developed, number of trained engineers and empowered home owners as detailed below:

- ***Safer houses*** is the number of new houses with improved living environment for the residents because of the projects inputs. Out of the target of 7,972 houses, a total of 7,000 houses have been completed, with the remaining under active construction and slated for completion by March-2017.
- ***Better builders*** is the number of builders and contractors who were trained and were involved in the earthquake resistant construction practices. A total of 1,000 masons and their assistants received hand-on training under this project and were actively involved in the earthquake resistant house construction.
- ***Trained engineers*** includes local engineers, architects and other construction professionals employed and mentored by the

Fig. 9.11: In tourist destinations, home owners invested wisely to model the new house as a lodge to link with the village tourism enterprise.

RMDD. More than 300 engineers got trained in earthquake resistant house construction techniques.

- ***Empowered home-owners*** includes home-owners who were involved in driving the process of house construction. About 7,000 home-owners comprising of 35,000 individuals were empowered by the home-owner driven construction strategy.

It is hoped that these learnings from the devastating Sikkim earthquake 2011 will add to the growing body of literature on post-disaster reconstruction and reduce the learning curve for other agencies and governments.

References

Barenstein, J. D., & Iyengar, S., (2010) India: From a culture of housing to a philosophy of reconstruction. *Building Back Better, 163.*

Build Change, Haiti Post-Earthquake Housing Reconstruction Programme. (2013) available link at http://www.buildchange.org/locations/haiti/(accessed on 15th April, 2016).

Freeman, P. K., (2004) Allocation of post-disaster reconstruction financing to housing. *Building Research & Information* 32.5 (2004): 427-437.

Hidayat, B., & Egbu, C.O., (2010) A literature review of the role of project management in post-disaster reconstruction. In *Procs 26th Annual ARCOM Conference* (2010), (pp. 1269-1278). Association of Researchers in Construction Management.

Jordan, E. & Javernick-Will, A. (2014) Successes and Failures of the Post-Tsunami Housing Reconstruction Programme in Tamil Nadu, India. *American Society of Civil Engineering* (ASCE), 1199-1208.

Martha, T. R., Govindharaj, K. B., & Kumar, K.V., (2015), Damage and geological assessment of the 18 September 2011 M w 6.9 earthquake in Sikkim, India using very high resolution satellite data. *Geoscience Frontiers,* 6(6), 6793-805.

Ophiyandri, T., Amaratunga, D., Pathirage, C., & Keraminiyage, K., (2013), Critical success factors for community-based post-disaster housing reconstruction projects in the pre-construction stage in Indonesia, *International Journal of Disaster Resilience in the Built Environment*, 4(2), 236-249.

Pinto, J. K., (2013) Lies, damned lies, and project plans: Recurring human errors that can ruin the project planning process. *Business Horizons*, *56*(5): 643-653.

Rai, D. C., Mondal, G., Singhal, V., Parool, N., Pradhan, T., & Mitra, K., (2012)

Reconnaissance report of the M6. 9 Sikkim (India – Nepal border) earthquake of 18 September, 2011. *Geomatics, Natural Hazards and Risk*, 3(2), 99-111.

Schilderman, T., (2010) "Putting people at the centre of reconstruction." *In Building Back Better*, edited by Michal Lyons, Theo Schilderman and Camillo Boano, Practical Action, London South Bank University, and International Federation of Red Cross and Red Crescent Societies, U.K.

Silva, J. D., (2010) Lessons from Aceh. *Key Considerations in Post-Disaster Reconstruction.*

Tambe, S., Kumar, R., Arrawatia, M.L. & Ganeriwala, A. (2012). How safe are our rural structures? Lessons from the Sikkim Earthquake 2011. *Current Science*, Vol. 102(10): pp. 1392-1397. 25 May, 2012.

Yourdon, E., (2004) Death March (2nd edition), Upper Saddle river, NJ, Prentice Hall.

10

Nepal Earthquake 2015: Lateral Analysis Factoring Vulnerability Attributes in Risk, Emergency Response, Recovery – Sustainability

Anil K. Gupta

Introduction

Countries in Asia-Pacific continue to suffer disproportionately from disasters caused by natural hazards. With 60 per cent of the world population, the region is highly vulnerable to the impact of hazards and has experienced major and minor disasters throughout the past decade. During 2002 to 2011, 40 per cent of all reported disasters (1,524) occurred in Asia, causing 63 per cent of all global disaster deaths (6,69,263), affecting 2.2 billion (90% of all those affected globally) and causing US$691 billion (48% of the global) damage (Davies, 2015). In the Global Risk Hotspots Analysis (GRHA), the first eight globally ranked countries with "relatively high mortality risk from multiple hazards" were all within the Asia-Pacific region (Reinhard, 2015). In recent past, the region suffered a range of major disasters, for example, earthquakes in Pakistan, Indonesia, the People's Republic of China and New Zealand; cyclones in the India, Philippines and Myanmar; floods across Pakistan, Myanmar and India; Indian ocean tsunami; a complex disaster in Japan involving an earthquake, tsunami and nuclear disaster; and unprecedented urban floods in India and Thailand. Reportedly, most Asian nations have been in the lower strata of socio-economic indices and frequently received international aid in post-disaster relief and recovery (Sharma, 2015).

Earthquakes are common major disaster risk in Asia Pacific region, known to also bring incidences of tsunami, landslides, fire, chemical spillage and radiation, etc. in some of the past cases as secondary, complex of consequential risks. A list of largest and deadliest earthquakes from 1990 to 2014 has been developed by the United States Geological Survey (Table 10.1). Though it shows some trend in number of fatalities with respect to magnitude of the earthquake, but no conclusion can be drawn on this basis particularly on outcome of global and local awareness through many earthquake safety programmes. This understanding calls for policy analysis on "underlying causes of vulnerability to earthquake risks", the unattained agenda of Hyogo Framework of Action (HFA Priority 4). The transition from HFA to Sendai Framework for DRR brings paradigm shift in focus on "reducing risk" from "reducing disaster losses". A focus on disaster losses means minimizing the impacts of disasters. A focus on disaster risk puts more efforts to reduce the size of disasters, which would then have an overall effect of reducing its impacts.

Nepal's location along the active Main Himalayan Thrust arc, where the subducting Indian plate and the overriding Eurasian plate interact, with approximately a half of the tectonic convergence between these two plates, i.e., about 20 mm/year (Avouac, 2003; Ader *et al.*, 2012). The locked part of the subduction interface has a low-dip angle (about 10°) and is located at depths of 4-18 km (Bilham, 2004) and has potential to generate M_w8+ earthquakes (Gupta, 2006). Nepal has a history of several large earthquakes (Ambraseys and Douglas, 2004; Bilham, 2004). A map of Nepal and locations of major historical seismic events are shown in Fig. 10.1. The 2015 Gorkha – Kodari earthquakes have ruptured a fault section that overlaps with the fault rupture plane of the 1934 earthquake.

Based on the seismic record of the number of earthquakes that occurred since 1255, earthquakes of magnitude greater than 8 occurred on average once every 80 years. The last great earthquake of magnitude 8.3 occurred in 1934. The seismic record of Nepal is available since 1255 A.D. in which 7.7 Richter scale in Kathmandu valley king Avaya Malla and one third of population lost their lives in this event. After that, a series of earthquake occurred in Nepal. Major are in 1260, 1408, 1681, 1767, 1810, 1823, 1833, 1834, 1866, 1934, 1980 and 1988 A.D. (Pokharel *et al.*, 2007).

Two severe earthquakes hit Nepal on April 25 and on May 12, 2015 with the first earthquake a most severe natural disaster to hit Nepal in the past 80 years (VanTassle, 2015). This was not unexpected as a build-up of stress between the Eurasian Plate and the Indian plate in the earth's crust was well-known and reported. However, prediction and forecast of

Table 10.1: List of Largest and Deadliest Earthquakes by Year: 1990-2014

Largest Earthquakes					Deadliest Earthquakes				
Year	**Date**	**Magnitude**	**Fatalities**	**Region**	**Year**	**Date**	**Magnitude**	**Fatalitie s**	**Region**
1	2	3	4	5	6	7	8	9	10
2014	04/01	8.2	6	NW of Iquique, Chile	2014	08/03	6.2	729	Near Wenping, China
2013	05/24	8.3	0	Sea of Okhotsk	2013	09/24	7.7	825	61km NNE of Awaran, Pakistan
2012	04/11	8.6	0	Off the west coast of northern Sumatra	2012	02/06	6.7	113	Negros-Cebu region, Philippines
2011	03/11	9.0	20896	Near the East Coast of Honshu, Japan	2011	03/11	9.0	20896	Near the East Coast of Honshu, Japan
2010	02/27	8.8	507	Offshore Maule, Chile	2010	01/12	7.0	316000	Haiti
2009	09/29	8.1	192	Samoa Islands region	2009	09/30	7.5	1117	Southern Sumatra, Indonesia
2008	05/12	7.9	87587	Eastern Sichuan, China	2008	05/12	7.9	87587	Eastern Sichuan, China
2007	09/12	8.5	25	Southern Sumatera, Indonesia	2007	08/15	8.0	514	Near the Coast of Central Peru
2006	11/15	8.3	0	Kuril Islands	2006	05/26	6.3	5749	Java, Indonesia
2005	03/28	8.6	1313	Northern Sumatra, Indonesia	2005	10/08	7.6	80361	Pakistan

(Contd.)

Table 10.1 (*Contd.*)

1	2	3	4	5	6	7	8	9	10
2004	12/26	9.1	227898	Off West Coast of Northern Sumatra	2004	12/26	9.1	227898	Off West Coast of Northern Sumatra
2003	09/25	8.3	0	Hokkaido, Japan Region	2003	12/26	6.6	31000	South-eastern Iran
2002	11/03	7.9	0	Central Alaska	2002	03/25	6.1	1000	Hindu Kush Region, Afghanistan
2001	06/23	8.4	138	Near Coast of Peru	2001	01/26	7.7	20023	India
2000	11/16	8.0	2	New Ireland Region, P.N.G.	2000	06/04	7.9	103	Southern Sumatra, Indonesia
1999	09/20	7.7	2297	Taiwan	1999	08/17	7.6	17118	Turkey
1998	03/25	8.1	0	Balleny Islands Region	1998	05/30	6.6	4000	Afghanistan-Tajikistan Border Region
1997	10/14	7.8	0	South of Fiji Islands	1997	05/10	7.3	1572	Northern Iran
1997	12/05	7.8	0	Near East Coast of Kamchatka	1997				
1996	02/17	8.2	166	Irian Jaya Region, Indonesia	1996	02/03	6.6	322	Yunnan, China
1995	07/30	8.0	3	Near Coast of Northern Chile	1995	01/16	6.9	5530	Kobe, Japan
1995	10/09	8.0	49	Near Coast of Jalisco, Mexico	1995				
1994	10/04	8.3	11	Kuril Islands	1994	06/06	6.8	795	Colombia
1993	08/08	7.8	0	South of Mariana Islands	1993	09/29	6.2	9748	India
1992	12/12	7.8	2519	Flores Region, Indonesia	1992	12/12	7.8	2519	Flores Region, Indonesia
1991	04/22	7.6	75	Costa Rica	1991	10/19	6.8	2000	Northern India
1991	12/22	7.6	0	Kuril Islands	1991				
1990	07/16	7.7	1621	Luzon, Philippine Islands	1990	06/20	7.4	50000	Iran

Source: United States Geological Survey website, accessed 10 January, 2016.

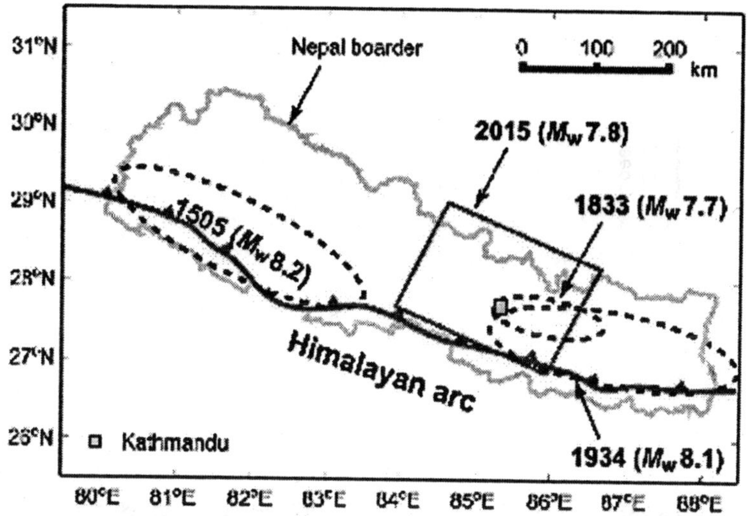

Fig. 10.1: Major historical earthquakes in Nepal along the Himalayan arc. The locations of three historical earthquakes (1505, 1833, and 1934) are approximate. For the M_w7.8 mainshock, the fault plane model by the USGS is shown (Goda *et al.*, 2015).

the time or the magnitude of an earthquake disaster to occur is not yet been achieved.

Earthquake Safety Initiatives in Nepal

Despite the availability of knowledge about historical earthquakes and the continued geological research on the Nepal Himalayas (Bilham *et al.*, 1994; Thapa, 1988), public awareness of earthquake hazards and risks were minimal until some years back, and ground efforts of earthquake risk management were almost non-existent. Udaypur earthquake of 1988 marks the beginning of planned activities on earthquake safety in Nepal. A number of international organizations and funding agencies have put in the efforts and joined hands on disaster safety initiatives in Nepal. Some of them focused on school safety, for example, the Disaster Preparedness for Safer Schools in Nepal (DPSS-2) Project with support of The American Red Cross, implemented in two phases starting 2008 until 2014. In May 2009, the Government of Nepal launched the comprehensive Nepal Disaster Risk Reduction Consortium (NRRC). The NRRC is a unique institutional arrangement, bringing together financial institutions, development partners, the Red Cross/Red Crescent Movement, and the UN in partnership with the Government of Nepal. The NRRC identified and emphasized on following five flagship areas (NRRC, 2011):

(i) School and hospital safety – structural and non-structural aspects of making schools and hospitals earthquake resilient;
(ii) Emergency preparedness and response capacity;
(iii) Flood management in the Koshi River basin;
(iv) Integrated community-based disaster risk reduction/management; and
(v) Policy/Institutional support for disaster risk management.

A Municipal Disaster Risk Reduction Programme (MDRIP) was implemented in Ilam and Panauti municipalities under the Global Risk Identification Programme (GRIP) of UNDP/Bureau for Crisis Prevention and Recovery (BCPR) with the three-year estimated budget of US $146.8 million funded through the United Nations Office for Project Services (UNOPS) starting 2008 were also available (NRRC, 2011). A Comprehensive Disaster Risk Management Programme (CDRMP) with the cost of USD 16.55 million was launched by the United Nations Development Programme (UNDP) Nepal in 2011 for a period of 5 years. CDRMP partnered with five municipalities in the Kathmandu Valley as well as with key Government authorities to develop Risk Sensitive Land Use Plan aiming at disaster resilient urban-renewal to build on existing transport, housing, and infrastructure master plans as well as emergency response scenarios. The programme broadly covered 39 districts (Mountain 6, Hills 21, and Terai 12) bringing lessons from 2011 earthquake and across following seven thematic issues (Rothenberger, 2015):

(i) Institutional and Legislative Systems (ILS) for disaster risk management, National Building Code (NBC) and Risk Sensitive Land Use Planning (RSLUP);
(ii) Strategic Linkages with other Sectors and disaster risk management mainstreaming;
(iii) Climate Risk Management (CRM);
(iv) Community Based Disaster Risk Management (CBDRM);
(v) Emergency Preparedness and Response (EPR);
(vi) Early Recovery (ER); and
(vii) Cross cutting themes – Gender inclusion, Monitoring and Evaluation; and Knowledge Management.

In Nepal, the World Disaster Reduction Campaign for 2006-2007 was initiated and many initiatives such amendment in school curricula for disaster risk education, community-based disaster management in village level, disaster mitigation plans in district-level, etc. have been undertaken. Raising awareness within school communities is the well implemented programme in Nepal (Tuladhar, *et al.*, 2015). Such initiatives of Disaster risk reduction in schools and communities of Nepal were well documented (ActionAid, 2011a, b). Recently, Nepal has also started to include disaster risk reduction into secondary and higher education system and the curricula.

Besides above examples, there were several indigenous, regional, multi-lateral and bilateral initiatives with national and international funds. Nepal Earthquake Engineering Society (a non-governmental organization) has been involved in many of these activities, along the Nepal Consortium for Disaster Risk Reduction (NRRC). The NRRC is a unique arrangement that unites humanitarian and development partners with financial institutions in partnership with the Government of Nepal in order to reduce Nepal's vulnerability to natural disasters (NRRC, 2011). However, disaster management in Nepal, like in most countries, has been relief centric, as also Natural Calamity Relief Act, 1982 (also known as the Natural Disaster Relief Act) which established a tiered institutional set-up for relief management at central, regional, district and local level. However, most of these initiatives had least emphasis on prevention and mitigation and focused primarily on developing plans, institutions, and training interventions in communities and schools, for example the National Action Plan for Disaster Management (1996) which has been developed and implemented by the Nepal Government's Ministry of Home Affairs (Eriksson, *et al.*, 2007). Whereas there has been increasing efforts to address disasters through appropriate mechanisms, including adoption of National Strategy for Disaster Risk Management (October 2009), concern was growing to strengthen the DRR framework in Nepal (Action Aid, 2010). National Water Plan (2005), an important initiative, also set primary targets around emergency relief, early warning and mitigation related infrastructure and to arrive at reducing socio-economic losses at par with developing nations. Journey of disaster management legal framework in Nepal is depicted in Fig. 10.2.

Apart from the aforementioned legal and policy frameworks, disaster risk management in Nepal is also provisioned, indirectly or directly, by other related acts, rules, regulations and guidelines, such as the Nepal Building Act, the Nepal Building Code, Environmental Protection Act,

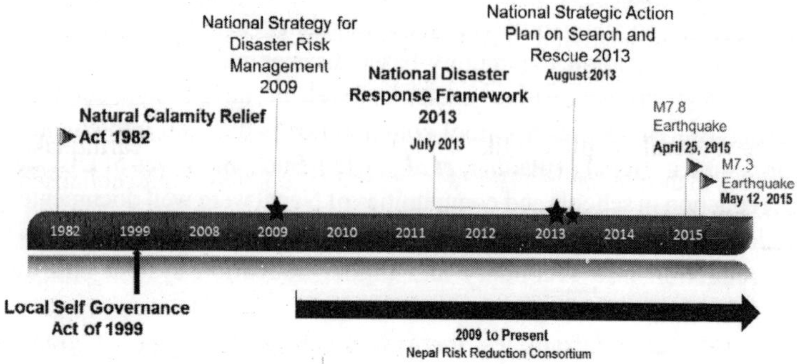

Fig. 10.2: Timeline of the Legal Framework for Disaster Management before the 2015 Gorkha Earthquake (*Source*: Madamba, *et al.*, 2015).

National Agriculture Policy (2004), National Shelter Policy (1996), National Urban Policy (2006), National Water Plan and Water Resource Policy, National Water Resource Strategy (2002), and the Water Induced Disaster Management Policy in 2006 (ADRC, 2014).

Quests on past and ongoing earthquake safety initiatives in and around Nepal especially in terms of their approach and methodologies arise with the incidence of this earthquake which caused heavy damage and losses. The nature and extent of damage along the dimensions of environmental, socio-economic and governance in backdrop of pre-and post-earthquake development settings in Nepal calls for a lateral introspect, to help focus on the underlying causes of disaster vulnerability. This is equally important for aiming safer and sustainable post-disaster recovery activities.

A requirement of paradigm shift in approach to earthquake risk mitigation in Nepal, therefore, calls for redesigning the programmes and actions aligning with the understanding brought in by the lessons of recent earthquake and the background of transition from HFA to the Sendai Framework of DRR. Thus, the approach of risk and vulnerability assessment, emergency preparedness and sustainability issues in recovery and reconstruction need to integrate lateral viewpoints. It will influence the design and will ensure success of earthquake disaster risk management programmes in Nepal.

Nepal Gorkha Earthquake: Vulnerability and Effects

The April 25 earthquake was felt across areas of at least five nations: Nepal, India, China, Bangladesh, Bhutan, and Pakistan. In Nepal alone, the earthquakes were responsible for at least 8000 deaths, 25,000 injuries, and up to 2 million people were left homeless. Half a million houses were completely destroyed, and almost 2,70,000 damaged, and avalanches and landslides altered the landscape and ended lives all across the region ("M_w7.8 - 36km E of Khudi, Nepal," 2015). There is big number of people missing. Several people are likely buried forever given post-earthquake landslides in the mountains. Heritage sites and religious temples collapsed to rubbles, turning centuries-old icons into so much land fill (Ehrlich, 2015). Behind these statistics are terrible human miseries of earthquake caused damage and losses. In some areas, up to 90 per cent of schools and health facilities have been severely damaged. In a country with limited resources such as Nepal, these are only estimates (Binns and Low, 2015).

Poverty is both cause and consequence of disasters in under-developed or developing countries (Tuadhar, *et al.*, 2015) and effects of past non-seismic disasters on their vulnerability to the recent earthquake is an important research question. Poverty drives people to live in high risk marginal areas of mountains and river valleys, which make them vulnerable to disasters. On the other hand, heavy disaster losses such as during earthquakes and tsunamis or landslides and flood unexpectedly create poverty among a large number of people by destroying their houses, productive lands, other personal assets, and livelihood (Yamin, *et al.*, 2005; Takeuchi, *et al.*, 2011). It is important to realize that Nepal is one of the poorest countries on the planet, with an average per capita income of less than $1500 (Stark, 2015). Tourism is a major economic substrate, as people's main economic activity is "services" contributing over half of the national GDP. Tourism includes adventure seeking mountain climbing and experiencing Nepal's culture and religious history. However, agriculture supports to income of more than 70 per cent population, but contributing just over one third of the GDP. Up to one fourth share of country's GDP comes from remittances (The *World Factbook: Nepal*, 2015).

Building construction in Nepal is predominantly unreinforced brickwork and un-coared rubble stone masonry with piecemeal foundations made out of mud- or concrete-mortar and fieldstone. It was very unlikely for these constructions to withstand the forces generated in even moderate earthquakes, and the Gorakha earthquake been a major one. However, some of the constructions are slightly better in urban and semi-urban areas, where a good proportion of buildings are lightly reinforced frame construction with solid concrete foundations. Rural constructions primarily of mud and stones, with over 90 per cent failed to withstand, were inhabited by mostly old aged as young members remain outside for work. For several decades Nepal constructions were not tested by a major earthquake and, therefore, turned to rubble this hard time.

Physical, environmental and social dimensions vary among populations displaced by the recent earthquake. Such disasters can cause long term displacement of populations or even in some cases permanent migration. Disruption of employment opportunities and livelihood resources can drive people to move away even from their undamaged homes. Economic changes after a disaster can cause both in and out migration among different groups (Cutter, *et al.*, 2011) and this was observed in Nepal as well as the Kathmandu city witnessed post-earthquake huge but both out and in migration.

The earthquake that struck Nepal on 25 April resulted in huge devastation across 14 districts in the country. Six districts – Dhading, Dolokha, Gorkha, Nuwakot, Rasuwa and Sindhupalchock – were particularly badly hit and were further affected by several aftershocks including a particularly big one measuring 6.8 on the Richter scale on 12 May. Due to the bumpy topography, limited roads in rural areas and being a landlocked country, transportation in Nepal is challenging at times and depends on India for transit facilities (CFE-DMHA, 2015). Rapid, unplanned and haphazard development of urban agglomeration characterized with non-compliance with building codes, failure to use qualified engineers or trained masons, encroachment of buildings on open space, mindless alteration of landscape and natural drainage and depletion of the water table is known to have increased multi-hazard vulnerability of people, their resources and infrastructure. Kathmandu's critical infrastructure and essential services were already considered extremely vulnerable before the earthquake (URD, 2014).

There are several facets of urban vulnerability, of which weak governance and poverty are key underlying drivers that contribute to urban disaster risks (UNISDR, 2012). Weak governance has magnified impacts in cities, for example land-use flaws, poorly designed and constructed housing, drainage, deficits in services, infrastructure, etc. Urban poverty drives large numbers of people (especially displaced persons) to live in overcrowded areas with informal settlements or occupy marginal or low cost, low lying lands that are usually unsafe (Le, 2013). A peculiar syndrome of inhabiting people and buildings occupying urban space in Nepal contrary to be basic principle is shown in Fig. 10.3.

The majority of the populations in Nepal live in the Central Highlands, and in recent years there has been migration of a significant part of the population to the *Terai* region. Nepal is predominately a rural country, but is urbanizing rapidly (CFE-DMHA, 2015). In addition to specific urban disasters, the rapid growth of cities means that regional disasters tend to have both rural and urban components, and therefore also negatively impact the linkages between urban and rural areas (Le, 2013). A critical component of urban resilience is that, despite the short-term nature of humanitarian aid, emergency interventions must also contribute to long-term risk reduction and development goals (Lewis, 2012).

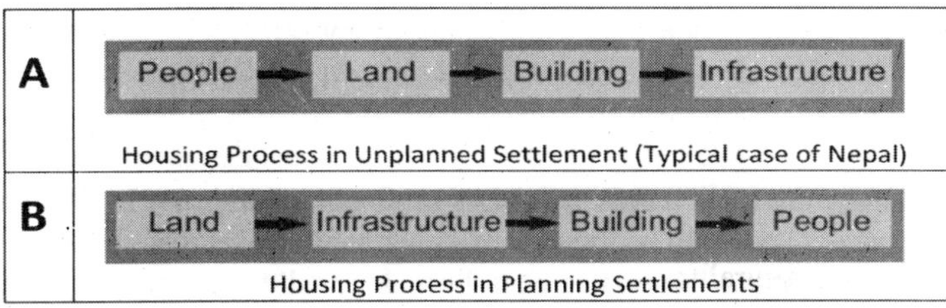

Fig. 10.3: Urban settlement process in Nepal contrary to planned approach (Rana, *et al.*, 2007).

Damage to structures and buildings are immediately visible, reported immediately and often outweigh complex, more challenging and long-lasting impact on livelihood support and natural resource system. This is important in case of Nepal as well, and the effect on natural resource management systems has affected not only their livelihood, health, economy and thereby people's capacity to withstand and/or recover but reinforced new layers of vulnerability. Damage to storage facilities, stored crops including seeds, irrigation systems, rural transport, agricultural tools, crisis of agricultural labour availability, has been serious and beyond the local coping capacity.

On average 80 per cent of households in Nepal own some animal but in limited numbers which is a major contribution to agricultural livelihoods. Losses due to the earthquake are significant for animals, with 20 per cent for cattle and 42 per cent for poultry and more animals injured and sick. Animal health was also affected due to lack of shelter and feed and limited access to veterinary services (NFSC, 2015). Production of animal products has been reduced due to stress syndromes, lack of feed and deteriorated health conditions. This affects households both for own consumption and income earning.

Looking Earthquake Risk in Multi-hazards Context

First recorded earthquake Valley dates back to eight centuries ago in 1255 that killed one-third of people in Kathmandu Valley. Nepal suffered several earthquakes since then. Prior to the 2015 Gorkha earthquake, there have been serious earthquakes over the past century in 1934, 1980, 1988 and 2011 (Simkhada, *et al.*, 2015). Apart from earthquakes, landslides are also common and annually 12,000 big or small landslides occur in Nepal (DPNet, 2015) and are becoming more frequent as over 3,000 major landslides have been recorded after the first earthquake in April (UNOCHA, 2015). According to government records, Nepal has experienced over 14 large landslides since 1967 (CFE-DMHA, 2015). Landslides incidences are exacerbated due to the instability of the soil after the earthquake. Landslides are generally known to be induced by either natural or human factors, or both. Some natural factors that contribute to landslides are high relief or steep slopes, unstable geology, and concentrated rainfall. Human factors can be deforestation, improper land-use and construction, and agricultural activities on hill slopes. Additional factors causing landslides are removal of lateral support, surcharge loads, transitory stress caused by earthquakes or blasting, and factors causing low shear strength such as weak soil, high pore-water pressure, and so on. Earthquakes and heavy rainfall are the landslide triggers in most cases. Landslides often give rise to debris flows (UNISDR, 2003).

Table 10.2: Year-wise disaster scenario loss of lives by major types of disasters in Nepal (2000-2011)

Year	*Flood and Landslide*	*Earth-quake*	*Thunder-bolt*	*Fire*	*Hail-tone*	*Wind-storm*	*Epidemic*	*Avalanche*
2000	173	0	23	53	1	2	141	–
2001	196	1	39	26	1	1	154	–
2002	441	0	3	14	0	3	0	–
2003	232	0	42	16	0	20	–	–
2004	131	0	10	10	0	0	41	–
2005	141	0	18	28	0	0	34	21
2006	141	0	17	28	1	0	34	–
2007	216	0	35	34	18	1	9	9
2008	134	0	14	11	0	2	10	0
2009	135	0	7	35	0	0	462	2
2010	201	0	39	42	0	2	34	2
2011	269	6	95	46	2	6	9	0

Source: Ministry of Home Affairs, Government of Nepal.

As a consequence many rural communities remain isolated and do not benefit from relief and recovery activities. The direct impact of the earthquake and its secondary effects such as landslides and avalanches has crippled the transportation networks across central Nepal. Displaced people at sites where road connectivity is either insufficient and/or cutoff by landslides are more vulnerable. Much of the hill and mountain areas are very fragile and vulnerable to landslides. Terai lands are regularly threatened by flooding and sedimentation (Karkee, 2004). Heavy rain has added to the hardship of thousands of people, and water, food and power are scarce, raising fears of waterborne diseases (Khazai, *et al.*, 2015).

Population displacement, crowding, limited quantities of safe water, inadequate hygiene and toilet facilities, and unsafe practices in handling and preparing food contribute to disease transmission. In the backdrop of Nepal earthquake, risk of an increase in communicable diseases, including diarrhoea, respiratory infections, and mosquito borne diseases, particularly when the rainy season likely approaching was significant (Bagcchi, 2015). Likelihood of outbreaks and insufficient healthcare services caused a bad combination. When an earthquake happens in a high altitude area, some special issues need to be noted. Due to the low temperature, great temperature difference, changeable weather, inconvenient transportation and lack of medical security, lung infection has a high incidence (Ding *et al.*, 2015). This further complicates the medical response and care of victims as was also seen in Yushu earthquake in China (Kang *et al.*, 2010).

Nepal is exposed to multiple recurrent hazards. Nepal loses more than 300 lives every year due to water induced disaster. During the period of 1971 to 2007, more than 50,000 people have been reported injured; about 27,000 deaths were recorded, which reveals a persistent threat to huge loss of human lives due to natural disasters (UNDP, 2008). An annual account of major disaster incidences during 2000-2011 is given in Table 10.2. It is evident from the disaster typology and scenario that a programme of earthquake safety cannot yield desired result if the programme is designed without a multi-hazard risk consideration. Recurring hydro-meteorological and epidemic disasters have their bearing, separately and in combination, on vulnerability of landscape, constructions and people's socio-economic capacity.

Transition from Conventional Risk and Damage Analysis

A wider range of theories in disaster studies reflect on the need to review key concepts that situate natural hazards within the vulnerability context (Yasir, 2009). Current methodologies of vulnerability analysis have widely recognized the need for developing more comprehensive approaches that shift attention from threshold-based methodologies to functional-based frameworks focusing more on processes rather than the static threshold limits of the social system (McFadden, 2007). The PAR Model (Fig. 10.4) developed by Blaikie, *et al.* (1994) addresses the inadequacies of the Risk-Hazard (RH) framework by illustrating the ties between the causal forces of vulnerability and the natural hazards. The idea of 'release' focuses on reducing the impacts of disaster by releasing pressure through a reduction in vulnerability (Wisner, *et al.*, 2004). In this explanation, root causes were defined as the interconnected systems of processes within a society and the world economy.

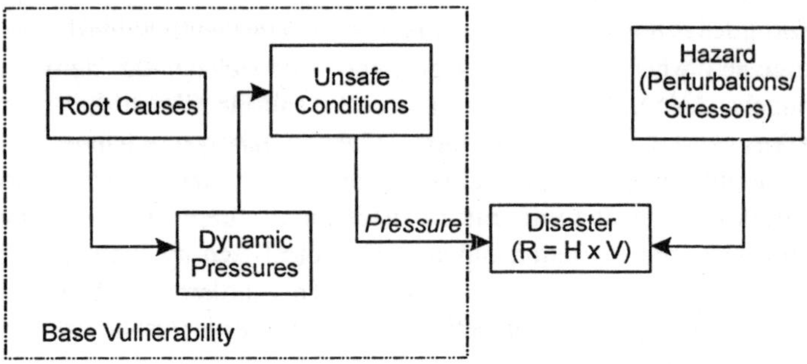

Fig. 10.4: The Pressure and Release (PAR Model) of Progression of Vulnerability.

Source: Turner *et al.* (2003).

Gorkha earthquake disaster or Nepal 2015 has triggered a wide range of thoughts and interventions on scientific and policy platforms. Conventional perspectives of earthquake risk mitigation narrowly comprising of earthquake safety behaviour, engineers and masons training, mega mock drills and school safety drills, are now under cross-quest. Perspectives that make the natural phenomenon 'earthquake' realised into a 'disaster' are, therefore, need to be integrated into the risk assessment process through adequate emphasis on underlying vulnerability factors, local organized-preparedness, trans-boundary cooperation and 'sustainability' consideration in post-disaster recovery actions. Integration of climate change adaptation and ecosystem services resilience addressing underlying vulnerability agents and, thereby, its role in community resilience is an important consideration.

Earthquake related disaster risk reduction remained primarily based on loss estimation (Chaulgaini *et al.*, 2015a, as in Chaulgaini *et al.*, 2015 b). While scientific investigations are mooted to track geo-environmental precursors to enable some level of earthquake forecasting (Freund, 2009; Wu *et al.*, 2015) as many scientists around the world have reported the occurrence of atmospheric anomalies prior to earthquakes, researches interrogating the underlying agents of people's vulnerability to earthquake risks are inadequate. Estimating the seismic disaster risk by means of vulnerability, hazard and response capacity terms has been discussed well (Hajibabaee *et al.*, 2014). However, more recent discussions of natural disasters have shifted their attention towards social factors, elevating the importance of political economy to other methods of explanations (Wisner *et al.*, 2004; Cohen and Werker, 2008). Studies on incorporating the social vulnerability analysis into disaster management's planning process by the administrative institutions is significant in achieving a versatile evaluation of the existing situation (Fernandez *et al.*, 2006; Kuban and MacKenzie-Carey, 2001 among others). These causes of disaster vulnerability relate to land-use, planning and tenure in a number of respects. The impact of natural disasters on land and human land-use is shaped by the nature of vulnerability within a particular land governance context (UNHSP, 2010).

Interaction of earthquake risk with other hazards present scenario of complex emergencies, na-tech (naturally induced technical disasters) and domino effects, especially the urban areas present heightened risk of an earthquake triggering other secondary disasters. The potential for an earthquake to trigger fires, chemical contamination, social unrest and mass displacement should be at the heart of all preparedness and response planning (URD, 2014). Improvement of the disaster risk management system has been considered as one of the most important priorities in Iran for the related organization during the recent years and especially after the Bam Earthquake of 2003. Earthquake loss estimation has been practiced by the selected municipalities using combination of seismic hazard, structural vulnerability, and exposure data (Binns and Low, 2015b). In order to evaluate the vulnerability of urban tissues and structures to potential earthquake, following three indices were put in the practice (Hosseini and Hosseini, 2008):

(i) Building Damage Index (Ratio of possible collapsed buildings to the total buildings in three scenario earthquakes);

(ii) Evacuation Index (Includes open space area, narrow road ratio, number of evacuees and number of disaster weak); and
(iii) Secondary Damage Index (include hazardous facility, gas pipeline damage and electric power cable damage).

A range of research studies on probabilistic risk assessment and its different components (inventory creation, vulnerability curves, hazard modelling) were conducted, but most models used the current condition of infrastructure. These static models suffer with the underestimation of risk in most cases and, also constrict policy-makers to a hopeless catch-up mode. Their scope of action remain limited to mitigating risk to existing assets rather than proactive actions to reduce future risk arising from a larger than present-day asset base (Lallemant *et al.*, 2014). Vulnerability to a large earthquake in Nepal is further compounded by the likelihood that international response mechanisms may be compromised, as risk scenarios reveal likely damage to airport and access roads to the Kathmandu Valley in event of an earthquake. In such situation, the weak national systems, such as the military, police and health services, may be forced to deal with the consequences of a disaster unaided for a significant period of time and, significantly, beyond the typical time span of search and rescue efforts.

Studies manifest community institution's capacity of response to environmental shocks and stresses, but often overlook the fact that these institutions and their resources are also vulnerable to the impacts of shocks and stresses (Allen, 2006). Getting ready for future disasters is a multifaceted process which attracts attention of the public as much as local and central authorities (Fisek, *et al.*, 2003). There is need of a multidisciplinary evaluation of the term risk, and to cover land and ecological fragility as underlying factor to socio-economic fragility as aggravating factors besides physical risk. Conditions caused by social fragility and lack of resilience are determined by the ecosystem services to a large extent, to constitute the higher order impacts of a disaster (Sungay *et al.*, 2012). As concluded by the Wilton Park (2010) Conference Report, though the "impact of disaster and humanitarian crises escalate when disaster management fails", this is also inextricably linked to the "failure of development policies to enhance governance and institutional capacity compounded by unsuccessful efforts to address economic and social redistribution" (Field, 2010). Approach of root cause analysis for arriving at policy interventions as suggested by GCDR (2012) is given in Fig. 10.5.

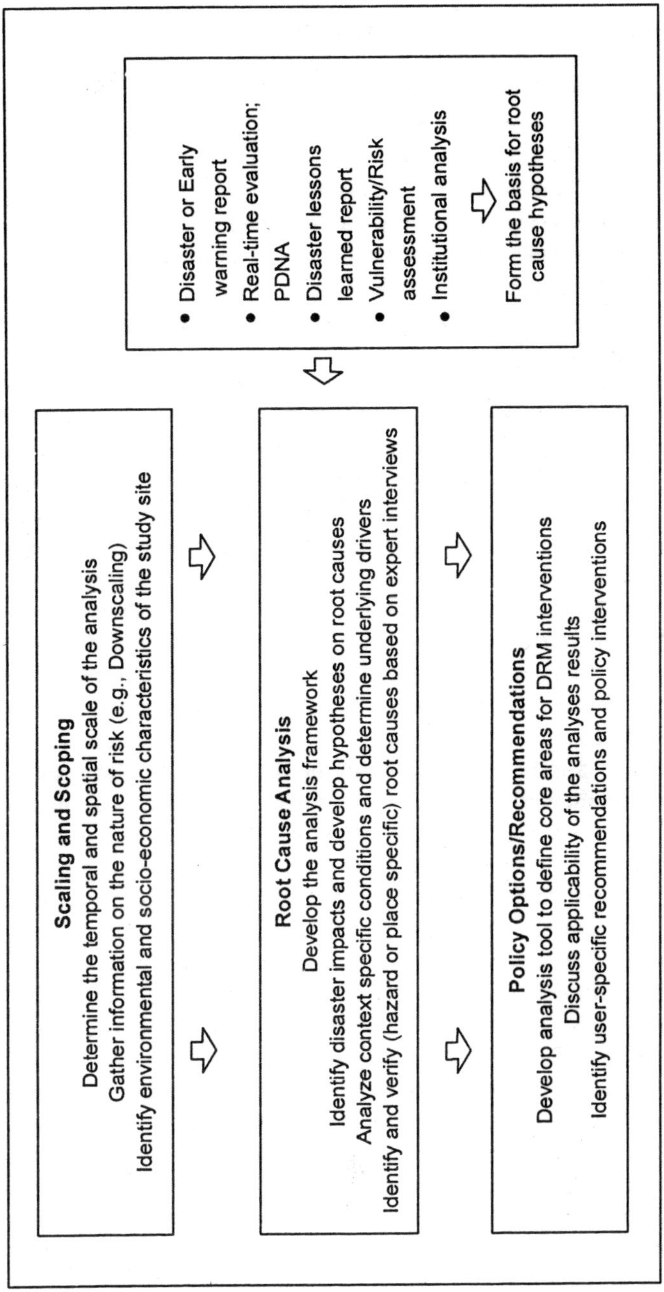

Fig. 10.5: Analytical approach for understanding disaster root causes.

Emergency Response and Humanitarian Assistance

Currently, over 80 million people globally require humanitarian assistance (WHO, 2015) and has gave rise to an awakened network of agencies, institutions and resources for disaster response and relief from outside the nations as well which was evident in case of Nepal earthquake. International aid started within few hours of the earthquake hit Nepal on 25 April. The post-disaster relief and recovery support from international aid piled in huge in terms of amount, projects, people and socio-cultural and political complexities much beyond the native carrying capacity (VanTassle, 2015).

Rapid and intensive support interventions from culturally related and capable trans-boundary capacity has been evident in emergency cooperation, as witnessed from the tasks undertaken by Indian Army and Indian Air Force, especially in providing aid to inaccessible and difficult to reach areas of Nepal. Presence of the Indian National Disaster Response Force and its senior envoys at most operational and strategic levels helped build confidence in disaster search and rescue and primary relief operations. Followed by China which brought in the prudent technical strength to the operations, other neighbouring countries and then many international agencies and developed nations extended their hands to back relief operations in Kathmandu and far off areas affected by earthquake, the aftershocks and landslides.

A near 1.5 million population in the Kathmandu Valley – one of the world's most earthquake-prone areas live with limited local capacity to carry out search-and-rescue missions despite of Nepal having earthquake history and the countless prior warnings from scientists and risk assessment studies. Reportedly, the rescuers used their bare hands to dig out bodies. This underlines the need of robust disaster management plans particularly at local level, backed by an effective national coordination, and concerned global and regional humanitarian cooperation mechanisms (Caballero-Anthony *et al*., 2015). The delivery of aid and relief services to the affected areas was further complicated by the landlocked nature of Nepal with extremely challenging geography and inadequate road infrastructure. Damage to the road infrastructure, debris, and logistics continued to hamper relief operations and remote settlements at high altitudes remain isolated. A study of the Nepal earthquake and emergency response on site (Khazai *et al*., 2015) concluded that the National government and in particular the local administration outfits were clearly unprepared, and overwhelmed by the sudden intense devastation, has no option then to appeal for international assistance. Rapid assessment of the situation, damage and needs to rationalize and optimize resources and operations, besides efficient cooperation of foreign militaries within themselves and with civilian agencies was a critical requirement.

The earthquake response has a strong regional dimension, with India and China in particular playing a central role. International actors should seek to align and coordinate with and mutually support these actors. Despite the fact that the South Asian Association for Regional Cooperation (SAARC) Secretariat is based in Kathmandu and is headed by the Secretary General, its absence from the operational ground actions of pre-disaster risk mitigation and/or preparedness was reportedly realised during this phase of emergency response where international cooperation was much evident (Khazai *et al.*, 2015). It was also realised that SAARC level cooperation cannot sustain if given thrust only on emergency response, but rather continual activities with two-way feedback mechanisms for strengthening prevention-mitigation and preparedness capacity building including education and research would needed through a joint platform. It has been suggested crucial to promptly activate a regional disaster prevention and preparedness cooperation mechanism, on the lines of the AHA Centre, that can complement not only the international relief assistance and provide a mechanism to coordinate between civilian agencies and militaries (Caballero-Anthony *et al.*, 2015), but would strengthen all time and intense cooperation towards the established goals of sustainable development including climate change adaptation, environmental safeguards and livelihood resilience in larger perspective of SAARC's objectives.

Disaster response is dependent on planning and the availability of capacity to restore infrastructure. For countries that are struggling to develop economically, diverting resources to planning and to provide reserve capacity is difficult (Chaulgaini *et al.*, 2015). According to the seismological centre of Nepal medium and small size earthquake event occur in a different part of Nepal frequently. However, analyzing vulnerability does not simply serve the purpose, its proper communication to the concerned stakeholders is equally important and forms the core of the risk-reduction strategies (Wisner *et al.*, 2004). Experience from disasters indicates the need for preparedness also at the individual level. Efforts to withstand a disaster and its consequences at the local level depend on risk mitigation activities and preparedness together with individual and institutional capacities (Sungay *et al.*, 2010).

Interestingly, the Ministry of Home Affairs in Government of Nepal used a mock scenario for earthquake response preparedness that if an earthquake of the 1934 magnitude is reported at that time, an estimated 40,000 death, 90,000 injured and 6,00,000 to 9,00,000 homeless can be expected (DPNN, 2007). However, disaster responses resemble military operations in their heavy reliance on command and controls. The sense of urgency when lives are at stake sometimes discourages participatory processes. In particular, the perceived need for haste makes it easy to bypass local power structures. People and institutions that might help rebuild affected communities are left out of the relief response, often because the external support agencies have limited knowledge of the communities (IE, 2015). Leadership remains vital as key decision-making needs to be swift and clear. But the value of beneficiary participation is also clear, for example in issues of livelihood restoration or relocation of residences and businesses.

Participation often brings out least cost and sustainable solutions. Transparency and honesty in the use of resources is a grave concern in emergency recovery operations. The vulnerability to corruption is presumed greater in situations where large accounts of resources are made available and where urgency calls for by-passing slower processes of checks and balances. Given some nascent return to full democracy in Nepal, it will be all the important to have clear criteria to share responsibilities among the various actors above and below the local government level to assess local needs and monitor interventions (IED, 2015).

Large amounts of rubble constitute an urban disaster phenomenon that presents a challenge, but which can also be a resource (IASC, 2010). Interestingly, a strategic plan for post-earthquake debris management for Kathmandu Valley has been prepared during 2014 by the Ministry of Federal Affairs and Local Development of Government of Nepal with the support of International Organization of Migration (IOM) and USAID (GoN, 2014). Poorly managed disaster waste is threat to health, safety and the environment, and can be a major impediment to post-disaster rescue operations. Experience shows that disaster waste is often managed in an *ad hoc* manner; however, substantial improvements can be made in response efforts with a clear coordination structure and management plan (GoN, 2014). Lack of local capacities and local emergency preparedness to such big challenge has also been pointed out by WHO (Sharma, 2015).

Land Management – Fundamental to Risk Reduction

Good land-use and planning are essential for the prevention of disasters.

In addition, land is fundamental to the recovery from disasters. It provides a site for shelter, a resource for livelihoods and a place to access services and infrastructure. Therefore, land issues – such as security of tenure, land-use, land access and land administration – are important to key humanitarian sectors after a disaster (UNHSP, 2010). A mock scenario of sheltering 9 million persons in a major earthquake used by the International Organization of Migration (IOM) during 2010, identified 83 potential shelter locations assigned for specific uses. This was further updated in 2014 (MoHA and IOM, 2013; and Shelter Cluster Nepal, 2014, as in Khazai *et al.*, 2015). A comparison of the M_W7.8 earthquake occurred on April 25th, 2015 with the scenario event by IOM is given in Table 10.3. The earthquake on April 25 was not the worst-case scenario postulated

Table 10.3: A comparison of the M_W7.8 earthquake occurred on 25th April, 2015 with the scenario event by IOM

Scenarios	*Contingency Plan Scenario Event (Shelter Cluster 2014)*	*Gorkha Earthquake 25th, April 2015 (UN OCHA Situation Report No. 10)*
Fatalities	44,000	7,367 official (as of 4th May); 7,560 modeled median (Daniell *et al.*, 2015)
Injured	1,03,000	14,355 official (as of 4th May)
Affected	1 to 1.5 million	Over 5 million live in the most affected districts
Displaced	9,00,000	37,500 IDPs officially in Camps. Estimates based on building damages are around 1 million in the most affected districts and another 4,00,000 in affected districts
Shelter capacity and management	64 designated large shelter sites with a total capacity of 7,10,000 persons	58 camps in the Kathmandu Valley 17 are managed as 'Formal Camps'
Outmigration (KV, and outside)	Up to 6,25,000 people will attempt to leave Kathmandu Valley	3,00,000 are estimated
Physical Impact	Large amounts of debris, airport unusable	Airport temporarily shut-down for large cargo planes on Sunday 3rd May
Building damage	60% of buildings destroyed, another 20% of buildings damaged or inhabitable	Official count: 1,91,058 homes destroyed and 1,75,162 damaged. 90% buildings destroyed in Gorkha and Sindupal Chowk District (most stone and mud houses)

in the contingency plan, but serves as a major first event testing the response planning framework for the Government and partner agencies (Khazai *et al.*, 2015).

The building damage in Kathmandu was localized to specific areas. It appeared that the building collapse sites were affected by local soil characteristics and/or structural deficiencies. In this regard, microzonation studies provide valuable insights into earthquake damage occurrence (Goda *et al.*, 2015). Land degradation is major challenge of Nepal (Acharya and Kafle, 2009). More than 90 per cent of the population in Nepal is dependent upon the land for their fulfilment of basic needs (food, fodder, fuel, fiber and timber) (LRMP, 1986). Rural livelihoods in the hills of Nepal are directly linked with forest ecosystems for human needs, animal rearing, crop production, and providing environmental and spiritual needs. As a result, there is greater human pressure on the hill forest ecosystems due to which about 200 hectares per day of forest conversion in non-forest land, or degradation and fragmentation into shrub/bush lands. These cause loss of plant species and high levels of erosion resulting in further loss of soil nutrients. Lowering agricultural productivity from loss of soil nutrients has lowered rural communities' income and livelihood support. This has adversely affected poverty levels, resulting in 45 per cent of hill population having to survive below the poverty line in Nepal (Gautam, 2000).

Both the natural conditions and human activities have contributed to the degradation of land in Nepal. Some of the major causes of land degradation are fragile geological structure, forest fire, avalanches and dry landslides in which increasing population, fragile economy and sometimes farm policies add fuel to it in its natural condition. Natural calamities like landslides in the hills, drought in the most of the areas of the country and flooding in the foothills and the Terai have frequently occurred (Karkee, 2004). The heavy grazing pressure in the mountain areas has speeded-up the soil erosion, which lead to increase run-off and compaction of soil. Cultivation on steep slope without taking considerations of improved farming such as terracing. Development activities such as construction of roads, buildings, dams have added effect to it (Neupane and Thapa, 2001).

In meeting the agricultural needs of communities, interventions should be phased and designed appropriately to support and promote resilient livelihood recovery. This implies to not only focus on the effects of this earthquake but rather have a comprehensive approach to reduce the vulnerability of households to other more frequent hazards, such as landslides, floods, droughts, pests and diseases. If not repaired quickly, damage to small-scale irrigation will have significant negative consequences on crop production in the winter cropping season. Damage to Agricultural and Livestock Service Centre buildings and facilities will seriously affect the ability of extension staff to provide technical services to farmers (NFSC, 2015). The interaction between vulnerability, disaster and resilience may be illustrated in simple terms in the Fig. 10.6. Planning early recovery responses to land issues should begin immediately after a disaster, or at the latest upon completion of the rapid land assessment (Mitchell, 2010). Early planning is essential because land issues can be a time-critical barrier to early recovery, particularly in relation to following:

(i) Security of tenure as necessary to facilitate housing reconstruction;
(ii) Access to land for livelihoods, infrastructure and, where necessary, relocation; and
(iii) Improved land-use and settlement planning for prospective hazard risk reduction.

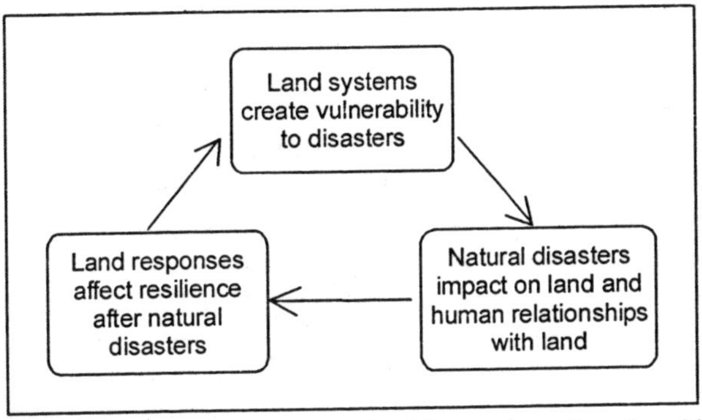

Fig. 10.6: Understanding post-disaster land issues through vulnerability and resilience analysis (UN Habitat, 2010).

Sustainability Issues for Recovery Framework

Post-disaster recovery after a major earthquake has a natural focus on reconstruction and recovery in terms of housing and infrastructure and some kind of "bringing back" functional status in towns and social life. Of later the issues of extended relief like trauma and psychosocial care, livelihood, and concept of built back better, especially the schools and hospitals, have also been integrated. However, sustainability of recovery efforts and with the aim of addressing underlying causes of vulnerability calls for a more holistic and cross disciplinary framework that incorporates interrelations between environment and livelihood with socio-economic and physical vulnerability of the people, besides the influence non-seismic disasters can have on the society and their built environment.

"The ability to withstand, recover from, and reorganize in response to crises so that all members of society may develop or maintain the ability to thrive" is a working definition of social resilience offered through the discussion on the evolution of resilience theory (Benson *et al.*, 2012). This definition reflects the growing consensus among development and humanitarian partners that the definition of resilience needs to go beyond the definition traditionally used within the disaster risk management community that frames resilience as the ability to "cope or bounce back" from shocks or extreme events. Within this perspective, a rethinking of natural disasters has shifted focus from reactive actions of measuring risk (to external physical processes) to a pro-active approach of understanding and modifying social actions that shape vulnerability of internal structures of the society (Yasir, 2009).

A key aim of disaster management should be the focusing of interventions on equity to help reduce existing inequalities and ensure that these are not made worse post-disaster (Ramirez and Peek-Asa, 2005). People living in seismically active regions like Nepal will see another earthquake sooner or later. Whilst many non-seismic disasters like landslides are affected more by environmental aspects such as land-use and climate change, a caution is necessary related to future earthquakes in Nepal because the 2015 earthquake is not necessarily the worst-case scenario (Goda *et al.*, 2015).

An inventory of past-disastrous events during 1971-2005 (Allen *et al.*, 2009) reveals that epidemics take the largest toll of life every year, and that landslide, flood (including the flash floods) and urban or rural fire are the principle hazards in terms of their extent and frequency of occurrence as well as the spread and intensity of physical and socio-economic impacts. Earthquake is a major potential hazard to reckon with – the country is located on an active seismic belt and the exponential urbanization trend over the past decade with general disregard of earthquake-resistant measures in building construction is the cause of ever-increasing earthquake risk (ALNAP, 2015).

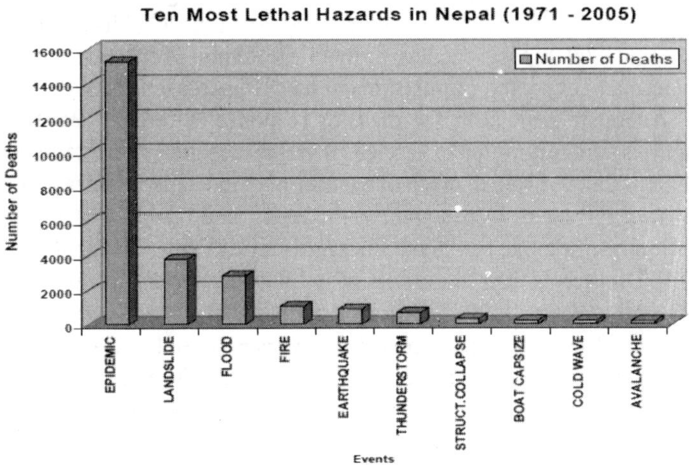

Fig. 10.7: Inventory of disastrous events during 1971-2005 (Allen *et al.*, 2009).

Environment is equally exposed to damage in post-disaster situations, when people are relocated from the affected area or forced to move from their place of origin to the vicinity of protected areas, natural forests, riverbanks or hill slopes vulnerable to landslides. Severe damage is caused to environment from this kind of temporary settlements where the migrant community mostly depends on environmental resources for their livelihood. Normally, in lack of law enforcement capacity of the government and alternatives provided to these people, the temporary relocation sites gradually become sites of permanent settlements, and loss of environment is forgone forever Environmental degradation makes especially poor communities more vulnerable to hazards because their livelihoods are more often fully dependent on natural resources (NSET *et al.*, 2008). Good environmental management can lessen the frequency and impacts of a natural disaster. Conversely, poor environmental management weakens ecosystems, increasing the frequency of disasters and exacerbating disaster impacts. In a cyclical fashion, the shocks of sudden onset disasters or stresses of slow onset disasters further contribute to diminishing an ecosystem's resilience and capacity to meet human consumption needs (UNDP, undated). Therefore, considering natural disaster management within the larger scope of environmental management is essential if recovery efforts are to reduce the risk of future disasters. Yet, funding for post-disaster environmental initiatives still largely focuses on the immediate impacts of disasters such as waste management and water quality issues. In the post-disaster situations, the massive reconstruction process can have serious environmental impacts causing further degradation of critical ecosystem services and exposing populations to new or increased risks.

Adequate provision for disaster response is rare in developing countries, and restoration of services is greatly dependent on international aid. In the case of Nepal, much of the transport and logistics infrastructure has been damaged. Consequently, the repair and resupply of essential public amenities, like health facilities, are very difficult (Chaulgaini *et al*., 2015). Disasters in their framework of sustainable recovery are now viewed differently (Yasir, 2009). At first, it argues that disasters are socially constructed and, secondly, it places the interactions of large-scale natural forces with local political-economic settings in the broad context of vulnerability to contend that disasters are consequences of unresolved development challenges. However, the enhanced understanding and emphasis on underlying causes has given rise to recognition of ecosystem services and land stability (Young and Potschin, 2010). For example, interventions should be phased and designed appropriately to support and promote resilient livelihood recovery by meeting the agricultural needs of communities. This implies to not only focus on the effects of this earthquake, but rather have a comprehensive approach to reduce the vulnerability of households to other more frequent hazards, such as landslides, floods, droughts, pests and diseases. Particular awareness should be given to the needs of women farmers and elderly headed households (NFSC, 2015).

Five main issues and challenges are evident in the context of rural communities of South Asia for reducing their disaster vulnerability through building local knowledge and capacities, as following (Jigyasu, 2002), (i) Loss of material and land resources (from rural communities); (ii) Loss of Traditional Skills; (iii) Cultural Incompatibility of external interventions; (iv) Increasing Social and Economic inequity; and (v) Weakening of Local Governance. Lack of cultural continuity and compatibility is certainly a key issue resulting in increasing disaster vulnerability. The existing notions of decision-makers as well as local people on development consider 'modernity' and 'urbanization' as panacea for development (Jigyasu, 2002). However, these "images of development" are seldom comprehended in reality because of the four main reasons:

(a) Ignorance of the local people on what 'modernity' implies in reality.

(b) While the images are created, culturally deep-rooted thinking processes may remain unchanged, thereby creating a mutually contradictory dichotomy.

(c) Lack of education, because of which local people may not be conscious and confident to be aware of their assets (resources), rights and duties.

(d) Inability of the local people to afford and sustain whatever is perceived as 'modern'.

A human rights compliant approach to the disaster response will be critical to ensuring that the quest for equality, justice and accountability in Nepal does not lose ground as the country struggles to recover from the devastation. Protection and respect for human rights has been severely weakened by Nepal's unsettled political climate at the national level and the resulting governance vacuum at local levels, and also impacted by the armed conflict between Government forces and Maoist insurgents between 1996 and 2006 (AIL, 2015). In Aceh-Nias, after the Asian Tsunami 2004, local communities were involved in designing the building standard of social housing in a way that respected the local culture and tradition (IE, 2015). Furthermore disasters, though associated with negative outcomes, must be viewed positively through a developmental perspective. They provide opportunities for better planning and innovation in improving safety, enhancing equity and rebuilding safer communities with sustainable livelihoods for people (Bolin and Stanford, 1998). Tourism in Nepal is a growing industry and is generally confined to the Kathmandu Valley. The tourism sector is a key contributor for the country's economic growth and provides over 7,50,000 jobs. In 2012, Nepal hosted almost 6,00,000 foreign tourists which contributed to 3 per cent of the country's GDP (CFE-DMHA, 2015).

Climate change is known to exert more stress on the already overstressed human-environmental system of Nepal. Findings from recent studies (FAO, 2014; ADB, 2011) suggest that infrastructure and livelihoods of the Nepali population will be impacted by climate change, as climate related risks will multiply the stresses that households and communities already face. Nepal has some of the most spectacular natural areas and biodiversity in the world with 118 ecosystems, 75 categories of vegetation, and 35 types of forests. Nepalese people, mainly the rural poor are dependent on these resources for survival. A large portion of Nepal's economy is derived from climate-sensitive businesses such as agriculture, forestry, and ecotourism (CFE-DHMA, 2015). Altogether

2,315 glacial lakes have been identified in Nepal and, about 14 GLOFs are recorded to have occurred between 1935 and 1991 in Nepal. In total, 20 glacial lakes have been identified as being potentially dangerous at present (UNISDR, 2003).

Soil structure is major factor for all forms of degradative processes and also affects the provision of ecosystem services (Acharya and Kafle, 2009). Human activities are responsible not only for the degradation of land, but also important for improvement of land through prevention, rehabilitation and reclamation (MoEST, 2008). Because the livelihoods of a large proportion of Nepali population depend upon agriculture, forestry, pastureland and water, the impacts of climate change will negate development gains and increase multifaceted vulnerabilities facing the poor and marginalized communities (MoSTE, 2015). Unfortunately only a small number of programmes run by government agencies and development organizations focus on integrating Indigenous Knowledge and Local Practices (ILKP) in a meaningful way though they have supported communities in Nepal build their adaptive practices and local level resilience for generations (GoN, 2011). Disaster Risk Reduction (DRR) and Climate Change Adaptation (CCA) have become national priority and being institutionalized to support sustainable development in Nepal. The Tenth Five Year Plan (2002-2007) and the There-Year Interim Plan (2007-2010) emphasized disaster risk management as an integral component of sustainable development and accorded priority to pre-disaster preparedness.

Conclusion and Recommendations

Sendai Framework for DRR which is built on the lessons of HFA and regional experiences of practice including policy and research is at doorstep with message of national and local strategy transformation towards addressing underlying risk factors to some significant yardsticks. The conventional approach of earthquake safety programmes which prevailed over past few decades need to be redesigned with a holistic vision of safer and sustainable development to be built upon the integration of technological, environmental, socio-economic and governance facets of sustainability. Case of earthquake risk reduction conventionally revolves around safe housing design and construction, school and hospital safety, personal safety behaviour and emergency preparedness for dealing with mega-disasters or mass casualties, etc. which have proved if not inappropriate then certainly inadequate in the background of Nepal's earthquake disaster. Since, the current period coincides with the onset of recovery programmes, following lessons are drawn for future strategy of risk reduction towards sustainable development in Nepal:

- Earthquake safety need to be looked in the multi-hazard context and the structures and people are exposed to recurring hazards, most of which are non-seismic, but more frequent. These hazards affect landscape and ground stability, drainage, weaken the constructions and reduce people's capacity, for example floods and epidemics are more common.
- Land management should be treated as fundamental to risk assessment and vulnerability reduction, incorporating ecological, built/constructions and governance aspects as key context of risk sensitive land-use planning. Land is equally important in post-disaster shelter, reconstruction, reclamation and rehabilitation contexts.
- There is no substitute to local level preparedness to deal with emergencies and to host external assistance. Systemic design of regional and trans-boundary cooperation in pre-disaster risk reduction and coordinated response resource programme need to augment the country's local capacities of risk reduction and response coordination.
- People's capacity to cope with "all type environmental risks", seismic, climatic or health related, is crucial, and the programmes of structural development – housing, infrastructure, industry, need to ensure they do not increase risk, but reduce vulnerability of people's livelihood by effectively providing for land, ecosystems and other natural resources.
- A major paradigm shift is anticipated in approach to risk (and post-disaster damage) assessment which should aim at capturing the root causes (underlying factors) of vulnerability. This may form part of strategic planning process not only of pre-disaster development in urban, rural, industrial and tourism areas, but also in post-disaster reconstruction programmes.
- Safe and sustainable development and behavioural aspects in safety are important facets of cultural capital, and the transition from research-technology-planning *via* legal and monitoring mandates need to be infused in community's ethos and personal ethics. This may require folk strategies along social resilience

concerns with programmes on poverty, gender, health, education and equity.

- Over and above, a composite programming of DRR based on structural safety and emergency preparedness along these lateral dimensions could be enabled through an appropriate mechanism, such as drawing-up national, provincial and district-level DRR roadmaps for implementing Sendai framework, as woven with current and proposed post-quake recovery programmes.

References

Acharya, A.K., & Kafle, N. (2009). Land degradation issues in Nepal and its management through agro-forestry. *Journal of Agriculture and Environment, 10*, 133-143.

ActionAid, A Report on Launching of DRR Toolkit for Constituent Assembly Members of Nepal. Launch Programme Report, 10 March, 2010. *Action Aid Nepal*, Kathmandu, Nepal, p.10.

ActionAid. Disaster Risk Reduction through Schools: A Groundbreaking Project. 2011b. http://www.actionaid.org/sites/files/actionaid/disaster_risk_reduction_through_schools.pdf. Accessed on June 2013.

ActionAid. Disaster Risk Reduction through Schools: Learning from our experience 5 years on. 2011a. http://www.actionaid.org/sites/files/actionaid/drrs_final_report_to_dfid.pdf. Accessed on June 2013.

ADB (2011). *Technical Assistance Report*. Capacity development technical assistance, Nepal: Mainstreaming climate change risk management in development. Project number: 44168. November 2011, Asian Development Bank, Manila, Philippines.

Ader, T., Avouac, J.P., Liu-Zeng, J., Lyon-Caen, H., Bollinger, L., Galetzka, J., *et al*. (2012). Convergence rate across the Nepal Himalaya and interseismic coupling on the Main Himalayan fault: implications for seismic hazard. *J. Geophys. Res.* 117, B04403. doi:10.1029/2011JB009071

ADRC, (2014), *Disaster Management Institution and System in Nepal*. Kathmandu, Nepal. Asian Disaster Reduction Centre, Kobe, Japan.

AIL, (2015), Earthquake Recovery Must Safeguard Human Rights, Nepal 2015-12-22, Index: ASA 31/1753/2015. Amnestry International Ltd., London, UK.

Allen, K., (2006), Community-based disaster preparedness and climate adaptation: Local capacity building in the Philippines. *Disasters*. **30(1)**:81-101.

Allen., L., Mehling. K.C., Hasnain, M., Ree. A., Selim, N., and Yoshino, A. (2009). Assessing UNFPA's Humanitarian Response in Nepal. Final Report—May 8, 2009. A Joint Initiative of Columbia University and the United Nations Population Fund (UNFPA). School for International and

Public Affairs (SIPA) Columbia University, New York, USA. p.77. https://sipa.columbia.edu

ALNAP, (2015), Nepal Earthquake Response: Lessons for Operational Agencies. ALNAP Lessons Paper. London: ALNAP/ODI.

Ambraseys, N. N., and Douglas, J., (2004), Magnitude calibration of north Indian earthquakes. *Geophys. J. Int.* 159, 165-206. doi:10.1111/j.1365-246X.2004.02323.x

Avouac, J. P., (2003), Mountain building, erosion and the seismic cycle in the Nepal Himalaya. *Adv. Geophys,* 46, 1-80. doi:10.1016/S0065-2687(03) 46001-9.

Bagcchi, S., (2015) Risk of infection after the Nepal earthquake. *Lancet Journal.* 15:770-771. www.thelancet.com/

Benson, Charlotte, Margaret Arnold, and Alejandro de la Fuente (2012). "Financial Innovations for Social and Climate Resilience." Unpublished framework paper. World Bank, Washington, DC. (as in Margaret *et al.*, 2014).

Bilham, R., (2004), Earthquakes in India and the Himalaya: tectonics, geodesy and history. *Ann. Geophys,* 47, 839-858. doi:10.4401/ag-3338.

Bilham, R., Bodini, P., Jackson, M., (1994). "Entertaining a Great Earthquake in Western Nepal: Historic Inactivity and Geodetic Test for the Development of Strain". In *Journal of the Nepal Geologic Society*, Volume 11, Special Issue.

Binns, C. and W. Y. Low, (2015) Nepal Disaster: A Public Health Response Needed. *Asia-Pacific Journal of Public Health*, 27(5): 484-485.

Blaikie, P., Cannon, T., Davis, T., and Wisner, B., (1994), *At Risk: Natural Hazards, People's Vulnerability, and Disasters*. London: Routledge, (1994).

Bolin, R. and Stanford, L., (1998). *The Northridge Earthquake: Vulnerability and Disaster*, London: Routledge Publications.

Caballero-Anthony, M., Cook, A.D.B., & Trajano, J.C. (2015). Nepal earthquake: Enhancing international humanitarian cooperation. (RSIS Commentaries, No. 100). RSIS Commentaries. Nanyang Technological University, Singapore. http://hdl.handle.net/10220/26001

CFE-DMHA. (2015). Nepal Disaster Management Reference Handbook. Centre for Excellence in Disaster Management & Humanitarian Assistance (U.S. Department of Defense), Ford Island, Hawaii.

Chaulagain, H., Rodrigues, H., Silva, V., Spacone, E., and Varum, H. (2015a). Earthquake loss estimation for the Kathmandu Valley. *Bull Earthq Eng. (in review).*

Chaulagain, H., Rodrigues, H., Silva, V., Spacone, E., and Varum, H. (2015b). Seismic risk assessment and hazard mapping in Nepal. *Natural Hazards*, 78(1):583-602.

Cohen, C. and Werker, E.D., (2008). The Political Economy of Natural Disasters. *Journal of Conflict Resolution*, 52(6): 795-819.

Cutter, S.I., (2011) Migration and Global Environmental Change. CSI: The Katrina Exodus: Internal Displacements and Unequal Outcomes. Hazards and Vulnerability Research Institute. University of South Carolina. SC, USA. p.12. Available at: http://www.bis.gov.uk/assets/foresight/docs/migration/case-studies/11-1156-cs1-katrina-exodus-internal-displacements.pdf

Davies, I., (2015). Introduction. In: Disaster Risk Management in Asia and the Pacific (ed.: I. Davies). New York, USA: Routeledge Publications, and the Asian Development Bank Institute, Tokyo, Japan, pp. 3-32.

Ding S.I., Hu, Y.H., Zhang, Z.K., Wang T., (2015), A contrast study of the traumatic condition between the wounded in 5.12 Wenchuan earthquake and 4.25 Nepal earthquake. *Chinese Journal of Traumatology*: 18(3):157-60., http://dx.doi.org/10.1016/j.cjtee.2015.08.001

DPNet, Disaster situation Report, Nepal. [online] 2015, June 22 last update. [cited 2015, Jun 29]. Disaster Prevention Network, (2015). Available from: http://www.dpnet.org.np/index.php?pageName=disaster.

DPNN, (2007), Preparedness in Practice. Disaster Preparedness Network-Nepal, and UNDP Nepal with assistance from European Commission Humanitarian Aid Department. Souvenir-2064. Disaster Preparedness Network-Nepal, Kalimati, Nepal, p.101.

Ehrlich, R.S., The state of Nepal's historic sites after major earthquake, (2015), Report – 27 April, 2015. Retrieved 25 August, 2015, http://www.cnn.com/2015/04/26/travel/nepalearthquake-landmarks/index.html.

Eriksson, M.G., Rana, G. M., Mendez, J. M. and Pradhan, B.K., (2007). National Policy and Strategy for Disaster Risk Management. The International Centre for Integrated Mountain Development (ICIMOD), p. 280.

FAO, (2014). *Managing climate risks and adapting to climate change in the agriculture sector in Nepal*. Climate, Energy and Tenure Division (NRC), Food and Agriculture Organization of the United Nations (FAO). Rome. Italy, (2014).

Fernandez, J., Mattingly, S., Bendimerad, F., Cardona, O. (2006). Megacity Indicators System Implementation in Metro Manila. EMI Topical Report TR-07-01, Earthquakes and Megacities Initiative.

Field, S., (2010). *Urban risks: moving from humanitarian responses to disaster prevention. Wilton Park Conference Report. Monday 22 - Thursday 25 November 2010 | WP1059* Wilton Park.

Fisek, G., Müderrisoglu, S., Yeniçeri, N., and Özkarar, G., (2003). Informed Ownership, Training, and Organization: Ingredients of Successful Disaster Preparedness by the Public. *World Bank Meeting on Disaster Preparedness, Istanbul.* Available: www.cendim.boun.edu.tr

Freund, F. T., (2009). Stress-Activated Positive Hole Charge Carriers in Rocks and the Generation of Pre-earthquake Signals. In: *Electromagnetic Phenomena Associated with Earthquakes and Volcanoes*, M. Hayakawa (ed.), pp. 41-96, Research Signpost, India.

Gautam, M.K., (2000). Social impact assessment of South Asia Poverty Alleviation Programme: Nepal. A pilot study. Impact Assessment Technical

Report. SAPAP/UNDP/UNOPS/RAS United Nations Office for Project Services, Kuala Lumpur, Malaysia.

GCDR (Ed.), (2012). Detecting Disaster Root Causes – A Framework and an Analytic Tool for Practitioners. DKKV Publication Series 48, German Committee for Disaster Reduction, Bonn, Germany, p. 62.

GIWA, (2002). GIWA Methodology. Detailed Assessment, Causal Chain Analysis, Policy Option Analysis. *Global International Waters Assessment*, UNDP.

Goda, K., Kiyota, T., Pokhrel, R.M., Chiaro, G., Katagiri, T. Sharma, K. and Wilkinson. S. (2015). The 2015 Gorkha Nepal earthquake: insights from earthquake damage survey. *Front. Built Environ.* 1:8. doi: 10.3389/fbuil.2015.00008

GoN, (2011). *Priority framework for action (2011–2020) Climate change adaptation and disaster risk management in agriculture*, Kathmandu Government of Nepal: Kathmandu.

GoN, (2014), Kathmandu Valley Post-Earthquake Debris Management: Strategic Plan. Ministry of Federal Affairs and Local Development, Government of Nepal: Kathmandu.

Gupta, I. D., (2006). Delineation of probable seismic sources in India and neighbour-hood by a comparative analysis of seismotectonic characteristics of the region. *Soil Dynam. Earthquake Eng.* 26, 766-790. doi:10.1016/j.soildyn.2005.12.007.

Haines-Young, R. and Potschin, M., (2010), The links between biodiversity, ecosystem services and human well-being. In: Ecosystem Ecology: A New Synthesis (Eds., David., G. Raffaelli and Christopher, L. J. Frid). BES Ecological Reviews Series. Cambridge, UK: Cambridge University Press, pp. 110-138.

Hajibabaee, M., Amini-Hosseini, K., Ghayamghamian, M.R., (2014) Earthquake risk assessment in urban fabrics based on physical, socio-economic and response capacity parametres (A case study: Tehran city). *Natural Hazards*, 74(3): 2229-2250.

Hosseini, M. and Hosseini, K.A. (2008). *Recent Development in Earthquake Risk Management Plans and Programmes in Tehran.* The 14th World Conference on Earthquake Engineering. October 12-17, Beijing, China.

IASC, (2010). Meeting Humanitarian Challenges in Urban Areas, Geneva: IASC. (www.alnap.org/resource/6196.aspx).

IED, (2015). Response to Nepal's Earthquake: Ten Lessons from Evaluations. Independent Evaluation, Independent Evaluation Department, *Asian Development Bank*, Manila, Philippines.

Jigyasu, Rohit, (2012). "Reducing Disaster Vulnerability through Local Knowledge and Capacity – The Case of Earthquake-prone Rural Communities in India and Nepal", Dr. ing thesis, *Norwegian University of Science and Technology, Trondheim*,.

Kang, P., Zhang, L., Liang, W., *et al.*, (2012). Medical evacuation management and clinical characteristics of 3,255 inpatients after the 2010 Yushu earthquake in China. J. *Trauma Acute Care Surg.*, 72:1626-1633.

Karkee, K., (2004). *Land Degradation in Nepal: A menace to economy and ecosystems international Master's Programme in environmental science*, Sweden: University of Lund.

Khazai, B., Anhorn, J., Girard, T., Brink, S., Daniell, J., Bessel, T., Mühr, B., Flörchinger, V. and Kunz-Plapp, T. (2015). Shelter response and vulnerability of displaced populations in the April 25, 2015. Nepal Earthquake. Centre for Disaster Management and Risk Reduction Technology of the Karlsruhe Institute of Technology, and the South Asia Institute, Heidelberg University, 05.05.2015, *Nepal Earthquake: CEDIM Report* No. 2, Focus on Shelter, p.31.

Kuban, R., MacKenzie-Carey, H., (2001). Community-wide Vulnerability and Capacity Assessment. Government of Canada: Office of Critical Infrastructure Protection and Emergency Preparedness.

Lallemant, D., Wong, S., Morales, K., Kiremidjian, A., (2014). A Framework and Case Study for Dynamic Urban Risk Assessment. *Proceedings of the 10th National Conference in Earthquake Engineering*, Anchorage, AK: Earthquake Engineering Research Institute.

Le, G. (2013). Scaling up urban resilience and disaster risk reduction: preparing for a major earthquake in Kathmandu. Masters of Art in Development and Emergency Practice 2011-2012. Dissertation thesis for the Degree of M.A., Oxford Brookes University Centre for Development & Emergency Practice (CENDEP), *School of Architecture, Faculty of Technology, Design and Environment*, p. 69.

Lewis, D. (2012). Key Note at the 27th ALNAP Annual Meeting, Chennai, India. The Urban Challenge - adapting humanitarian response to a changing world. 17 January, 2012 [Homepage of ALNAP], [Online]. Available: http://www.alnap.org/resource/6277.aspx.

LRMP, (1986). Forestry land-use report Mimeograph, Topographical Survey Branch, Land Resouce Management Programme, Kathmandu, Nepal.

Madamba, C. A., Gourraud, C. and Crozier, R. (2015). 2015 Nepal Earthquake. M_W7.6 Gorkha Earthquake Response and Early Recovery Case Study – First Five Months. Earthquakes and Megacities Initiative, Manila, Philippines. p. 38. http://emi-megacities.org/

McFadden, L., (2007). Vulnerability Analysis in Environmental Management: Widening and Deepening its approach. *Environmental Conservation*, 34(3): 195-204.

Mechler, R., (2014). Financing and risk financing disaster risk reduction in Asia and the Pacific. In: *Disaster Risk Management in Asia and the Pacific* (Ed: I. Davis): Roultege – Taylor and Francis Group, New York, USA and Asian Development Bank Institute, Tokyo, Japan, pp. 168-208.

Mitchell, D. (2010). Land tenure and disaster risk management. *Land Tenure Journal*, *1* (1) : 121-141.

MoEST, (2008). Thematic assessment report on land degradation. Ministry of Environment, Science and Technology; Government of Nepal, Kathmandu, Nepal.

MoHA and IOM, (2013). *Kathmandu Valley Open Spaces*, Government of Nepal, Ministry of Home Affairs, Kathmandu, and International Organization for Migration, Nepal. Available from: https://sites.google.com/site/kathmanduopenspaces/home (Accessed 3 May 2015)

MoSTE, (2015). Indigenous and Local Knowledge and Practices for Climate Resilience in Nepal, Mainstreaming Climate Change Risk Management in Development, Ministry of Science, Technology and Environment (MoSTE), Kathmandu, Nepal, p. 90.

Neupane, R.P. and Thapa, G.B. (2001). Impact of agro-forestry intervention on farm income under the subsistence farming system of the middle hills, *Nepal. Agroforest. Syst.*, 53: 31-37.

NFSC, (2015). Nepal Earthquake: Agricultural Livelihood Impact Appraisal in Six Most Affected Districts. Nepal Food Security Cluster, Food and Agriculture Organization of the United Nations. Kathmandu, Nepal. p.53. https://www.humanitarianresponse.info

NRRC, (2011). Disaster Risk Reduction in Nepal Flagship Programmes. *The Nepal Risk Reduction Consortium*, April 2011, p. 61.

NSET, National Strategy for Disaster Risk Management in Nepal. March 2008. National Society for Earthquake Technology, Kathmandu, Nepal, UNDP, Government of Nepal and European Commission Humanitarian Aid.

Pokharel, J.R., Wonta, T.R., and Neupane, R.C., (2007). *Preparedness in Practice*. Souvenir. Disaster Preparedness Network – Nepal. Kathmandu, Nepal.

Ramirez, M., Peek-Asa, C. (2005). *Epidemiology of Traumatic Injuries from Earthquakes*. Epidemiol Rev. 2005: 27:47-55, http://dx.doi.org/10.1093/epirev/mxi005 PMid:15958426

Rana, G., Beatrice Murray, A., Maharjan, D.R. and Thaku, A. K. (2007). *Kathmandu Valley Environment Outlook*. International Centre for Integrated Mountain Development, Kathmandu, Nepal.

Rothenberger, B. and Stolz, N. (2015). Risk Assessment Nepal – After the Earthquakes in April and May 2015. A desk study undertaken by the Swiss NGO Disaster Risk Reduction Platform, August 2015. Caritas Switzerland, Geneva, Switzerland, p.22. http://www.drrplatform.org/

Sharma, D.C.,(2015). Nepal earthquake exposes gaps in disaster preparedness. *The Lancet Journal*, 385(9980):1819-1820.

Shelter Cluster Nepal, *Shelter Contingency Plan for the Coordination of Shelter Preparedness and Response in Nepal*, Update 2014.

Simkhada, P., van Teijlingen, E., Pant, P.R., Sathian, B, Tuladhar, G. (2015). Public Health, Prevention and Health Promotion in Post-Earthquake Nepal. *Nepal J. Epidemiol.* 5(2):462-464.

Stark, C. (2015). "Nepal earthquake: A tragedy waiting to happen" – April 27, 2015 CNN.com. Retrieved August 25, 2015, from http://www.cnn.com/2015/04/25/opinions/stark-nepalearthquake-geology/index. html

Sungay, B., Cakti, E. and Erdik, M. (2012). Discussing Vulnerability, Capacity and Resilience of the Community in the face of Earthquakes at a Microscale. Bogazici University, Kandilli Observatory and Earthquake Research Institute, WCEE 2012.

Sungay, B., Cakti, E., & Erdik, M. (2010). Assessment of the Coping Capacity of a Community Under Earthquake Threat. In Proceedings of the 14th European Conference on Earthquake Engineering, Ohrid.

Takeuchi, Y., Mulyasari, F., Shaw, R. (2011). Chapter 4 Roles of Family and Community in Disaster Education. In *Community, Environment and Disaster Risk Management*, vol 7. Edited by Shaw, R., Takeuchi, KSY. Emerald Group Publishing Limited, UK. 77-94. OpenURL.

Thapa, N. (1998). "Bhadau Panchko Bhookampa 2045"(The Earthquake of 1988). Kathmandu: Niranjan Thapa.

The World Factbook: Nepal, Retrieved, (2015), available link at https://www.cia.gov/library/publications/the-world-factbook/geos/np.html

Tuladhar, G., Yatabe, R., Dahal, R.K., and Bhandary, N.P. (2015). Disaster risk reduction knowledge of local people in Nepal. *Geoenvironmental Disasters* 2:5 DOI 10.1186/s40677-014-0011-4

Turner, B.L. II, Kasperson, R.E., Matson, P., McCarthy, J.J., Corell, R.W., Christensen, L., Eckley, N., Kasperson, J.X., Luers, A., Martello, M.L., Polsky, C., Pulsipher, A. and Schiller, A. (2003). Framework for vulnerability analysis in sustainability science. *Proceedings of the National Academy of Sciences* 100, 8074-78.

UN Habitat (2010). Land and Natural Disasters: Guidance for Practitioners. United Nations Human Settlements Programme (UN-HABITAT), P.O. Box 30030, Nairobi 00100, Kenya.

UNDP, (2008). Nepal Country Report – Global Assessment of Risk. ISDR Global Assessment Report on Poverty and Disaster Risk 2009. United Nations Development Programme, Kathmandu, Nepal, p.193.

UNDP (undated). Guidance Notes on Recovery – Environment, Internatioal Recovery Programme, UNDP India, New Delhi, and UNISDR.

UNHSP, (2010) Land and Natural Disasters Guidance for Practitioners. United Nations Human Settlement Programme, UN Habitat, Nairobi, Kenya, p.140.

UNISDR, (2011). *Global Assessment Report 2011: Revealing Risk, Redefining Development.* UNISDR.

UNOCHA, Weekly Situation Update; 26.06.2015; [online] 2015, June 26 last update. [cited 2015, Jun 29], UN Office for the Coordination of Humanitarian Affairs, (2015) – Nepal Earthquake Assessment Unit. Available from: http://reliefweb.int/report/nepal/nepal-earthquake-weekly-situation-update-26-june-2015

URD (2014). Urban Preparedness: Lessons from the Kathmandu Valley. British Red Cross, *Nepal Red Cross and Urgence Rehabilitation Development*.

WHO (2015) Policy and technical topics: Response to emergencies and outbreaks. World Health Organization, Regional Office for South-East Asia,

Sixty-eighth Session SEA/RC68/10 Dili, Timor-Leste 7–11 September 2015. Regional Committee Provisional Agenda item 8.1.

Wisner, B., Blaikie, P.M., Cannon, T. and Davis, I., (2004). *At Risk:Natural Hazards, People's Vulnerability, and Disasters*. (2nd ed.), London: Routledge Publications.

Wu, H., Tikhonov, I.N., and C′esped, A.R. (2015). Multi-parametric analysis of earthquake precursors. *Russian Journal of Earth Sciences*, 15:1-6.

Yasir, A. (2009). *The Political Economy of Disaster Vulnerability: A Case Study of Pakistan Earthquake 2005*. Munich Personal RePEc Archive. London School of Economics & Political Science. Online at https://mpra.ub.uni-muenchen.de/20762/MPRA Paper No. 20762, posted 17. February 2010 23:41 UTC.

11
Chemical Disasters and Their Management – An Overview

S. V. S. Rana

Introduction

Chemicals are an integral part of everyday life. Over 1,00,000 chemical substances are used by man today for different activities. They play a significant role in economics, industry and human well-being. Yet they endanger human health and environment if not managed properly. The health related effects range from acute poisoning to long term effects, such as cancer, birth defects, neurological problems and endocrine disruption. Environmental effects include effects on sensitive species/ ecosystems to large scale issues such as acid rain, stratospheric ozone depletion and eutrophication of water bodies. People are exposed through occupational activities as well as daily life through air, water and food to a variety of chemicals. In turn, they manifest into several occupational diseases. International Labour Organization (ILO) organized two important conventions on occupational safety and health, i.e. Radiation Protection Convention (No. 115) in 1960 and Benzene Convention (No. 136) in 1971 (http://www.ilo.org). The Occupational Safety and Health Act or Williams-Steiger Act was signed by President of the United States in December 1970. On May 1, 1975, the Japanese Government promulgated the Working Environment Measurement Law in 1955. A Special Commission (Commission for the Investigation of Health Hazards of Chemical Compounds in the Work Area), was formed in Germany – known as Deutsche Forschungsgemeinschaft. Later on several agencies like Occupational Safety Health Association (OSHA), National Institute of Occupational Safety and Health (NIOSH), American Conference on Governmental Industrial Hygienists (ACGIH) and others were inducted with a primary objective of safeguarding human health in work environment. The concern of American citizens towards threat of hazardous substances and chemicals led the U.S. congress to enact the Superfund Legislation in 1980. Superfund created Agency for Toxic Substances and Disease Registry (ATSDR) within the framework of Public Health Service.

Global economy foresees a rapid increase in generation of hazardous wastes. Although most of the conventional hazardous wastes are produced in industrial and manufacturing units, significant amounts are generated in non-industrial sectors including sludge from waste water treatment plants, waste oils and waster batteries. Hazardous wastes contaminate non-hazardous wastes. History has witnessed several catastrophic events during recent past. A brief review of these events signifies the environmental threats and exposes consequences demanding sound management policies.

Acid Rain

It was identified in mid, 1970s as an ecological problem linked to emissions of oxides of sulphur, nitrogen, fuel combustion that are oxidized in the atmosphere to form acids that make the precipitation as acidic and referred as acid rain. It affected forests, food crops, soil health, ground-water quality, surface waters, aquatic biota, materials and human health. In Sweden alone 15,000 lakes turned acidic and so were thousands in Norway, the US and Canada. India too experienced acid rains in Trombay, Chembur, Pune and Mumbai (Krug and Frink, 1983).

London Smog

The Great Smog or Big Smog was a severe air pollution episode that affected London in December 1952. Until 8th December 4,000 people had died prematurely and 1,00,000 fell sick due to respiratory problems. It is known as the worst air pollution event in the history of United Kingdom (Berridge Virginia, 2005).

Meuse River Valley (Belgium) Episode

In 1930, Meuse valley fog killed 60 people in Belgium due to a combination of industrial air pollution and climatic conditions. Cattle in the area were also affected. Fluorine gas from the nearby factories was found to be the killer (Nemery *et.al.*, 2001).

Sevenso Disaster

It was an industrial accident that occurred on July 10, 1976 in a small chemical manufacturing plant approximately 20 km north of Milan. It resulted in the highest known exposure to 2, 3, 7, 8-tetrachlorodibenzo-p-dioxin (TCDD) in a residential population (Hombergerer, *et.al.*, 1979).

Minamata Disease

It was first discovered in Minamata Bay in the Kumamoto prefecture of Japan in 1956. It was caused by the release of methyl mercury in the industrial waste water by Chisso Corporation Chemical Industry which continued from 1932-1968. As of March 2001, 2265 people have been officially recognized having Minamata disease. 1784 of whom had died and over 10,000 have received compensation from Chisso. A second outbreak of Minamata disease occurred in 1965 in Nigata prefecture (George, 2001).

Chernobyl Accident

It was a catastrophic nuclear accident that occurred on 26th April, 1986 at Chernobyl Nuclear Power Plant in the town of Pripyat in Ukraine. It was the worst nuclear power plant accident in history in terms of cost and casualties. It was level 7 accidents in the International Nuclear Event Scale (Abbott, 2006).

Three Mile Island tragedy

It was a partial nuclear meltdown that occurred on March 28, 1979 at reactor no. 2 of Three Mile Island Nuclear Generating station (TMI-2) in Dauphin County, Pennsylvania, United States. It was the worst accident in commercial nuclear power plant industry. It was rated five in the international nuclear event scale with wider consequences (Samuel, 2004).

Love canal episode

Love canal is the neighbourhood of Niagra Falls, New York. In the late

1970s, love canal received national attention for ensuing health effects that originated from the disposal of 22,000 barrels of toxic waste. Numerous families were displaced. Many of them indicated leukemia (Blum, 2008).

Fukushima Episode

Several nuclear power facilities were affected during the Great East Japan Earthquake occurred on 11th March, 2011. A series of large tsunami waves reached the TEOCO's Fukushima Dai-ichi site. The earthquake and tsunami waves caused widespread devastation across a large part of Japan killing more than 14,000 of people. About 10,000 were reported missing (IAEA, 2011).

Bhopal Gas Tragedy

The worst industrial tragedy occurred on the night of December 2-3, 1984. Over 5,00,000 people were exposed to deadly methyl isocyanate and other chemicals leaking from the pesticide plant of Union Carbide India Limited, Bhopal (India). The gas killed 8,000 people and injured 5,58,125 of which 3900 were permanently disabled (Banerjee, 1987).

Exxon Valdez Oil Spill, Alaska

On March 24, 1989, Exxon Valdez, an oil tanker targeted to Long Beach, California hit the Bligh Island Reef, Prince William Sound Alaska, spilling 2,60,000 to 7,50,000 barrels of crude oil over the next few days. Immediate effects of spill are the death of 2,50,000 birds, at least 2800 sea otters and hundreds of other sea creatures as per reports of 2010, there was still an estimated 23,000 gallons of crude oil in Alaska soil, breaking down only 4 per cent per year (Sarah, 2003).

Halifax Explosion

The deadliest industrial disaster in Canada happened on December 6, 1917, when a cargo ship loaded with wartime explosives collided with a Norweign vessel in the Halifax harbour causing a massive explosion that devastated Halifax (MacDonald, 2005).

The Kuwait Oil Fires

Around 6 million barrels of oil were lost from January to November 1991, 600 oil wells were set ablaze as part of the second earth policy by the retreating Iraqi military forces. $ 1.5 billion was spent by Kuwait to extinguish the fires that caused heavy pollution to the air and soil (Suzanne, 2004).

Gulf of Mexico Dead Zone

The most infamous hypoxic zone in the United States, the Gulf of Mexico dead zone is the dumping area of nitrogen and phosphorus. The substances come from the Mississippi river which is the drainage area for almost half of continental America (Potera, 2008).

E-Waste in Guiyu, China

Guiyu is the largest electronic waste site on earth. As a result 88 per cent of the children suffer from lead poisoning. The province is referred as electronic graveyard. None of these horrifying examples of chemical/ nuclear disasters are natural but man made. Keeping the environment and people safe from harmful substances and hazardous wastes goes beyond management. However, for more than 30 years UNEP's work has supported initiatives related to specific chemicals or to critical elements of their life cycles. A number of international treaties on chemicals and waste have been hosted by UNEP (Johnson, 2006).

International Treaties on Chemicals and Waste

Basel convention

This treaty on the control of trans-boundary movement of hazardous waste and their disposal became effective from 5th May, 1992. One hundred and eighty two states and EU are the parties of convention.

Rotterdam convention

Rotterdam convention is a multilateral treaty to promote shared responsibilities in relation to impact of hazardous chemicals. The 6th meeting of the Rotterdam convention was held from 28th April to 10th May, 2013 in Geneva, Switzerland.

Stockholm convention

S C on POPs is an international environmental treaty signed in 2001 and effective from May 2004, that aims to eliminate or restrict the use and production of POPs.

UNEP Minamata Convention

It is a global treaty to protect human health and the environment from the adverse effects of mercury. It was signed on 19th January, 2013 and adopted on 10th October, 2013 in Kumamoto, Japan. Major highlights of convention include a ban on new mercury mines and phase out the existing ones.

SAICM (The Strategic Approach to International Chemical Management)

It was adopted in February, 2006. It was supported by recommendations of 2002 Johannesburg Summit on sustainable development. It includes 175 governments, 85 NGOs and broad range of representatives from industry and civil society.

GPA (Global Programme of Action for protection of marine environment)

It aims at protecting the marine environment from land based activities addressing the connectivity amongst terrestrial, freshwater, coastal and marine ecosystems.

Montreal Protocol

For the first time, the world's major producers and consumers of pollutants accused of destroying the ozone layer met at Montreal on September 16, 1987. Twenty four countries signed the protocol that came into force on January 1, 1989. The protocol sets out a schedule of freeze on five most severe CFCs. In August 1989, 44 countries and the EEC ratified the Montreal protocol.

Saving the Ozone layer Conference, London

One hundred twenty three countries and the EU attended this conference held from March 5-7, 1989 at London. It was universally agreed that the Montreal protocol which calls for 50 per cent reduction of the use of chlorofluorocarbons by 1998, should be accepted and implemented worldwide.

International Agencies involved in Safety against Chemicals and Hazardous Wastes

In delivering policy and technical assistance for the sound management of chemicals, UNEP builds and strengthens partnerships with governments, international organizations and non-government organizations. It also works closely with agencies within UN family including WHO, FAO, UNIDO, ILO, UNITAR, UNDP and the World Bank, and with the secretaries of the Basel, Rotterdam, Stockholm and the Minamata Conventions.

The WHO hosts a number of bodies specializing in hazardous chemicals and waste activities including –

- International Programme on Chemical Safety (IPCS),
- Inter-Organization Programme for the sound Management of Chemicals (IOMS),
- Intergovernmental Forum on Chemical Safety (IFCS); and
- Health and Environment Linkages Initiative (HELI).

A series of regional consultations was held in Indonesia, Zambia, Czech Republic and Uruguay in early 2016 in preparation for the 7th Session of the Intergovernmental Negotiating Committee (INC7) in the Dead Sea Area in Jordan from 10-15 March, 2016.

UNEP Initiatives

The United Nations Industrial Development Organization (UNIDO) undertakes activities on chemicals through its Energy and Environment Programme.

The Food and Agriculture Organization of the United Nations (FAO) has activities in the field of pesticides, a major chemicals sector including many hazardous chemicals.

The United Nations for Training and Research (UNITAR) provide support to governments and stakeholders through its chemicals and waste management programme.

The International Labour Office (ILO) contains references to the safe use of chemicals in the workplace and prevention of major chemical accidents.

The United Nations Development Programme (UNDP) helps countries to improve their chemicals management programmes and attain the Millennium Development Goals (MDGs) by providing MDG support services through the chemicals and waste management programme.

The Organization for Economic Co-operation and Development (OECD) hold a wealth of information on the topic of Chemical safety and Biosafety.

The Global Chemicals Outlook

The Global Chemicals Outlook report concludes a two year long process that has brought together the governments, industry, academics and civil society to provide for the first time a comprehensive environmental understanding and up to date assessment of trends and changes affecting the production and use of chemicals throughout their life cycle, their health and environment effects, economic implications and policy options.

This report is expected to provide a stimulating and convincing set of scientifically-based economic arguments to elevate chemicals management to the top of the international policy agenda as an essential condition to the achievement of sustainable development. Published in 2012, a weeks before ICCM3, it also is a very strong policy document designed to support the SAICM process and to contribute to the revitalization of its partnership spirit.

Agency for Toxic Substances and Disease Registry

ATSDR based in Atlanta, Georgia is a federal public health agency of the US Department of Health and Human Services. ATSDR serves the public by using the best science taking responsive public health actions and providing trusted health information to prevent harmful exposure and diseases related to toxic substances.

International Union of Toxicology (IUTOX)

Mission of IUTOX is to improve human health through the science and practice of toxicology worldwide. IUTOX achieves its vision by fostering international scientific cooperation for the global acquisition and utilization of knowledge in toxicology for improvement of health of humans and their environment. Founded in 1980, IUTOX now has 63 affiliated societies including India representing all six continents and over 25,000 toxicologists from industry, academia and governments as members: offering a diverse and challenging perspective on every issue and development related to the profession.

Regulatory Measures

Environmental laws and policies in India provide significantly for disaster risk reduction in the context of natural disasters, but the environment sector narrowly recognize chemical disasters and their management. However, Disaster Management Act, 2005 provides significant consideration to environment. National Disaster Management Authority (NDMA) has been entrusted the responsibility of developing policies and guidelines on various aspects of disaster management. Ministry of Environment and Forests has been identified as a nodal agency for management of chemical disasters in the country. Laws and policies for environmental protection in India are summarized as follows :

Acts

- The Indian Forest Act, 1927
- Factories Act, 1948
- Factories Amendment Act, 1987
- Wildlife Protection Act, 1972
- The Water Prevention and Control of Pollution Act, 1974
- Forest Conservation Act, 1980
- The Air Prevention and Control of Pollution Act, 1981
- Environment Protection Act, 1986
- The Public Liability Insurance Act, 1991
- Biological Diversity Act, 2002
- Forest Rights Act, 2006
- The Cultural Heritage Conservation Bill, 2010
- Mine and Minerals Act, 2010
- National Green Tribunal Act, 2010

Rules

- The Manufacture, Storage and Import of Hazardous Chemicals Rules, 1989
- Manufacture, use, import, export and storage of hazardous micro-organisms, genetically engineered organisms or cells Rules, 1989

- Emergency preparedness, Planning and Response to chemical accidents Rules
- Dumping and disposal of fly ash discharged from coal or lignite based thermal power plants on land, Rules 1999
- Biomedical waste management and handling, Rules 1998
- The Hazardous wastes management and handling, Rules 1989
- Environment sitting for industrial projects, Rules 1999
- The Municipal Waste management and handling, Rules 2000
- Hazardous Waste management and handling and transboundary, Rules 2008
- Plastic Waste management and handling (Amendment), Rules 2011

Polocies

- National Environmental Policy, 2006
- National Disaster Management Policy, 2009

Role of Toxicology in Regulatory Programmes

Current programmes for controlling human exposure to toxic chemicals are concerned with the burden of proof which is the responsibility for demonstrating whether a substance is safe or hazardous. For carcinogenic chemicals, regulators generally rely on the concept of acceptable daily intake (ADI). The ADI for a chemical is derived by applying a safety factor – usually 100 – to the human equivalent of the lowest "No Observed Effect Level (NOEL)" revealed in animal experiments. When the estimated human exposure to a chemical falls below the ADI, it is considered "safe". There are other concepts *viz.*, no risk, negligible risk etc.

In USA, several agencies like FDA, EPA, Occupational Safety and Health Association (OSHA) and the Consumer Product Safety Commission (CPSC) are involved in regulating human exposure to chemicals including human drugs, medical devices and cosmetics. No pesticide can be marketed unless it has been registered by the EPA. The Toxic Substances Control Act (TSCA) covers all chemical substances manufactured or processed in or imported into the United States except for substances already regulated under other laws.

Several statutes administered by the EPA regulate land disposal of hazardous materials (those which are ignitable, corrosive, reactive or toxic). In 1976, the Resource Conservation and Recovery Act (RCRA) established a comprehensive federal scheme for regulating hazardous waste. RCRA directs the EPA to regulate the activities of generators, transporters, and those who treat, store or dispose of hazardous waste to protect human health and environment.

Modern Toxicology has developed in substantial part in response to the information needs of contemporary regulation. Regulatory agencies often prescribe the specific objectives and design of studies that are conducted to satisfy regulatory requirements.

The National Toxicology Programme (NTP) was established in 1978 as an administrative umbrella for coordinating federal efforts to improve test methods and coordinate toxicological studies then underway. Health risk assessment research techniques have been improved accordingly.

Conclusion

The ubiquitous presence of a variety of chemicals in the environment has given rise to the concept of chemosphere. It is that part of the environment which is dominated by chemicals. Chemosphere is composed of essential and non-essential chemicals. Essential chemicals play a vital role in human and ecosystem health. Whereas non-essential chemicals pose serious risks to ecology. Their management has been treated at priority by federal agencies as well as society. Several international treaties have been signed to manage hazardous chemicals. UNEP has taken initiatives to manage chemical wastes and safeguard the ecosystems. In addition, regulatory agencies in India and elsewhere have constituted policies, rules and Acts to manage chemical disasters. Honest implementation of these rules may help in keeping our planet chemically safe. Recent activities like 7th Session of the Intergovernmental Negotiating Committee held in Jordan in March 2016 on Minamata and similar events are expected to be helpful in attaining Millennium Development Goals (MDGs).

References

Abbott, P., (2006). *Chernobyl: Living with Risk and Uncertainty. Health Risk and Society*, 8.2, pp. 105-121.

Banerjee, B.N. (1987). *Environmental Pollution and Bhopal Killings*, New Delhi: Gyan Books.

Berridge, Virginia (Ed.). (2005). *Big Smoke. Fifty years after the 1952 London Smog.* Institute of Historical Research. London: University of London.

Blum, E.D., (2008). *Love Canal Revisited: Race, Class and Gender in Environmental Activism*. Kansas: Kansas University Press.

George, T. S., (2001). *Minamata: Pollution and the Struggle for Democracy in the Post-war Japan*, Harvard University, Asia Centre. ISBN 0-674-00785-9.

Graham, S. (2003). Environmental effects of Exxon Valdez Spill still being felt. *Scientific American*. Archived from the original on 29th March, 2006.

Homberger, E., R. Eggiani, G., Sambeth, J. and Wipf, H.K. (1979). The Seveso Accident: Its nature, extent and consequenes. *Ann OccupHyg*., 22, 327-370.

Krug, E.C and Frink, C.R., (1983). Acid rain and acid soil: A new perspective. *Science*, 221, 520-525.

MacDonald, L. (2005). *Curse of the Narrows. The Halifax Explosion of 1917*. Harper Collins. ISBN 978-0-00-200787-0.

Nemery, B., Peter, H.M. and Hoet, A.N. (2001). The Meuse Valley Fog of 1930: an air pollution disaster. *The Lancet*., 357, 704-708.

Potera, C. (2008). Corn ethanil revives dead zone concerns. *Env. Health Perspect*., 116, 242-243.

Suzanne, J.M. (2004). *The Gulf War: War and Conflict in the Middle East*. Rosen Publishing Group.ISBN 9780823945511.

Tim, J. (2006). "E-waste dump of the world", *Seatle Times,* Retrieved 2007-03-09.

Walker, J.S. (2004). *Three Mile Island: A Nuclear Crisis in Historical Perspective*. Berkeley: University of California Press.

12
Social Media: A Tool for Disaster Management

Shyamli Singh and *R. Vijendran*

Introduction

The term "social media" refers to Internet-based applications that enable people to communicate and share resources and information (Lindsay, 2011). It is a collaborative applications supported by Web 2.0 technologies that include, but is not limited to Twitter, Facebook, Myspace, wikis, and blogs. Blogs, wikis, and Myspace were the first applications becoming popular in the early 2000s while Facebook and Twitter are more recent creations. Social media provides many ways to disseminate information in a fast, inexpensive, and efficient manner. Social Media has the ability to not only to disseminate information to a network of people online, but also extend the information in a variety of other electronic and non-electronic ways. This helps to get the right information to the right people at the right time. This real-time environment helps support the decision-making needs of the public and emergency management during time critical/emergency situations (White, 2011).

The use of social media has become widespread and can serve a variety of purposes. In case of emergencies and disasters *social media* can be used somewhat passively to disseminate information and receive user feedback *via* incoming messages, wall posts, and polls. It can also be used as an emergency management tool which includes using the medium to conduct emergency communications and issue warnings; using social media to receive victim requests for assistance; monitoring user activities to establish situational awareness; and using uploaded images to create damage estimates, amongst others. However, many of these applications remain speculative, while other uses are still in their infancy

(Lindsay, 2011). Besides, social media can help people understand the residual disaster risks in their communities, and what is being done (structural and non-structural methods) to manage this risk. Several organizations around the world are using social media to engage with communities of interest to discuss ways to reduce disaster risk (Dufty, 2012). Applications like Facebook, Twitter and other Web 2.0 applications are especially suited for disaster response as they provide immediacy, two-way interactions and an opportunity for citizen journalists to provide up-to-the-minute information on what is happening on the ground.

A study was conducted at Indian Institute of Public Administration, New Delhi to understand the ways by which social media contributes in emergency response and risk reduction and the barriers in effective use of social media in Emergency Management and Disaster Risk Reduction. This chapter analyzes the contribution of social media in increasing the situational awareness for emergency management and the bottlenecks in embracing the use of social media for disaster management and a way ahead.

Methodology

In this study primary data was collected through questionnaires and google form which was circulated to the personnel of National Disaster management agency, National Disaster Response Force and Training, capacity building institutes in emergency management like National Institute of Disaster Management (NIDM) and various other line departments such as fire, police, hospitals etc. Besides, the inputs and opinions of officers of the various governmental departments, Armed Forces officers of Integrated Defence Staff (HQ IDS), Indian Army, Indian Navy and Indian Air-force were also taken. Inputs gained from informal discussions with officials from federal emergency management agencies were also used for arriving at the conclusions of the data analysis.

The questionnaire was so designed so as to cover three basic aspects of the social media viz., use of social media as a two way communication and information sharing tool, use of social media in emergency management and identify the barriers if any the effective use of social media and use of social media for better crisis response. There were a total of seventeen responses and not all of them attempted answering all the questions.

Result Discussion

Using social media as a two way communication tool

The advantage of social media as compared to traditional channels of communication is two way communications as well as direct communication with higher levels of organization in times of crisis (Dufty, 2012). Thus social media can be leveraged effectively by using it as a two way communication tool and build online network of communities. When asked if there is a web page of their organization, around 50 per cent of the people opined that their organization has a webpage (Fig. 12.1).

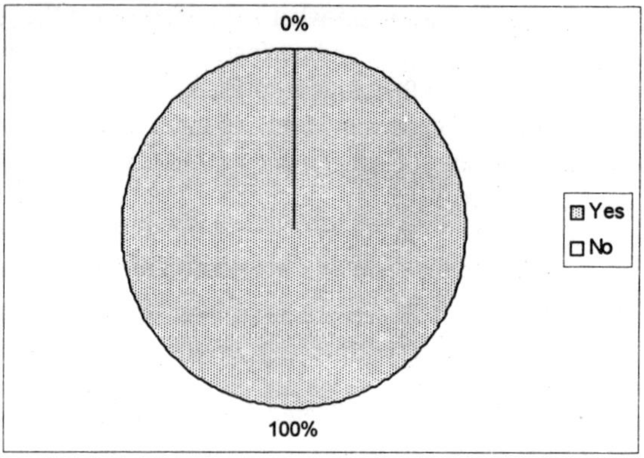

Fig. 12.1: Social media as a communication tool.

However, when asked if the question/answer page of the organization website is updated regularly, 47 per cent said it is updated regularly while 53 per cent of the respondents replied updates are not regular (Fig. 12.2). This would simply implies that around 50 per cent at least had their organizational web page.

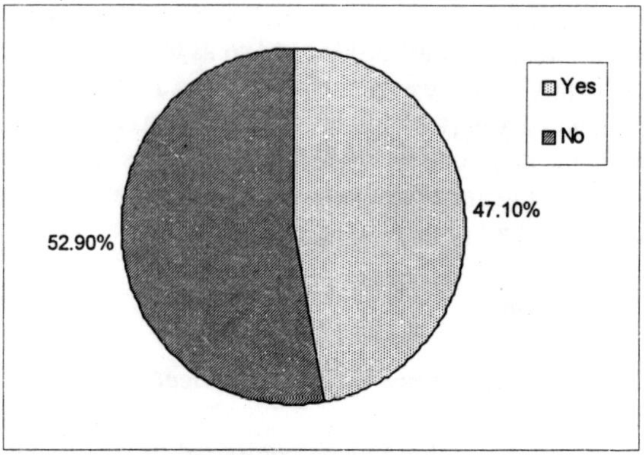

Fig. 12.2: Using Social media for regular sharing of information.

However, only one third (35%) of them use social media for two way interaction forming online network of communities sharing information. Sixty five per cent (Fig. 12.3) of the respondents negated that their organization receives and replies to input *via* social media indicating that only 35 per cent of them are involved in effectively building online network through two way communication.

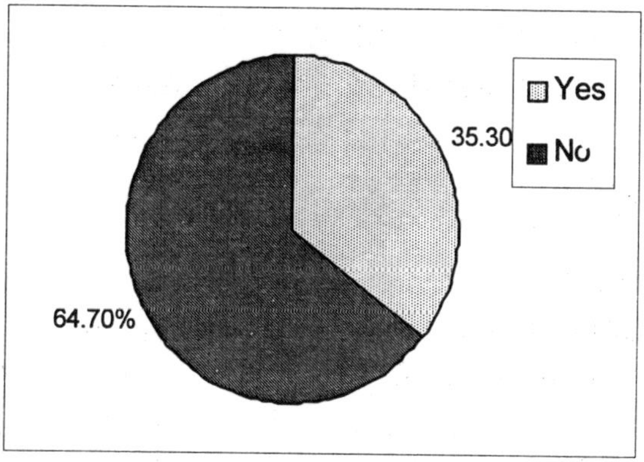

Fig. 12.3: Using Social media to build online communities by two way interaction.

A positive response of initiation of offline conversation and exchange with the audience was 24 per cent, indicating that most of them adopt passive mode for building up online community network (Fig. 12.4).

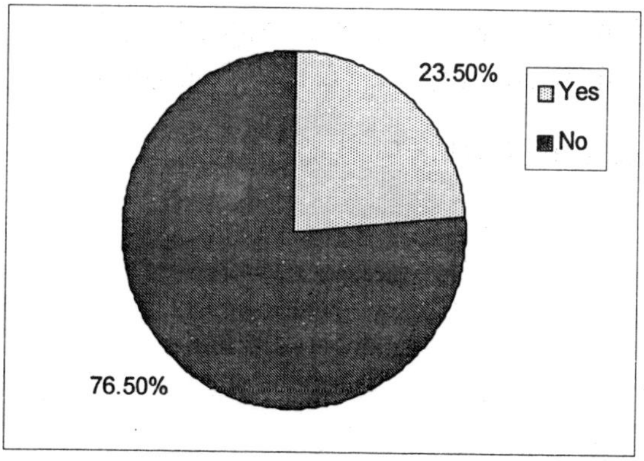

Fig. 12.4: Using Social media for building online community networks.

However, 30 per cent (Fig. 12.5) of the respondents had a forum to exchange two way communications with the population in real time during crisis.

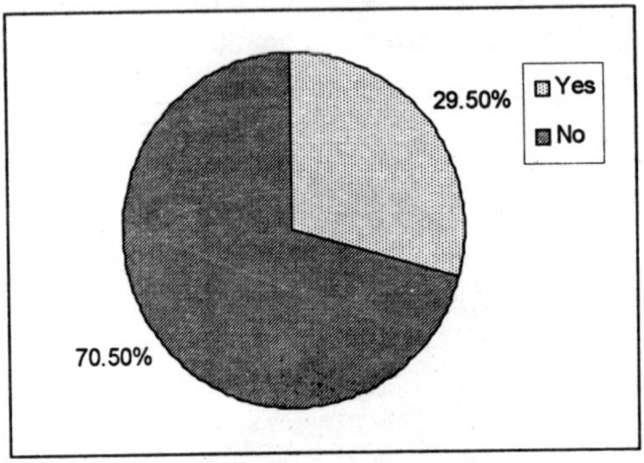

Fig. 12.5: Using Social media forums for receiving and sharing information in emergencies.

It is disheartening to note that 18 per cent (Fig. 12.6) of the respondents said they use online interaction risk awareness campaign to increase risk awareness through interactive games on social media. There seems to be a lack of utilizing cheaper crowd sourcing options readily available with the growing internet population. Building-up of social capital can lead to increased resilience amongst communities to respond and recover quickly in emergencies. The potential of social media is yet to be unleashed and leveraged successfully as a collaborative tool in managing crises effectively.

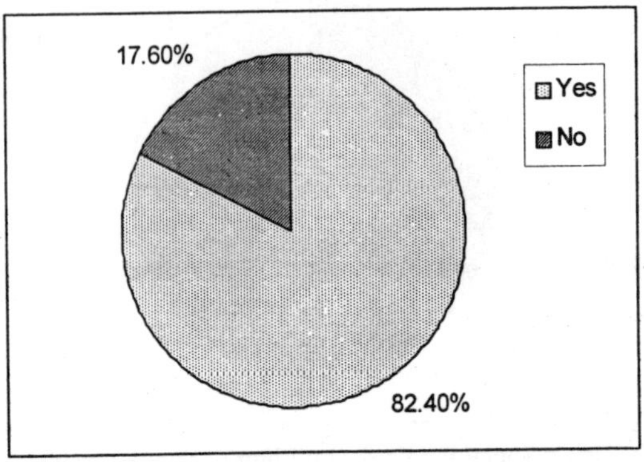

Fig. 12.6: Building-up community resilience and social capital.

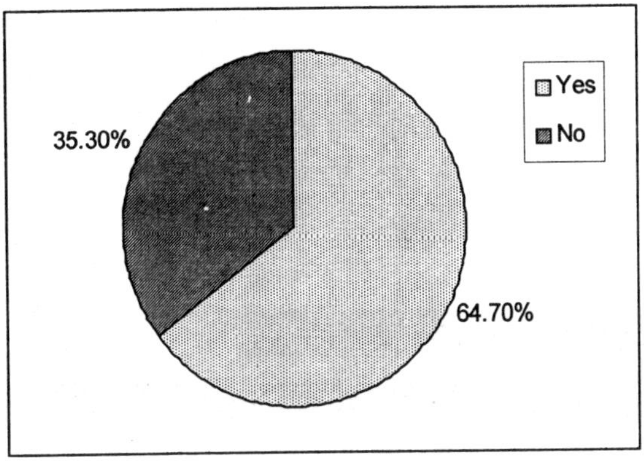

Fig. 12.7: Leveraging Social media in crises situations.

Fig. 12.7 clearly shows that 35 per cent of the respondents believe that citizens can use social media to request for assistance when in a crisis. Others do not believe that social media can be used in emergency situation due to the following reasons:

- Although, it is possible through social media to seek assistance in concerned area yet there is reliability and accuracy crisis. While it is possible to communicate through social media to seek assistance an area of concern in times of crisis is reliability and accuracy of information.
- In the aftermath of a crisis situation the communication channels are snapped due to power outages. This may further lead to discharging of mobile sets, computer etc. which act as conduits of information exchange.
- Some of the respondents did not feel the need to communicate through social media and use social media in crisis situations used or they simply did not have a presence on social media for interaction.

Use of social media by emergency managers

The visibility and presence of an organization on social media is important to engage communities and build-up their resilience by increasing their awareness towards achieving better response and recovery. The top down approach would be a significant influencing factor in increasing the mutual trust and engagement between the officials and public. In this regard 41 per cent (Fig. 12.8) of the respondents said they have an official page of their organization in social media websites and 29 per cent (Fig. 12.9) agreed when asked whether they used social media for emergency management.

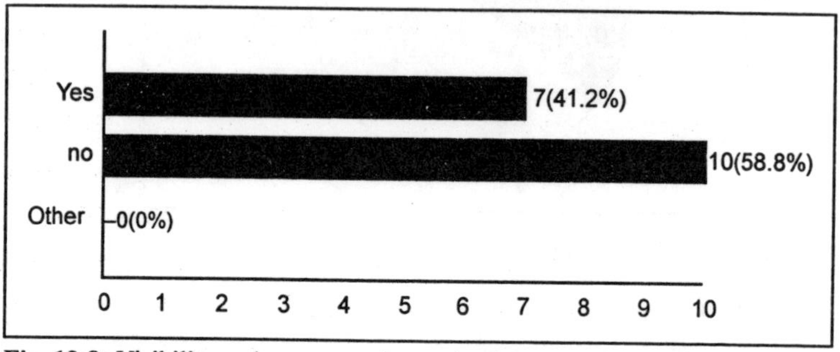

Fig. 12.8: Visibility and presence of organization on social media.

However, the uses of social media website were used for purposes such as helping during crises by information dissemination and give clarifications, interacting and to keep in touch with family and friends, informing public about our new services and resolving their problems, personal or mostly for advertising, publicity and developments, communicating the new initiatives taken by the department.

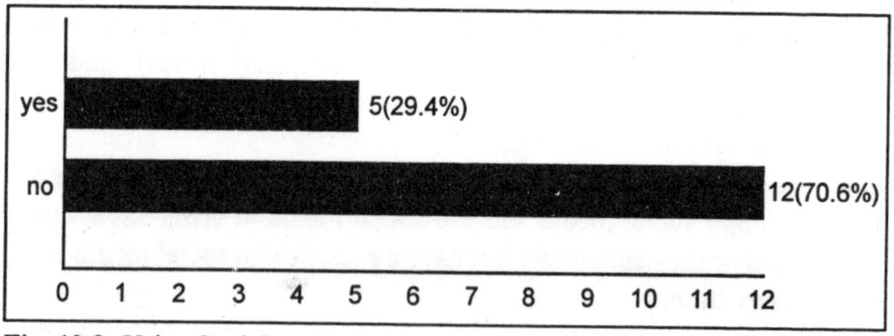

Fig. 12.9: Using Social media for emergency management.

The barrier in the use of social media for most of the respondents from various departments was security concerns (Fig. 12.10). Forty two per cent of the respondents replied security as the main issue. Eight per cent of the respondents believed that there is lack of trained manpower and resources which act as a barrier in use of social media for crisis response communication and risk reduction. Other reasons included lack of policy at departmental level and also lack of awareness of the existence of any such knowledge policy.

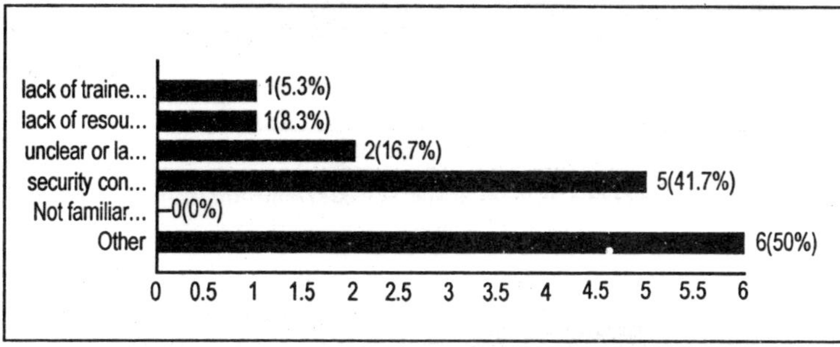

Fig. 12.10: Barriers in use of social media.

Another major barrier for the use of social media is the prevalence of ambiguous policies with no clear cut written guidelines on how to use social media in emergency situations as one of the reasons.

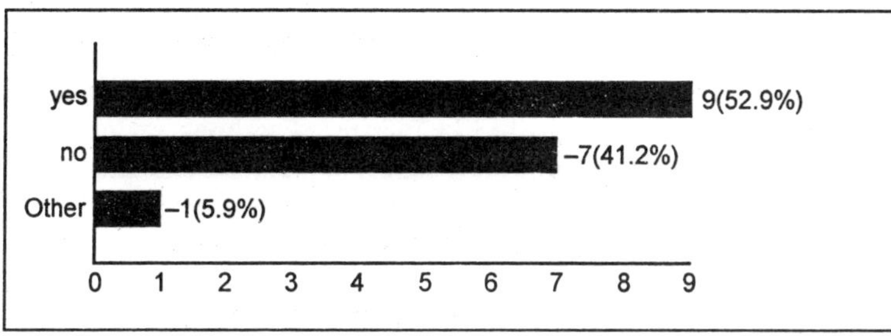

Fig. 12.11: Availability of policy and guidelines on the use of social media.

Forty one per cent of the respondents said no guidelines of social media exists for the employees or people involved in communication (Fig. 12.11). Twitter and Facebook seemed to be more popular than blogs, forums etc. 60 per cent of the respondents replied affirmative for having a organizational presence in Facebook (Fig. 12.12), while 33 per cent said they have a Twitter account page (Fig. 12.13).

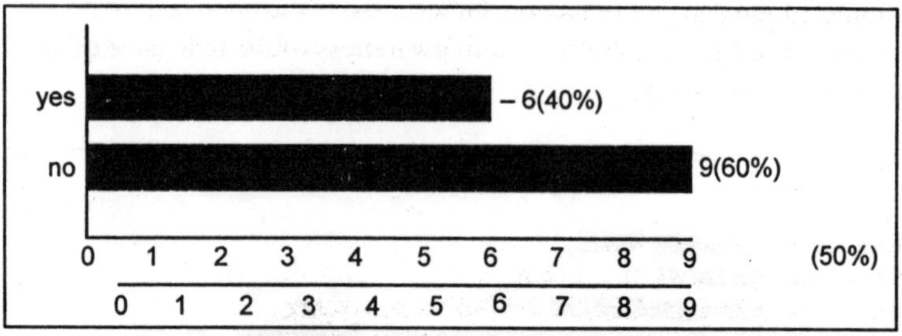

Fig. 12.12: Use of Facebook as popular social media platform by organizations.

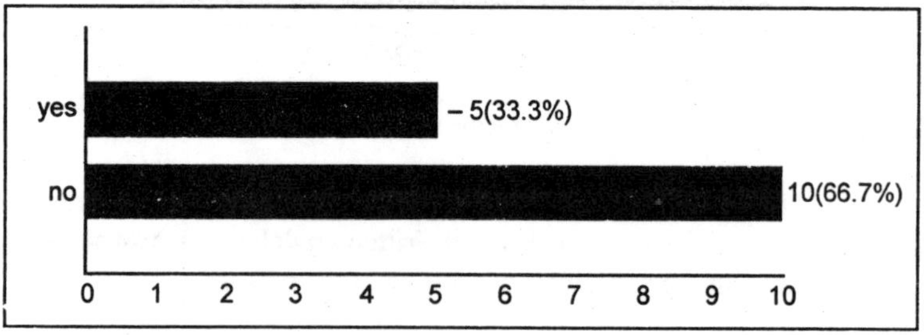

Fig. 12.13: Use of Twitter account as a media platform by organizations.

Though 43 per cent (Fig. 12.14) said that the head of the organization has a separate page on social media like Twitter or Facebook, majority of the organizations do not update posts regularly or publicize their presence in social media to enhance their visibility and trust amongst the users to gain followers.

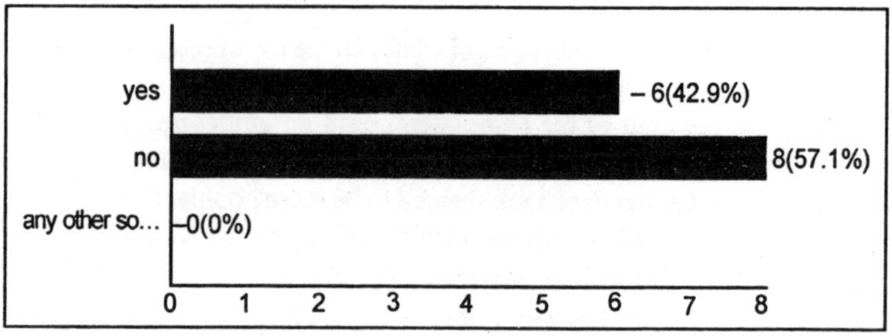

Fig. 12.14 Use of Social media by top emergency managers.

Only 12 per cent (Fig. 12.15) said they use social media to raise risk awareness by sending tips of the week or what to do in case of emergency through social media sites like Twitter, You tube, Facebook etc.

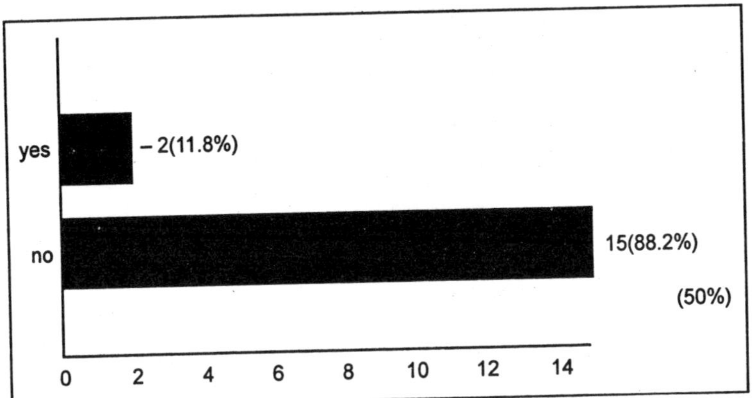

Fig. 12.15 : Leveraging Social media for enhancing community preparedness, response and recovery.

Use of social media to increase situational awareness

When asked how regularly does organizations monitor social media for increased situational awareness only 31 per cent (Fig. 12.16) respondents said they monitor despite 44 per cent of them responded that they possess the necessary human skills to use social media tc conduct situational awareness (Fig. 12.17).

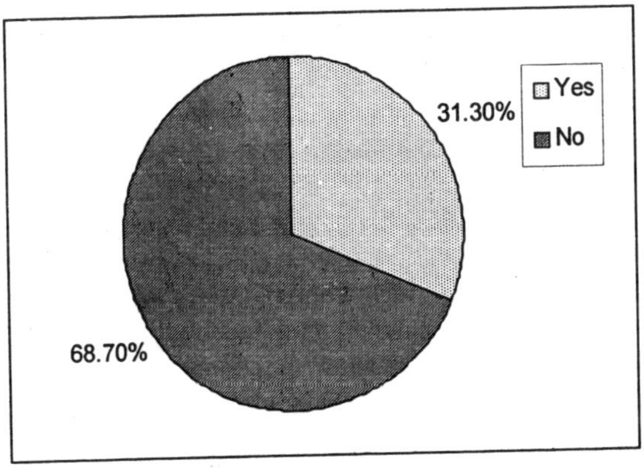

Fig. 12.16: Monitoring Social media to gain awareness of emergent conditions.

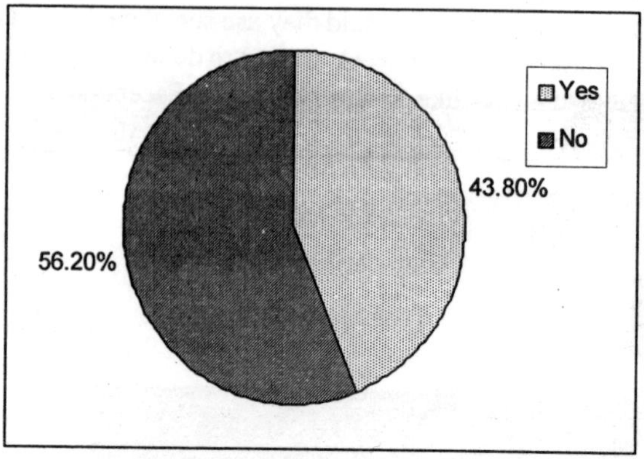

Fig. 12.17: Availability of human resources.

There is no policy to train their staff to use the social media as a situational awareness tool as 94 per cent (Fig. 12.18) said no in response to a question on training.

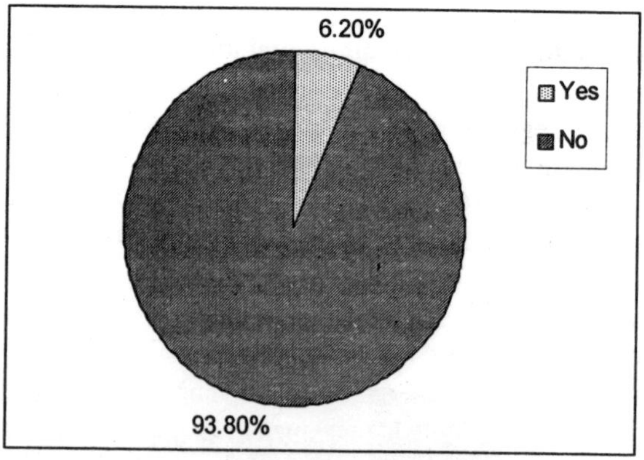

Fig. 12.18 : Policy on training and building capacity of human resource.

Also it seems there are no policies in place to use crisis mapping through crowd sourced social media data or integrating social media in emergency exercises. Seventy one per cent of the respondents said that they do not have partnership with community volunteer organization or NGOs in case of an emergency (Fig. 12.19).

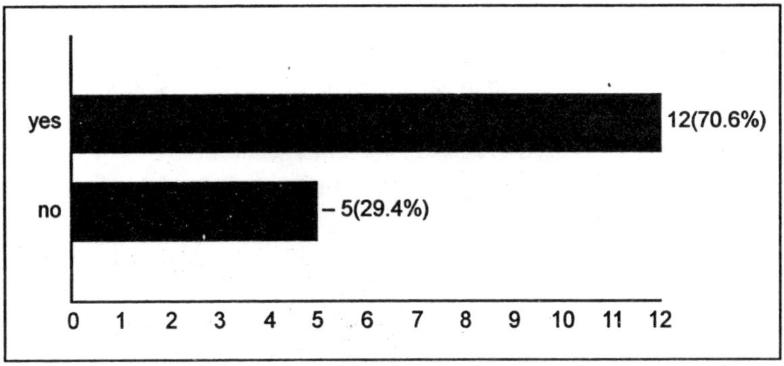

Fig. 12.19: Coordination of emergency response and recovery with other agencies.

Strengths of Social Media

Social media has played an increasing role in dissemination of information on emergencies and disasters and can be used as collaborative tool for accurate and timely information in an emergency because of the following reasons:

Reliable Form of Communication: The internet has proven that it is often a more reliable way to communicate during a disaster situation than traditional forms of communication. When phones fail, as they frequently do during major disasters, Social Media can be a reliable alternative form of communication.

Reaches a Broad Audience : Information reaches a much broader audience with social media. Sharing a link on Facebook or by "retweeting" it on Twitter will spread the information across the internet quickly.

Allows for Direct Communication: Social Media gives a disaster management organization, the ability to communicate directly with the public. This allows a disaster management organization to provide the public with the precise information that they want them to have, when they want them to have it.

Allows the Public to Participate: With Social Media the public can receive updates directly from those involved in a disaster situation.

Can Cross Organizational Lines: Social media allows emergency personnel on the scene to communicate directly across organizational lines when necessary. This can increase the speed and effectiveness of emergency personnel's response during a disaster.

Delivered Instantaneously: With social media people hear about news the instant it happens.

Limitations and Weaknesses of Social Media

But the use of social website in situations of emergency management is not flawless, the following limitations of the social media have to be considered when it is used in disaster and emergencies.

Non-use of Social Media: Older generations may not be as familiar with social media as younger generations. They may feel uncomfortable using these new technologies and prefer using traditional forms of media.

Non-use of Internet: Not all people use the internet. Whether because of where they live or because of other circumstances, without access to the internet these people will not have access to social media.

Rumours: False information and rumours can spread quickly over social media. This can lead to confusion during an emergency situation. It is important for disaster management organizations to counter any rumours or false information with the correct information. There is a need to monitor information and counter false rumours to prevent spreading panic amongst people.

Unrealistic Expectations: According to a University of San Francisco survey, one out of three Americans expect help from a disaster management organization within an hour of their posting information on Social Media, and 80 per cent of Americans expect disaster management organizations to be actively monitoring social media.

Electricity Required: During a natural disaster such as a hurricane or an earthquake electric power may fail. If people do not have access to electricity then they will not be able to keep a charge on their electronic devices such as cellphones and laptops.

Literacy Requirement: Though there is fast penetration of mobile in urban and rural areas a person needs to be literate in order to use most forms of Social Media. While majority of the urban population are literate this may not be the case in rural areas especially in some developing countries.

Poverty Areas: Regions of the world that have high levels of poverty will not have as much access to the internet as the more affluent regions of the world. These regions typically do not have the infrastructure necessary to support internet access (Huang, Chan and Hyder, 2010).

Unrealized Potential: Some governments have not yet seen the potential that social media has in disaster management. By not utilizing social media to its full potential these organizations are limiting the tools that they have in managing disasters (Boudreau, 2012).

Barriers in use of Social Media

Security Concerns: Security of information poses a constant threat in any online environment. Some of the concerns by the emergency managers is that some aspects of emergency management that require some degree of security, and these would require another avenue of communication. Also fear of viruses, Trojans and worms etc., of the infecting system. People who pretend to be someone they are not; who use social media for evil designs or for perpetrating terror activities.

Lack of clear guidelines on use of Social Media

This is one of the major reasons cited for non-use of social media. There are no clear guidelines to users on social media. There are no clear cut laws or regulations governing the use of social media.

Accessibility and Robustness: Another reason cited is about the openness of social media. Anyone has accessibility to social media. It is hard to limit who puts information on the system, which could lead to false information being provided.

Conclusion

To sum up, when utilized effectively social media provides benefits that are not seen when only using traditional media. It is invaluable when used in an emergency situation. Social media has the added value of being able to reach a larger audience and being able to communicate directly with the public. Whether emergency management organizations adopt it or not social media appears to be making inroads into emergency management for a variety of reasons. For one, accurate, reliable, and timely information vital to public safety is possible through social media. As people continue to embrace new technologies, use of social media will likely increase. Moreover, as its popularity grows, a significant number of people are likely to choose social media as their main source of information. They may also increasingly expect that agencies will also use social media to meet their informational needs. Many emergency managers and agencies in the West have already adopted the use of social media to meet this expectation. However, they started using social media because they also believed it provides another tool to disseminate important public safety information.

In addition, beyond informational purposes, the use of social media not only allows people to interact and communicate in ways that are not possible through other media, but in some cases it has allowed response organizations and victims to interact and communicate with each other when traditional media were unavailable. It could be said that social media can be used to improve emergency management capabilities and that the promise of such positive results merit further use of social media for emergencies and disasters. Before adopting Social media for emergencies and disaster preparedness the cost implications and future technological development should be further researched thoroughly.

References

Boudreau, J., (2012). When disaster struck Japan, Google and Twitter became tech first responders, San Jose Mercury News article.

Dufty, N., (2012). Using social media to build community disaster resilience. *The Australian Journal of Emergency Management,* 27 (1):40-45.

Huang, C.M, Edward C. and Hyder, A., (2010). Web 2.0 and Internet Social Networking: A New tool for Disaster Management? – Lessons from Taiwan. *BMC Medical Informatics and Decision Making article.*

http://bmcmedinformdecismak.biomedcentral.com/articles/10.1186/1472-6947-10-57 (accessed on 6th April, 2015).

Lindsay, B. R., (2011). *Social Media and Disasters: Current Uses, Future Options, and Policy Considerations*. Congressional Research Service.

http://www. fas.org/sgp/crs/homesec/R41987.pdf (accessed on 10th April, 2016).

White, C., (2011). *Social Media, Crisis Communication and Emergency Management*, Leveraging Web 2.0 Technologies. CRC Press.

13
School Safety Programmes for Seismic Risk Mitigation in Delhi

Amir Ali Khan

Introduction

Disaster safe education is a basic child right. Worldwide approximately 1.2 billion students are enrolled in primary and secondary schools every year; of these 875 million school children are living in high seismic risk zones and more than hundreds of millions face regular flood, landslide, and extreme wind and fire hazards.[1] These children spend a considerable amount of time in schools and are under constant risk due to hazards/ disasters. In the past, disasters have not only damaged school buildings, but also taken away precious lives of many children. One of the important aspects of risk reduction activities is to safeguard children from ill effects of disasters. Thus, school safety is an important component of overall risk reduction strategy which can play a significant role in safeguarding the lives of children. Additionally, children are the next generation of the society, who learn earthquake/disaster risk mitigation techniques through school safety programme, which can ultimately contribute (considerably) in making a safer society. Thus, through school safety programmes, a culture of safety among the society can be created.

Hazards like earthquake have critical influence on the schools throughout the globe exposing large numbers of school-going children to earthquake risk. There are several examples of adverse impact of earthquakes on schools not only in India, but also from other parts of the world specially the developing countries. Among natural disasters frequency of earthquakes that have struck school buildings affecting education of school going children at international level is much higher than any other type of disaster. Data analysis of previous years (1925-2008) indicates that earthquakes have caused the destruction of school buildings maximum number of times (Fig. 13.1).

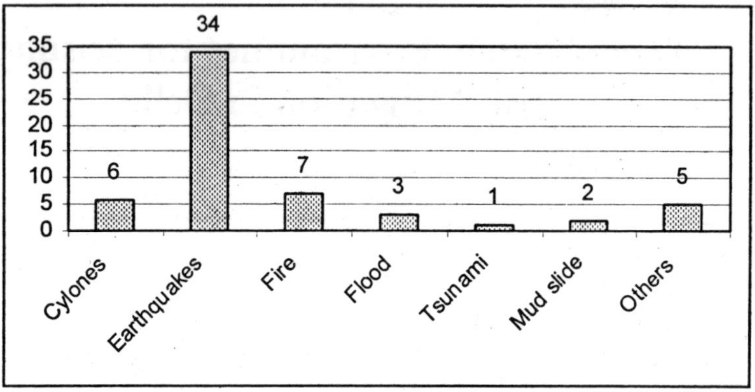

Fig. 13.1: Number of disasters affected the school buildings (1925-2008).

Source: Compiled from various sources

Schools can be made catalyst in developing the culture of preparedness and culture of prevention against earthquakes. Schools have tremendous resources in terms of teachers and students which form the basis of interaction with community on regular basis. Besides schools have buildings, which can be utilized for the purpose of emergency shelters. Similarly, schools have tremendous opportunities in terms of motivation of students and teachers to accept the challenge of seismic risk mitigation. The present chapter presents different aspects of seismic risk mitigation in context of urban areas with special reference to Delhi.

Earthquake Risk in Delhi

Delhi is situated in a highly earthquake prone zone (Zone IV as per seismic zoning map of India)[2] near the very active Himalayan seismic belt. Delhi and its surrounding regions have experienced earthquakes of magnitude 6 and above since historical times. Besides, its own seismogenic sources located in the National Capital Region of Delhi; it is also prone to possible future large earthquakes in the Central Himalayan seismic gap just 250-300 km north of it. The heavily populated city, with large number of man-made structures, could be prone to damages due to an earthquake

Box 13.1: Initiative for School Safety at National Level

School safety programmes have been taken up in India for quite some time. Few of the prominent programmes being carried out at national level include the following:

Sarva Shiksha Abhiyan (SSA) – The SSA focuses on 'useful' and 'quality' elementary education to children between 6-14 years. One third of SSA funds are spent on construction of schools buildings including additional classrooms etc. The new construction is done according to well established norms on school safety. The SSA "Framework for Implementation" has chapter on "School Infrastructure" highlighting the need and importance of disaster safety at school levels, which also describes the norms and codes to be referred for this purpose.

GoI-UNDP DRM Programme (2002-2007) – Under this programme school safety component was developed to build capacity of teachers and to create awareness among students and teachers about disasters. In addition, school disaster management plans (DMP) were also developed at many schools by involving all stakeholders.

National School Safety Project (2014-15) – NSSP had been implemented by NDMA in 22 states (covering 200 schools in 43 districts) of the country with an aim to promote a culture of disaster preparedness in the schools as fully centrally sponsored scheme with an outlay of Rs. 48.47 crore. The project had five components as:

- Formulation of draft National School Safety Policy
- Capacity Building (200 schools in each of the 43 districts)
- Information, Education and Communication
- Non-structural Mitigation Measures
- Demonstrative Retrofitting

Other Efforts – In addition several State Governments have very actively been involved in school safety activities. States like Assam, Bihar, Gujarat, Himachal Pradesh, Tamil Nadu, Haryana, Kerala, Maharashtra, Jharkhand etc. have taken a lead to initiate programmes on school safety. Activities undertaken in all such states include:

- Inclusion of a textbook on disaster management in different classes;
- Preparing school DMPs and to conduct school level mock drills;
- Capacity building of principals and teachers for disaster management activities;
- Development of audio-visual material on school safety aspects;
- Haryana has a State Policy on Safety Measures in Schools; and
- Many other such initiatives.

of considerable magnitude approximately 6 on the Ritcher Scale. The National Capital Region (NCR) of Delhi is characterized by several geological features like Delhi-Haridwar Ridge, Delhi-Lahore Ridge, Aravalli-Delhi Fold, Sohna Fault, Mathura Fault and Moradabad Fault.[3] All these features are capable of generating earthquakes of damaging intensities. Two lineaments, namely Delhi-Haridwar ridge and Delhi-Moradabad fault, have the potential of generating earthquakes of magnitude 6.5–6.7 in the region. The region has already faced seven earthquakes of magnitude 5.5 to 6.7 on Richter scale since 1720 A.D. A list of these earthquakes is given in Table 13.1:

Table 13.1: Major Historical Earthquakes in Delhi Region

Date	*Epicentre*	*Magnitude*	*Description*
July 15, 1720	Delhi	6.5	A dreadful earthquake in which walls of a fortress were damaged. Many houses were destroyed.
September 1, 1803	Mathura	6.5	A very violent shock, which destroyed the principal mosque. Felt at Calcutta, Kumaon and other far-off places. Caused intensive fissures in fields through which water rose with considerable force near Mathura.
January 16, 1842	Near Mathura	5.5	Felt extensively in Uttar Pradesh. Soldier's huts were damaged at Sultanpur.
January 14,1934	29.0^0 N-75.5^{0}E	5.0	Felt extensively and damage took place near old Delhi.
October 10,1956	28.15^0 N-77.57^0 E	6.7	Felt in a wide area. Twenty three people killed in Bulandshahr.
August 27, 1960	28.2^0 N – 77.4^0 E	6.0	Many houses damaged at Gurgaon. Fifty people hurt in Delhi.
August 15,1966	28.67^0 N 78.93^0 E	5.8	Near Moradabad, some people killed.

Source: IMD Catalogue and other sources.

Construction practices of Delhi are not appropriate from seismic safety point of view. Majority of buildings in Delhi are considered deficient in absence of non-implementation of safety standards on aseismic design and construction. The prevalent construction practices of Delhi include burnt brick wall with flat roof. This type of construction is classified under moderate damage risk.[4] Table 13.2 indicates the performance of different types of houses by predominant material of roof and wall and their expected performance for MSK VIII which is quite possible in Delhi considering its seismic hazard profile. It is not very difficult to conclude that the general condition of housing and other infrastructure facilities including schools (in Delhi) is vulnerable to earthquake induced damages.

Table 13.2: Distribution of Houses by Predominant Materials of Roof and Wall and Level of Seismic Damage Risk in Delhi

Wall Type with Flat and Sloping Roof		*%age of housing units*	*Seismic risk in Delhi*
Mud and Un-burnt brick wall		3.7	High
Stone wall		0.6	High
Burnt Brick wall		91.7	Medium
Concrete wall		1.6	Low
Wood wall		0.4	Low
Other material		1.9	Very Low
Total buildings		3,379,956	
Roof Category	Roof Combination	%age of total	
Light weight	Light weight sloping roof	13.1	Medium
Heavy weight	Heavy weight sloping roof	2.1	Medium
Flat roof	Flat Roof	84.9	As per that of wall supporting it

Source: *BMTPC* – Vulnerability Atlas on India 2006.

Earthquake Risk to Schools in Delhi

Government of Delhi is responsible for providing education up to secondary level. Different local bodies like Municipal Corporation of Delhi (MCD), New Delhi Municipal Corporation (NDMC), Delhi Cantonment Board (DCB) and Directorate of Education, Government of Delhi provide education in pre-primary, primary, middle, secondary and senior-secondary stages. The Local Bodies (Municipal Corporations) are responsible for providing education at pre-primary and primary levels, while Directorate of Education Government of Delhi provides education facilities for middle, secondary and senior secondary level education. There are 5043 schools in Delhi (2010). These schools include 2636 pre-primary and primary schools, 583 middle schools and 1824 secondary/sr.

secondary school with an enrolment of 37.39 lakh children and being taught by 1.10 lakh teachers; out of total number of schools 2666 are government schools and 2377 private schools.[5] Functioning of schools based on their management type can be categorized as government schools, schools run by local bodies, government aided school run by private organizations, government recognized schools run by private organizations and schools run by Central Government. There is large number of unauthorized schools in Delhi. Private schools play a significant role in providing school education in Delhi as they make significant contributions at secondary and higher secondary level. The government schools still play a dominant role in providing education at primary and middle school levels.

Many schools run by different agencies including government run schools have very poor infrastructural facilities with severe lack of basic facilities necessary for health and hygiene including the proper structural safety of buildings. Significant numbers of schools are being run from premises without a building or in dilapidated buildings or places like tents and partly or fully roofed with CGI sheets. Most of the unauthorized schools are functioning from sub-standard conditions like congested and crowded premises.

To improve the education environment in terms of health, hygiene and safety of government schools, Education and Technology Services Limited (ETS), the training and education arm of Infrastructure Leasing and Financial Services (IL&FS) conducted a survey of 202 schools in East, North-East, and North-West Districts of Delhi recently. According to this survey predominant building types used for school buildings in Delhi include the following:

Pucca structures refer to buildings that are designed to be solid and permanent. Such buildings are built by using material such as stone, brick, cement, concrete, or timber etc. However, the seismic performance of such structures needs to be evaluated.

Porta Cabin structures are pre-fabricated structures which are consisted of a series of panels and connectors interlinking internal and external walls including roof. The panels are made of specially formulated composite resins. Such structures are easy to build in comparison of *pucca* structures which takes long time to build.

Barrack Structures are multipurpose easy to install structures requiring limited technical expertise. Generally, such structures are made of CGI sheets. Such structures are easy to built in comparison of *pucca* structures.

SPS Structures – Structures made by using Sandwich Plate System (SPS), which is a structural composite material composed of steel and polyurethane elastomer.

The distribution of school buildings based on the prominent use of material is given in Fig. 13.2. Similarly, Fig. 13.3 shows school buildings indicating the situation which is not encouraging to face a severe earthquake. It may be clearly observed that the condition of the school buildings was not satisfactory and requires immediate attention for seismic safety point of view. To improve the condition of the government schools, Directorate of Education, Government of Delhi has initiated a series of measures to improve the overall quality of education. An important step taken in this regard is the improvement and rehabilitation of infrastructure facilities across all schools being managed by the government.

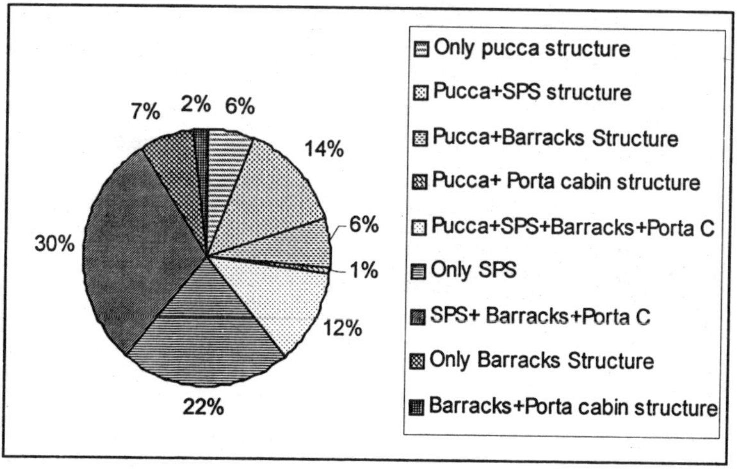

Fig. 13.2: Nomenclature of Building Types.

Source: IETS/IL&FS.

Schools in Delhi are being run in all sorts of buildings and premises constructed using all sorts of material and techniques with limited know-how about earthquake safe construction practices. There are many school buildings, specially in Old Delhi area, housing schools for more than 100 years. Based on the existing condition, many school buildings have been declared unsafe for running a school by the concerned authorities (as clearly shown in Fig. 13.3). It is not difficult to conclude that the seismic vulnerability of school buildings in Delhi is quite high.

Impact of Earthquakes on Schools

Disasters like earthquake had critical influence on the educational activities throughout the globe. There are several examples of adverse impact of earthquakes on educational facilities not only in India, but also from other parts of the world. There are several earthquakes which had severe impact on schools. A brief description of few of such earthquake events resulted in devastation of school buildings and having great bearing on functioning of schools is given in the following paragraphs.

Fig.13.3: Warning messages regarding the poor conditions of school buildings and actually very poor conditions of school buildings.

Source : IETS/IL&FS

Bhuj Earthquake, India (2001) – During Bhuj (Gujarat) earthquake educational facilities were affected severely in several districts of the state. Districts of Kutch, Banaskantha, Patan, Rajkot and Surendranagar were the worst affected. The damage to educational facilities in the earthquake affected areas of Gujarat has been shown in Table 13.3. In wake of the severe damage to these facilities, 42,000 school rooms had to be repaired/ renovated/rehabilitated. Besides the damage to physical infrastructure, about 971 students and 31 teachers were killed in the Bhuj Earthquake.[6] The severe impact of the earthquake on education sector paralyzes the entire education system in the affected areas resulting in delayed recovery and rehabilitation of the affected community. Bhuj earthquake is not the case in isolation; there are numerous other examples from other parts of the world where earthquakes had impacted on schools very severely.

Table 13.3: Damage to Educational Facilities due to Bhuj Earthquake

Sector	*Number of Institutions Affected*
Primary Education	
School Buildings	9593
Teacher Training Institutes	42
Kitchen for mid-day-meal programme	1871
Secondary/higher secondary education	
Government schools	127
Grant-in-aid schools	1913
Higher education (Universities & Colleges)	47
Technical education (polytechnic and engineering colleges)	58

Source: The Kutch earthquake 2001– recollections, lessons and insights.

Sichuan Earthquake, China (2008) – During the Sichuan earthquake about 7,000 classrooms were destroyed killing about 7,000 children and injuring another 15,000 students[7]. Prior to earthquake, schools in Sichuan, were not built to adequate standard to withstand such an earthquake, despite the fact China had building codes for aseismic design and construction of such buildings. Sichuan earthquake was a clear example of non-implementation of existing building codes. Improper construction of school buildings led to collapse of many classrooms contributing to the deaths of students. One of the remarkable finding was that in comparison to new school buildings older school buildings performed better during the earthquake.

Kashmir Earthquake, POK (2005) – During the Pakistan Occupied Kashmir (POK) earthquake, about 17,000 school buildings were affected, ranging from primary schools to institutions of higher education[8] including both government and private schools. Out of total schools damaged about 70 per cent were primary and middle schools. During this earthquake heavy human loss, including students, school teachers, and staff had been reported. About 19,000 students and 900 teachers were killed[9] in the worst affected areas of North-Western Frontier Province and Pakistan Occupied Kashmir provinces of Pakistan alone.

Bam Earthquake, Iran (2003) – In this earthquake, about 90 per cent of 300 existing schools (prior to earthquake) in Bam district were destroyed by the earthquake. The remaining schools sustained damages beyond repair. According to available reports, out of 32,000 students about 25-30 per cent were perished during the disaster. Similarly, 560 about one fifth of teachers were also killed in this earthquake.[10]

Spitek Earthquake, Armenia (1988) – The earthquake caused great damages to educational facilities where out of 131 schools, 105 were destroyed in Spitak and Leninakan areas only. The earthquake resulted in very high death rate of children and adolescents, which was almost two-third of the total deaths of about 25,000[11] students enrolled in schools. The main reason for such a high death rate was due to the fact that earthquake occurred at a very critical time when most of the children were in the schools and school buildings performed poorly during the earthquake due to lack of aseismic design and construction.

Here, it may be noted that majority of earthquake induced damages to school buildings do take place in developing countries where building codes are not being implemented seriously. Majority of damages to school buildings were due to improper design and construction practices. Such buildings could not withstand the shaking of an earthquake.

Another problem associated with the earthquake affected schools is that large number of surviving students and teachers usually have affected families as well, and thus, requiring special attention to bring them back to normalcy. Damaged schools usually are not in a position to provide this facility. It may also be noted that it takes a lot of time and efforts to develop a teacher in terms of his/her education, training, skills, attitude and experience; the death of a teacher thus represent not only losses to the teaching community of a particular school, but also represents a national loss.

Earthquake Risk Reduction Strategy for Schools

Strategy of earthquake risk reduction includes a mix of structural and non-structural measures. Broadly, the structural measures include engineering approach where built environment is designed and constructed to face earthquakes, e.g. facilities like bridges, flyovers, ordinary buildings, high-rise structures etc. are built to withstand earthquake forces. The non-structural measures include the efforts having limited use of engineering, e.g. risk sensitive land-use planning, implementation of building codes, development of disaster management plans and creating public awareness (through education and training). All such measures can be promoted by all stakeholders at all levels. Details pertaining to the distinctive components have been discussed in detail in the following paragraph:

Structural Measures of School Safety

All buildings are comprised of structural and non-structural elements. The structural elements of a building are constituents of overall structural system of the building. The structural system of a building defines its load path – means those elements which helps in carrying the load of entire building and transfers it to the ground (in RCC building elements like roof/slab, beams, columns and foundations are structural elements while in masonry buildings roof, sheer walls and foundation constitute the structural elements). In a building, besides structural elements all other elements are non-structural in nature which means these elements do not contribute in load transfer of the building to the ground (non-structural elements of a building include false ceiling, furniture, fixtures like gas and water supply lines, water tanks etc.). Non-structural elements play a critical role in overall functioning of the building. Thus, it is imperative that any comprehensive school safety programme must be based on strengthening of structural and non-structural elements of the school building.

Improving Structural Safety of School Building

Large number of buildings including school buildings, throughout the country, have been built using inappropriate design and construction procedures as per the prescribed building codes. Such buildings pose greater challenge to stakeholders trying to reduce the seismic risk of the built environment. The seismic risk reduction strategy for school buildings must be based on the following principles:

- All new buildings be constructed safe using appropriate building codes over a suitable and safe site as per planning norms/Master Plan regulations;
- All existing buildings must be retrofitted to make them safe to face future earthquakes; and
- School must get involved in activities like development of school disaster management plan, organising regular drills etc.

Incorporating earthquake resistant features in school buildings should be priority for safer schools at all stages of its construction which include proper site selection, architectural and structural design, and execution or construction of school building.

Site selection for school building must be carefully done as the school buildings constructed on a particular soil type can make big difference to the level of earthquake hazard. Soil profiles near high water tables, reclaimed lands (from water bodies) etc. can be highly unpredictable, which may lead to liquefaction of the soil and ideally be avoided. If not possible to avoid such sites, appropriate measures for soil treatment (site modifications) and foundation design must be taken into consideration.

There are school specific parametres notified in the National Building Code (NBC)-2005. Such norms need to be incorporated while planning a school building. Most important part of a school is classroom which need to be designed considering appropriate parametres as per the relevant IS Codes. Few of common parametres for classrooms design (as per NBC-2005) are as following:

- Height of classrooms should not be less than 3 metres measured at any point from the surface of floor to the lowest point of ceiling;
- The sill height for classroom with furniture arrangement should not be more than 800 mm from finished level of floor and with squatting arrangement not more than 600 mm;
- Ventilation and light – for light and air, windows opening direct to external air or into open verandah should not be less than 20 per cent of the floor area, if such openings are located on one wall and not less than 15 per cent of the floor area in case such openings are on both side walls at the same level. The percentage can be increased depending upon site location;
- Doors – each classroom should have two doors;
- Doorways – no exit doorway shall be less than 100 cm in width and 200 cm in height. Similarly, the door ways for WC, bathroom shall not be less than 75 cm wide;
- Verandah – not less than 1.5 metre wide;
- Plinth protection – for improving the environment and saving the foundation of the built infrastructure, it is necessary to provide plinth protection, with locally available cost-effective building material. This will enhance the life of the building and shall save

it from sudden collapse because of ingress of rain water into the foundation;

- Size of classroom should be calculated as given in Table 13.4; and
- Boundary wall/green fencing: every school should have a boundary wall or a proper green fencing for security of the children and school property and also prevent unauthorized access to the school campus.

In addition there are several Building Codes, which are relevant and need to be referred to while designing and constructing a school. Few of prominent codes are listed in Table 13.5. A very common secondary hazard associated with earthquakes is fire. All schools must incorporate fire protection measures in addition to seismic safety provisions. Few of the most common things to be kept in mind for fire safety include:

- All School buildings must be designed for fire protection as per NBC-2005;
- Avoid thatched roof/inflammable material as roofing material;
- Avoid storage of inflammable and toxic material in school premises building without appropriate safety provisions;
- Ensure adequate water supply for fire-fighting purpose; and
- Ensure appropriate number of fire extinguishers. Also ensure adequate capacity to handle these extinguishers. Identify critical locations to place them.

Table 13.4: Area Requirements for Classrooms

Category	*No. of Students*	*Gross Area of Classroom*
Pre School	20/25	2.00 Sq metre per child
Primary School (With furniture)	40	1.11 Sq metre per child
Primary School (With Squatting)	40	0.74 Sq metre per child
Secondary and Higher Secondary School	40	1.26 Sq metre per child

Source: ssa.nic.in

Retrofitting of Existing School Buildings to make them Earthquake Safe

Throughout the country, large number of existing school buildings are unsafe from the seismic risk point of view due to lack of proper planning, designing and construction according to existing building code and guidelines available for this purpose. Improper maintenance and aging of buildings also weakens the critical elements of the structure which may lead to failure with or without an earthquake. Thus, exerting school buildings need to be evaluated for their requirement of retrofitting. The Rapid Visual Screening (RVS) procedure is employed to assess the expected performance of the structures during an earthquake. The RVS utilizes a procedure that requires identification of the structural system to resist the earthquake loads of the building and other characteristics of the building which will influence the performance of the building during an earthquake. Generally, the RVS procedure is based on assessment of expected performance of the structure/building without going for detailed structural analysis calculations. Based on the results of RVS, buildings may be further analyzed for lapses and in case it is required such buildings must be retrofitted for better earthquake safety.

Table 13.5: Indian Standard Codes for Designing and Construction of School Buildings

Sl. No.	*Building Codes*	
National Building Codes Latest Edition		
1.	IS 1893 (Part 1) : 2002	Criteria for earthquake resistant design of structure
2.	IS 4326 : 1993	Practice of earthquake resistant design and construction of buildings
3.	IS 13828 : 1993	Guidelines for improving earthquake resistant of low strength masonry building
4.	IS 13920 : 1993	Ductile detailing of reinforced concrete structure subject to seismic force
5.	IS 456 : 2000	Structural design of buildings
6.	IS 14435 : 1997	Code of practice of fire safety in educational institutions
7.	IS 2440 : 1975	Guide for day lighting of building
8.	IS 4963 : 1987	Recommendation for buildings and facilities for physically handicapped
9.	IS 7662 (Part 1) : 1974	Recommendation of orientation of building
10.	IS 4837 : 1990	School furniture, classroom chair and tables recommendations
11.	IS 4838 : 1990	Anthropometric dimensions for school children age group 5-17 years
12.	IS 8827 : 1978	Recommendations for basic requirements of school buildings

Source: ssa.nic.in

There are well established guidelines and procedures available for carrying out retrofitting of buildings. Examples of retrofitting of school buildings have been discussed in the subsequent sections.

Improving Non-structural Safety of School Building

Based on their use and function in the building, the non-structural elements of a school building can be grouped into the following categories:

Contents of buildings include items like doors, windows, wall panels including partition wall and glass partitions, false ceiling, furniture, almirah, computer, photocopy machine, printer, fax, storage shelves (in library and labs), TV set, fridge, gas cylinder etc.

Appendages to buildings include cantilever projections (balconies), cladding (glass, stones, tiles etc.), parapets, water tanks, sign boards (including roof top antennas, satellite dishes advertisement hoardings and telecommunication towers) etc.

Utilities and services of the buildings like roof top water tanks, water supply pipes, sanitary and rain water pipes, gas pipelines, electricity cables, elevators, water coolers, and fire fighting system installations etc.

All non-structural elements have influence on the damageability of the building. All such elements need to be properly anchored/fastened with the structural elements of the building to avoid the potential damage from earthquake. The fixing/anchoring of most of the non-structural elements can be done at local level by the concerned teachers/students themselves using some basic techniques. However, for some more typical and complex items, it may require assistance from professionals/experts like structural engineers. It may also be considered that at school level (with the help of students and teachers) there is very limited scope for taking care of structural elements as it require professional engineering skills. However, non-structural elements can be fixed at local level itself with or without external assistance. Fig. 13.4. shows retrofitting of the non-structural elements in a Delhi school.

Non-Structural Measures of School Safety against Earthquakes

Non-structural measures to reduce the earthquake risk in schools include:

- ***Proper site selection and land-use planning*** – School building must be located on proper sites away from fault lines, dangerous slopes and liquefiable soils. Decision about the location and sitting

Fig. 13.4: Non-structural retrofitting include fixing of falling hazards like TV, wall clock, soft board, almirah etc.

of the school building should be based on the appropriate land-use and zoning regulations which must be based on the seismic hazard map, liquefaction map of the locality etc.

- ***Implementation of Building codes and guidelines*** – As mentioned in the earlier section there are several building and guidelines available for design and construction of earthquake safe school buildings. Proper implementation of such tools must be ensured for greater safety of school buildings.
- ***Disaster management plans of schools*** – There must be concerted efforts to develop disaster management plans at school level. Such plans must be developed by duly constituted committee comprised of school teachers, students and all other stakeholders involved in school safety. The SDMP must include appropriate linkages with all role players like police, hospitals, local civil administration (office of DM and SDM etc.). The SDMP so developed must be implemented and drill of such a plan must be conducted by involvement of all concerned to check the viability of the plan on regular basis.
- ***Public awareness*** – Public awareness is the key for mitigating

the impact of impending earthquakes. School have tremendous opportunities to mitigate the impact of an earthquake as they have significant resources in terms of students and teachers who are highly motivated to further carry forward the message of earthquake safety to larger community. The schools interact with the community on regular basis through parent- teacher meetings and the messages of earthquake safety and procedures can very easily be passed on to the community for further action. Moreover, children are a dynamic and powerful force of change and supporters of creating awareness in the community. They can contribute in a unique manner with energy and vision to find local solutions and enlighten their elders and parents urging them for safety against earthquakes. What needs to be done is to train the teachers to initiate activity based approach for earthquake risk mitigation. It is much easier to spread the message as teachers have to learn to properly teach the students. The students have to learn to enhance their performance while the society (parents) will learn with their wards over a period of time.

Construction of schools buildings being development activity of national importance, special efforts must be made for their proper design and construction. If properly designed and constructed, school buildings can be utilized not only as emergency shelters but also as disaster management centre as well after an earthquake. There are several countries in the world which are using school buildings as community shelters after earthquakes. Such experiences need to be replicated at local levels in the country.

School Safety Programmes in Delhi

For reducing the urban risk in Delhi through schools safety programme, Government of Delhi has adopted a two pronged strategy of non-structural and structural measures in the government schools.

The Non-structural Measures necessitate proactively working to create an environment of safety of schools through such measures. Through substantive efforts Government of Delhi is able to sensitize majority of government schools under its jurisdiction on non-structural aspects of earthquake disaster risk mitigation. In recent years, most common activities undertaken by the Government of Delhi include:

- Promoting awareness and education activities to sensitize

Table 13. 6: School Safety Programme in Delhi

Preparedness	*2008-09*	*2009-10*	*2010-11*	*Total*
No. of School Plans prepared in Delhi	789	963	896	2648
No. of awareness programme conducted	850	1009	1042	2901
No. of training Programme Conducted	1561	1983	2255	5799
No. of relief centres identified	48	50	50	148
No. of civil defence Volunteers trained	0	2800	3000	5800

Source: DDMA.

teachers and students through formal and non-formal education/ training methods like classroom teaching and IEC means. Details of different programmes undertaken in Delhi have been summarized in Table 13.6.

- Identification of hazards and vulnerabilities at school level and preparation of school disaster management plans (SDMP). The SDMPs include information about available resources at school level and identification of safe places within and around the schools. Constitution of teams within the schools to carry out specific tasks like awareness generation, warning and information dissemination, evacuation and safety against fire etc.
- To check the viability of SDMPs, Government of Delhi had made it mandatory to conduct mock drills at school level on regular basis targeting not only earthquake disaster but also other risks faced by the schools like fire etc. Such mock drills provide a reality check on school preparedness level; and
- Training and capacity building of teachers and other stakeholders involved in school safety programmes.

In addition to Government of Delhi, other agencies working in Delhi have also played significant role in earthquake risk mitigation by adopting non-structural measures. Few of the common activities taken out by other agencies include:

- The Central Board of Secondary Education (CBSE), Ministry of Human Resource Development, Government of India, which has 17,361 school affiliated (in India and abroad) including majority of schools in Delhi, is actively involved in disaster risk mitigation for quite some time. The CBSE has not only initiated disaster management educational programmes in all its affiliate schools at classes VIII, IX and X levels, but also has initiated schools' safety awareness towards structural and fire safety of schools buildings and management of risks due to natural and man-made hazards. The CBSE has instructed all schools to take appropriate action toward safety and security of students from all hazards at school-level.

- Building Material Technology Promotion Council (BMTPC), Ministry of Housing and Urban Poverty Alleviation, Government of India is an active role player in earthquake risk mitigation at national level. BMTPC has been instrumental in retrofitting number of schools for structural safety. The initiative of BMTPC is focused towards developing demonstration techniques for schools retrofitting and capacity building of the engineers and contractors involved in construction and maintenance of school buildings. BMTPC has been able to provide training to 200 municipal engineers in similar activities.
- The Delhi Disaster Management Authority has initiated a series of Training of Trainer (ToT) programmes on Earthquake Risk Mitigation and Preparedness in Schools to develop trainers from all the districts of Delhi to ensure sustainability of efforts. Under this initiative a team of trainers (including principals and senior teachers) from different sets of schools (e.g. government schools, public schools and central schools) from each district has been trained to further train the school teachers and other stakeholders in school safety.
- NGOs have played a significant role in facilitating all such efforts. Prominent NGOs like SEEDs and GHI have made significant contributions in building a culture of school safety in Delhi against earthquakes.

The Structural Measures have been carried out by the Government of Delhi through various programmes to make school buildings safe against earthquake by retrofitting (of structural and non-structural elements) of the existing buildings. There are several schools buildings, which have been retrofitted for seismic and other hazards so far. One of the very prominent school building retrofitted under this category is that of Government School at Shyamnath Marg (famously known as Ludlow

Castle School No.1), which has been retrofitted for structural and non-structural elements of the school building. The school consists of a three storey classroom block and a single storey multi-purpose hall; the classroom block is a brick masonry structure. Under the pilot programme of the Government of Delhi structural elements of the classroom block of the school and one of the multi-purpose rooms have been retrofitted as per the requirements of IS: 13935-1993 (Repair and Seismic Strengthening of Buildings-Guidelines). The walls of the buildings have been strengthened with wire mesh and a layer of micro concrete on both sides of the wall to provide sufficient strength and to develop the box action necessary for safety against earthquakes have been provided. The seismic belts were provided at appropriate levels. To strengthen corners, holes were drilled in the floor slabs in each corner of the room, and reinforcement bars were inserted from foundation till roof of the building. One additional door was also made in all classrooms as most of the classrooms in the school had single door.

Fig. 13.5: Outside views of the structurally retrofitted school at Ludlow Castle.

Similarly, provisions for retrofitting of non-structural elements and failing hazards of the school buildings have been made. One room has been retrofitted for non-structural elements as well in the school. After retrofitting the Government School at Ludlow Castle, Civil Line, Delhi has been designated as a relief centre for post-earthquake disaster management.

In another effort, Government of Delhi has initiated a project of structural retrofitting of one school in each of all nine districts of Delhi in collaboration with BMTPC. As of now, BMTPC has taken a lead in retrofitting of school buildings in Delhi. Through such efforts BMTPC is able to initiate projects to develop demonstrative techniques for retrofitting of school buildings in all zones of Municipal Corporation of Delhi. Many schools buildings have been structurally retrofitted so far under this programme. The structural retrofitting of masonry buildings is usually based on the provisions of IS: 13935 - 1993. One of recently retrofitted school building is of Municipal Corporation Model School Lajpat Nagar.[12] The school building is a two storeyed brick masonry structure, C shaped in plan. The walls are 400 mm thick in cement sand mortar. The floor and roof are 125 mm thick RC slabs. The building has continuous strip foundation. As such there were no specific elements provided for seismic safety point of view.

Fig. 13.6: Details of seismic strengthening techniques adopted at the school building retrofitted by BMTPC.

The building was retrofitted by incorporating the elements like seismic belts at lintel and sill levels; encasement of all openings like doors, windows and ventilators etc. with seismic straps; provided vertical seismic elements at wall intersections; room corners were strengthened by inserting reinforcement after drilling the corners and jacketing of masonry columns. School buildings retrofitted under this programme are being utilized as technology demonstration units for retrofitting of masonry buildings. Another interesting point to note is that the cost of retrofitting work (in 2009) in comparison to construction of a new school building has been worked out to be about 8.1 per cent of the total cost[13].

Directorate of Education, Government of Delhi has initiated a project on Integrated Infrastructure Development of Government of Delhi Schools, for about 966 government schools in Delhi. Under this project special provisions have been made to reduce risks due to earthquake and fire hazards while upgrading the overall condition of schools.

Looking Forward

Children have right to education which need to be delivered in safe, healthy and conducive environment; thus making it obligatory to provide sufficient school safety against all conditions, including earthquakes/disasters, which may harm them. It is clear that earthquakes occur without warning which restrict the coping mechanism against them by means of evacuation. The only way left to mitigate the impact of an earthquake is by taking preventive measures and getting ready to face the event in an appropriate manner.

Common aspect of the earthquake events of Spitek, Bhuj, Bam, POK, and Sichuan is that all these events had resulted in huge destruction of the built environment including school buildings and resulted in high deaths of students and teachers. Thus, it becomes more important to take preventive measure and getting ready in case of schools as children (one of the most vulnerable section of the society at the time of event) are at risk in these premises. As of now, schools pose a greater challenge due to poorly designed and constructed buildings and inadequate awareness to safeguard from earthquakes. Thus, earthquake safety of schools must be comprised of a combination of structural measures (structural and non-structural mitigation) and non-structural measures (capacity building and education and awareness).

The impact of damaging earthquakes on school buildings can be reduced by strengthening the buildings. To make school buildings earthquake safe these have to be constructed as per IS codes by adopting proper site planning norms; similarly, old buildings need to be retrofitted according to prescribed guidelines. In addition, capacity of all stakeholders including school administrator, teachers, students and community need to be enhanced.

These stakeholders (particularly educated children) carry the message of earthquake safety to their parents and help in building an earthquake aware society. There are encouraging examples which indicate that efforts made on these directions help children in not only carrying the message for life, but also ensure the overall safety and security of the society (Box 13.2). To bring about the much needed change in the perception, the school safety programmes require investment. Such an investment can be arranged by developing new partnerships, e.g. with the corporate sector. Time has come to bring about a change the way corporate sector had been engaged in disaster management activities at national level. Time is conducive to engage this sector in pre-disaster management rather than post-disaster relief, rehabilitation and reconstruction activities. It will be appropriate if the corporate sector can be roped in to make contributions for strengthening school safety programmes.

As children spend substantial amount of time in schools, in addition to earthquake safety, school buildings have to provide with adequate protection against the weather extremes, like cold and hot conditions, to make it more comfortable learning environment. When retrofitting a school building for earthquake safety, additional requirements for making them green can also be introduced, to improve the environment of such buildings. During the seismic retrofitting process different components of the buildings are worked upon; many of such components are same which need to be worked upon for making the buildings green. If the process of making the school buildings safe against earthquake and process of making them green go side by side, it will be highly cost-effective.

Box 13.2: Importance of Retrofitting of School Buildings

Probably, the Long Beach earthquake (USA) of April 10, 1933 was the trend setter for signifying the importance of earthquake safe school buildings. Since then school buildings, in US and elsewhere, are being constructed earthquake safe or retrofitted to required levels of earthquake safety. Once again, it has been observed that during recent Nepal earthquake (2015) the retrofitted school buildings had performed far better. The National Society for Earthquake Technology – Nepal (NSET) had retrofitted more than 300 school buildings throughout Nepal[14]. Almost all such school buildings performed very well during the earthquake shaking[15]. Most of the retrofitted school buildings were also used as emergency shelters by the people and also as emergency response coordination centres by response organizations after the earthquake (EERI-2016).

Box 13.3: School Education helps in Creating Awareness example

Children who are taught about natural hazard risks play an important role in saving lives and protecting members of community at a time of disasters.

On a beach in Thailand, when the December 2004 Tsunami struck, British schoolgirl Tilly Smith saved many lives by urging people to flee the shore: her geography class in Britain had enabled her to recognize the first signs of a tsunami.

Source: ISDR

The buildings so retrofitted are expected to reduce environmental impact, maximize efficiency and productivity, minimize operating costs and maximize overall functioning of schools.

By developing the demonstration school buildings by incorporating the retrofitting techniques for earthquake safety and energy efficiency will provide much needed impetus to spread the knowledge about the earthquake safe green buildings. The construction stage of the retrofitting process can very effectively be utilized for training of relevant stakeholders including local masons. The dual purpose of safety and training will go a long way in making earthquake safe society.

Notes

1. ISDR.
2. IS 1893 : 2002.
3. IMD.
4. Vulnerability Atlas of India, 2006.
5. Government of NCT of Delhi.
6. The Kutch Earthquake 2001– Recollections, Lessons and Insights.
7. Guidance Notes on Safer School Construction, GFDRR, INEE, ISDR.
8. Earthquake Engineering Research Institute.
9. UNESCO.
10. Earthquake Engineering Research Institute.
11. Reducing Vulnerability of School Children to Earthquakes, UNCRD.
12. BMTPC.
13. *Ibid.*

References

Bolt, B.A., (2006), *Earthquakes*, New York: W.H. Freeman and Company.

DDMA (2007), School Disaster Management Plan – a manual for school preparedness.

Education and Technology Services Ltd., Integrated Infrastructure Development of Government of Delhi Schools, (2007).

EERI (1986). *Reducing Earthquake Hazard: Lessons Learned from Earthquakes*; Publication No. 86-02, California: EERI.

EERI (2016). *Earthquake Reconnaissance Team Report*: M_W7.8 Gorkha, Nepal Earthquake on April 25, 2015 and its Aftershocks EERI, California.

EERI (2006). Learning from Earthquakes – The Kashmir Earthquake of October 8, 2005: Impacts in Pakistan – *EERI Special Earthquake Report*.

EERI, (2004). Learning from Earthquakes – Social and Public Policy Issues following the Bam, Iran, Earthquake – *EERI Special Earthquake Report*.

Fujieda, B.H. (2008). Pandey and S. Ando, Safe Schools to Reduce Vulnerability of Children to Earthquakes, *The 14th World Conference on Earthquake Engineering*, Beijing, China.

Gere, J.M. and Shah, H.C., (1984) *Terra Non-Firme: Understanding and Preparing for Earthquakes*. New York: W.H. Freeman & Co.

GSI (1996). *Killari Earthquake* – 30 September, 1993; Special Publication No. 37.

IITK-BMTPC Earthquake Tips (www.niccc.org)

Lagorio, Henry J., (1990) *Earthquakes–An Architect's Guide to Non-structural Seismic Hazards*, John Wiley & Sons Inc.

Mishra, P.K. (2004). *The Kutch Earthquake 2001 – Recollections, Lessons and Insights*, New Delhi: NIDM.

National Society for Earthquake Technology – Nepal (NSET), (2015); *Final Report on Post-Earthquake Rapid Damage Assessment of School Buildings*, Kathmandu.

National Society for Earthquake Technology – Nepal (NSET), (2014); Safer *Society: NSET Report 2014*, available at http://www.nset.org.np/nset2012/images/publicationfile/Safer_Society_2014.pdf.

National Society for Earthquake Technology – Nepal (NSET), (2016), School Earthquake Safety Programme (SESP) website, Kathmandu, Nepal, available at http://www.nset.org.np/nset2012/index.php/programmes/programdetail/programid-29

P.R. Bose and Amir Ali Khan, (2004), *Earthquakes in Delhi* – Are We Prepared?; ISET Delhi Chapter and Delhi College of Engineering.

UNCRD (2008). *Reducing Vulnerability of School Children to Earthquake*.

UNCRD & SEEDS India (2008). Preliminary survey and assessment of schools buildings.

UNCRD - SESI (2009). *Reducing Vulnerability of School Children to Earthquakes*.

http://www.quakesafedelhi.net

http://www.ilfsets.com/pdf/Delhi_Schoo_Link.pdf

www.cbse.nic.in

14
Extra Budgetary Resources for Sanitation in India

K.K. Pandey

Introduction

Financing the sanitation in recent one and half decade assumed special significance in line with global focus on adequate access to sanitation. Habitat Agenda (1996), United Nations Millennium Development Goals (UNMDGs) and UN sustainable development goals 2030 (UNSDGs) etc. have created global awareness and actions towards adequate access to sanitation. Goal-1 (poverty), 6 (water and sanitation), 7 (energy) and 11 (sustainable cities) do make a reference to improved sanitation with a range of specific targets for global community to follow. It is also noted that externalities of sanitation are fairly high in terms of environment, productivity, climate change and pro-poor and inclusive development. It is also recognized globally that a dedicated budgetary line of fund cannot meet the requirements and extra budgetary resources play a decisive role to ensure adequate sanitation for all.

Access to Improved Sanitation in India

India, as elsewhere, has also given special emphasis on improved sanitation. Total Sanitation Campaign (TSC) was initiated in 1999 to address rural sanitation whereas urban sanitation was addressed by Integrated Low Cost Sanitation (ILCS). The progress in rural areas was reported to be improved from 9 per cent in 1990 to 15 per cent coverage in 1999 to and 39 per cent in 2012, although 21 per cent toilets were found de-functional (MDWS website). It is also noted that urban areas show a relatively better coverage of improved sanitation covering 82 per cent HHs (58% HHs with Individual toilets and 24% with shared toilet) having access to safe sanitation,7 per cent unsafe access and 11 per cent show open defecation (Table 14.1).

The gap in the sanitation normally escapes attention unless something alarming takes place as happened in Surat (Plaque in mid-nineties), Srinagar (devastating floods in 2014), Heavy flooding in Chennai (2015) and Gurgram (massive traffic jam in 2016).But, this is not a result of one time mistake. It is a result of continuous neglect and ineffective approach to achieve safe sanitation covering waste disposal and management.

De-functional toilets are also linked with perception and mindset. In this regard Government of India is giving emphases on Community - led total Sanitation (CLTS) and School-led Total Sanitation (SLTS). These instruments have facilitated Open Defecation Free status to as many as 35,938 villages out of 6,11,753 villages in India (Website of MDWS, GoI). Therefore, Capacity building of local governments should specifically include funding to promote SLTS and CLTS approaches. At the same time development of appropriate cost-effective, affordable, local and pro-poor technology for toilet construction should also be duly covered under the financing system.

Table 14.1: Access to Improved sanitation in India

Access (%HHs)	*1990*	*2001*	*2012*
Rural India	9	15	39
Urban India	55	59	82

Sources:

(i) Ministry of Drinking Water and Sanitation;
(ii) Progress on DW&S, UNICEF, 2014; and
(iii) National Sample Survey-65th round.

Magnitude of Requisite Funds for Improved Sanitation in India

Water and sanitation have a basket of activities which involves different departments and agencies yet, there have been efforts to consolidate plans for a more effective follow-up. As may be noted from different projections, requirements of funds are fairly high by any standard:

- Water Aid India and UNICEF projected the requirements of US$ 11.8 billion and US$ 22 billion for (2002-2015) for rural and urban sanitation for meeting MDG targets.Rural sanitation figures are Rs. 676 billion.

- The requirement of funds for sanitation (2002-07) as per NIUA (National Institute of Urban Affairs) was Rs. 38 billion per annum whereas X plan document (2002-12) expected funds to the tune of Rs.108 billion per annum.
- UNICEF and WHO estimated a huge requirement of US $ 208 billion during 2005 to 2015 whereas Ministry of Urban Development had projected a requirement of Rs. 23 billion (2002-2007) during the same period to meet targets of millennium development goals.
- Similarly estimates for urban sanitation as per High Power Expert Committee Report was Rs. 5,22,301 crores at 2010 prices (for 20 years period). These include solid waste merge and sewage/ draining (HPEC, 2010).

Recent Estimates

Recent estimates by Government of India for rural and urban sanitation have placed a requirement of Rs.1,00,447 crore and Rs. 62,009 crore (1 crore=10 million) respectively under the Government of India's flagship programme of clean India mission (Swachh Bharat Abhiyan – SBM) to be accomplished by 2019 (Fig. 14.1).

Table 14.2 : Recent Estimates of Clean India Mission (2015-2019)

(*Rs. in Crore*)

Item	*Requirement*	*Annual Requirement*	*Funds Allocated (2014-16)*	*Average Annual Flow (GoI)*	*Average Annual Flow from Government of India as % of Annual Requirement*
Rural Sanitation	100447	20894	6975	3488	17
Urban Sanitation	62009	12002	1700	850	7
All	**162456**	**32896**	**8675**	**4338**	**24**

Sources: (i) Guidelines Clean India Mission (SBM), (ii) Ministry of Drinking Water and Sanitation, and (iii) Ministry of Urban Development Government of India. (Urban does not include sewage system.) Average annual flow from GoI is likely to have 40 per cent additional contribution from provincial and local governments.

Another important area of concern is resources for O & M of the assets at the disposal of local governments. Successive studies have indicated a huge gap and fiscal stress at ULG/RLG (Urban/Rural Local Governments) level leading to the occurrence of emergency and break down maintenance and failure to take-up repair and replacement of machinery and equipments as per requirements (Pandey, 2014-15a). This is reflected in a constant decline in the normative base of sanitation services. It is also noted that rural areas do not have adequate system of solid waste management whereas urban areas have wide gap in collection (25-50%), down time (3-5%), scientific disposal (10-20%).

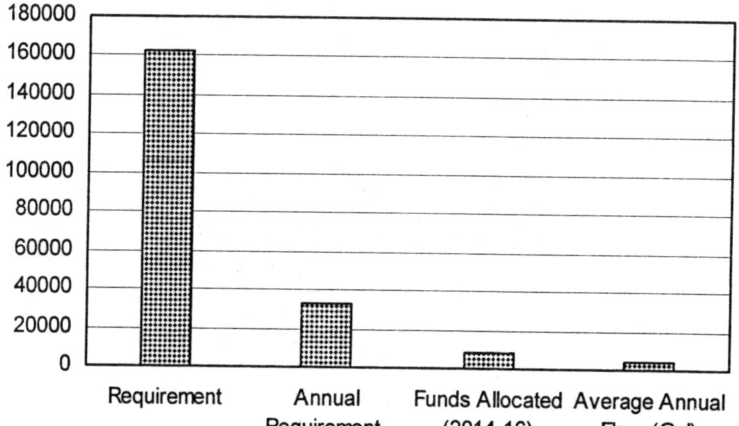

Fig. 14.1: Requirements for Clean India Mission.

Source: GoI documents.

Strategic Fiscal Gap in Sanitation

Difference between financial requirements to meet mandatory commitments on sanitation and investible (available) funds is called strategic fiscal gap in sanitation. The gap, as indicated earlier, is fairly high by any standard. The budgetary allocations for urban and rural areas as compared to requirements remain significantly low (Figs. 14.2 and 14.3). As seen from Table 14.2, annual flow of funds through budgetary allocation from Government of India is only 17 per cent and 7 per cent of annual requirements of funds for rural and urban sanitation confirming that budgetary allocation alone cannot deliver the desired results, although, it will have additional one fourth contribution from provincial/local governments. Therefore, it is realized by the Government of India that its budgetary allocation should be used as a seed capital to multiply flow of investments into sanitation sector.

Can the Country and Governments Afford the Gap?

Empirical evidence suggests that investment in sanitation have a multiplier

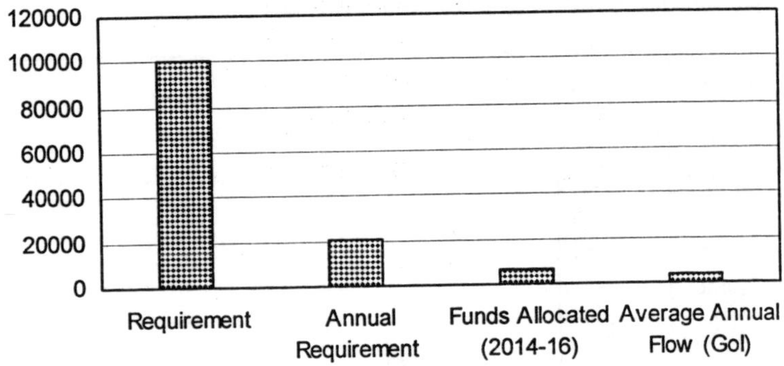

Fig. 14.2: Requirements and Flow of Funds for Rural Sanitation in India.

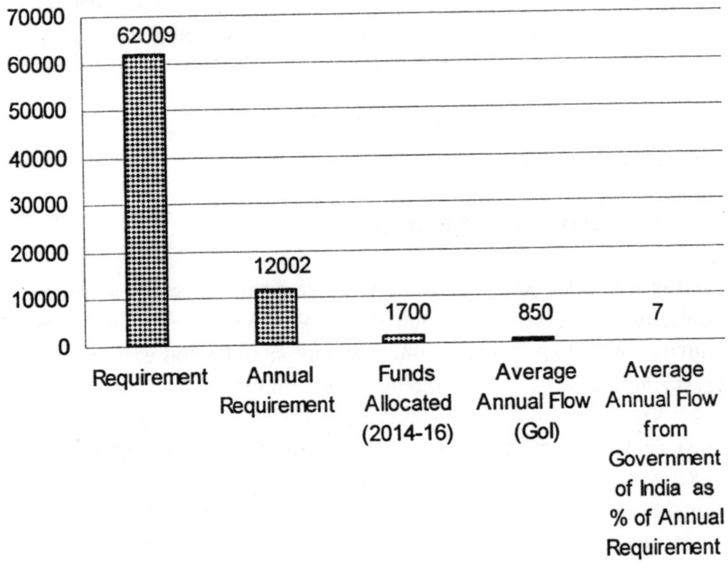

Fig. 14.3: Requirements and Flow of Funds for Urban Sanitation.

effect and can raise GDP by another 6.4 per cent in India (WSP, 2010). Therefore, the Indian economy (with a size of around Rs.1,30,000 billion as per recent estimates in the union budget) which can today gain Rs.8,320 billion from improved sanitation has the potential to spare resources for sanitation. Similarly, intergovernmental revenue will also undergo a substantial increase amounting to Rs.1,473 billion at the current rate of revenue to GDP ratio being (17.7% in 2014-15) in case backlog in sanitation is removed completely. Therefore, the government and country can afford the requisite investments in the sanitation.

Indian Funding Strategy

It was, therefore, realized that the entire amount of Rs.1,00,000+ crores needed for SBM-rural and Rs.62,000+ crore for SBM Urban cannot come from government alone although nearly 1/3 requirements were earmarked for budget allocation from Central and provincial government to achieve the objectives of the two missions by 2019. This pattern of allocation indicates that funds for sanitation have to come from multiple sources of financing. Accordingly nearly two third funds for clean India Mission (SBM rural) are expected to come from extra budgetary resources covering private sector (including CSR, NGOs/CBOs, community) and multilateral/bilateral support (Guidelines: SBM-Rural, GoI).

At the same time, it is also realized that actual disbursement remains further low as compared to allocation. Government of India's pioneering programme JNNURM (Jawaharlal Nehru National Urban Renewal Mission) with a budget of Rs. 50,000 crores (1 crore—10 million) to be spent during 2005-2012 could actually release nearly 40 per cent of earmarked amount. This was caused by inabilities of local bodies to prepare and implement projects accordingly (Pandey, 2016).

This magnitude of support is a difficult task to deliver/mobilize funds from respective sources. Therefore, liquidity of resources is a major issue and stakeholder participation has to be used through a well-designed strategy. In this regard local governments can play decisive role to carry out stakeholder mapping and involvement along with community contribution.

Second important issue is 'outreach' of dedicated resources caused by frozen demand for necessary investment in the sector. The requirements of funds are twofold: (i) individual households for construction of toilets; and (ii) local governments for putting in place a detailed network of waste collection, disposal and treatment. The local governments conventionally do not have effective demand to seek and absorb funds for respective task due to their historical weakness on technical ability and creditworthiness. UNICEF/Water Aid India have in their report indicated the need to ensure financing for equitable access to poor, special focus on bottom-up assessment, rural sanitation, and waste management by urban local bodies (Water Aid, 2005).

Improved Budgetary Resources

Extra Revenue Instruments include Cess and Funds known as cess on service taxes and Swachh Bharat Kosh (Clean India Fund) and Municipal reforms including Bonds.These are over and above the current budgetary practices. Important initiatives taken up in India are as follows:

- The government of India has since November 2015 introduced 0.5 per cent Cess on service taxes being collected by government across the country. These taxes fetch a huge sum of Rs. 200 billion per annum and may make available Rs.1000 crores (Rs.10 billion) per annum through the share of cess in the service tax. This amount is over and above the existing rate of service taxes and is fully dedicated to fiscal requirements for SBM.
- Government of India has also created clean India Fund to have on line individual and charitable contribution including CSR from firms and companies. This is a totally dedicated fund towards clean India mission, keeping a separate account, credibility, transparency and efficiency in the fiscal disbursement under SBM.
- P-Budget is used at local government level to have a dedicated flow of funds for poor which invariably includes sanitation.
- Similarly, benchmarking is used as part of budgeting exercise to focus on performance. It gives special attention on sanitation.
- Municipal Governments in India have also raised funds through municipal bonds. Cities of Ahmedabad, Bangalore etc. have raised nearly Rs. 10,000 million through bonds since 1997 (Pandey, 2016). In addition funds are also raised by provincial level institutions like to Tamil Nadu Urban Development Fund which raised Rs. 810 million for sanitation requirements of 11 small towns.

Emerging Extra Budgetary Resources in India

India is witnessing several innovations at different levels of governance to improve liquidity and outreach of resources for sanitation in urban and rural areas. This is twofold: Institutional arrangements and contribution in cash and kind. These are mobilized in a typology of instruments as follows:

(a) Institutional options/Special Purpose Vehicle (SPV)
(b) Resources from private sector
(c) CSR (Corporate Social Responsibility) funds
(d) Community resources
(e) Convergence and synergy
(f) Multilateral/Bilateral Support

Institutional Options/Special Purpose Vehicle

Special Purpose Vehicle (SPV) for sanitation related activities is gradually emerging as a tool to organize activities towards improved access to sanitation. Ahmedabad Municipal Corporation in Gujarat has created a fully municipal owned (100% equity) SPV to revive the Sabarmati River from a hazardous drain to a city life line. SPV is known as Sabarmati River Front Development Corporation (SRFDC) (Chart 14.1). It has included a range of activities such as (a) resettlement of low income HHs living on the river band; (b) Recreation and commercial development of river band area; (c) local treatment of sewage coming to river at respective

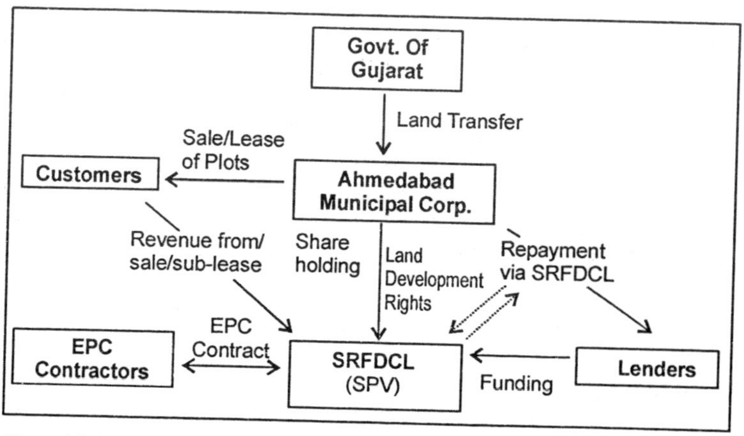

Chart 14.1: India's Municipal owned SPV of Ahmedabad.

places (bio-digesters); (d) organization of cultural event; and (e) turning river into a tourist attraction. The river now has a continuous flow of water drawn from Narmada Canal System and has provided a regular source for city water supply. It has also brought up the water table in the adjoining areas and has also contributed towards plantation and green areas in the city (Pandey, 2016).

These types of SPVs can also be created in a regional context covering rural and urban local governments on the basis of inter local body cooperation for improved sanitation. This manner can also include rural areas in the process to address a jurisdictional and distributional issues (Pandey, 2009).

Further nearly 4000 census towns which are still governed by RLGs (Rural Local Governments) too deserve special attention on a different type of support than SBM-G. These are the towns that have undergone structural readjustment (non-farm sector employment) in their economic profile to become urban from rural status. Their requirements for sanitation need similar attention as for urban.

Resources from Private Sector

Private Sector Participation (PSP) is emerging as a support in terms of resources, efficiency (in expenditure) and savings (as compared to potential municipal expenditure). PSP is used in terms of contracting out and divestiture. This enables local governments to get resources, management capacity, and technology without spending requisite amount or having incidence of expenditure.

Contracting Out

Some important case studies on contracting out include: Rajkot, Hyderabad and Bangaluru. Substantial savings (in a range of 25% to 50% of municipal expenditure) in expenditure are achieved through contacting out of solid waste. Bangaluru has achieved status of binless city for bulk generators through involvement of private sector (Box 14.1).

Divestiture/BOOT/BOO Projects

Divestiture is used as another tool to involve private sector to deliver SWM as per specific standards. It brings investments as resources are mobilized by private sector. Some important cases from Bangaluru, Anand and Hyderabad are given in Box 14.2.

Box 14.1: Contracting out for Sanitation

Rajkot

Street sweeping and transportation is contracted out for PSP. The city of Rajkot was one of the initial cities to apply PSP in early 1990s with nearly 30 per cent savings in the expenditure in municipal kitty. PSP was deployed on collection and transportation. Subsequently, several cities have followed the Rajkot experience.

Hyderabad

A recent case includes city of Hyderabad which outsourced three fourth of the city area for street sweeping in 2004-05 and the expenditure on this area was similar to the expenditure on 25 per cent area served by GHMC (Greater Hyderabad Municipal Corporation) directly (HSMI, 2006). This approach provided 50 per cent saving in expenditure and enabled GHMC to start innovative projects, systematic campaign on public awareness on sanitation, night sweeping and developmental litter free areas.

Bangaluru

Another important area is the practice of Bulk Service Providers (BSP) in Bangaluru. The city of Bangaluru has empaneled BSPs to collect waste from domestic bulk generators (>50 dwelling units, commercial establishments, hotels, cinema halls, eateries, shopping malls and academic institutions, colleges etc.). They are bound to either process the waste or use BSPs. These BSPs collect and segregate solid waste and recover cost from fee paid by bulk producers (Pandey, 2016).

Box 14.2: Divestiture for Sanitation

(1) Brihat Bangaluru Mahanagar Palike (BBMP)

BBMP has involved private sector to process kitchen waste through bio-methanization plant (5 tons capacity). The plant is operated by IKOs Environment Private Limited (IEPL) on management contract basis covering OT (Operate and Transfer) system of PSP. The plant is given on a 5 years contract @ Rs. 2.3 million per annum. The capital cost of Rs. 7 million is borne by BBMP.

BBMP is getting power for 25 street Lights in the city and manure generated from the plant. (There are 3 other bio-methanization units operating on similar pattern). It was told that BBMP is saving 50 per cent potential cost in this O & M contract (involving private sector).

(2) Anand Municipal Body

Anand Municipal Body (AMB) in Gujarat has identified a private operator to collect kitchen waste from bulk generators who are paid by contractor @ Rs. 0.90 per kg of kitchen waste. Nearly 300 academic institutions and 100 commercial establishments in the city are using this facility. City Government is benefiting from service without spending any money.

(3) Greater Hyderabad Municipal Corporation (GHMC)

GHMC has assigned scientific treatment to Ramkey Infrastructure on BOT basis to process the solid waste of entire city. The plant is generating manure and fuel. It is developed on DBOT (Design Build and Operate Transfer) basis. The project cost (Rs. 770 crore or Rs. 7.7 billion) is mobilized by the concessionaire who is paid a sum of Rs. 58 crore per annum towards O & M.

(4) BBMP

BBMP has assigned construction and processing of coconut waste through briquetting plant to CIPL Resurge Pvt. Ltd. The plant is operating since November 2015 and generating solid/carbon neutral fuel being used by farma industry. The plant is given on BOT basis for 5 years. CIPL has made investment of Rs. 7 million in the plant and is expected to recover capital cost and O & M through sale of products.

Community Resources

Community resources are also used to finance sanitation activities at different places in the country. Some important cases include Alandur (Tamil Nadu) and Bangaluru (Karnataka) (Box 14.3).These have shown ability of local community to come forward to provide resources for improved sanitation.

Box 14.3: Community Resources for Sanitation

(1) Alandur sewage treatment plant in Tamil Nadu was put up in early 90s through advance collection of connection charges from potential beneficiaries @ Rs. 5,000 per connection for domestic and Rs. 10,000 for non-domestic connection. A sum of Rs. 160 million was raised from community whereas Rs. 260 million was raised through loans against an ESCROW account which covered property tax and interest from community contribution of Rs. 160 millions. The plant was put up within time-limit.

(2) BBMP has identified NGOs to segregate garbage at Dry Waste Collection Centres (DWCC) in Bangaluru. These NGOs are known as *Kartavya* (Duty). The corporation provide door to door collection of garbage up to DWCC for NGOs to segregate. These NGOs do the segregation and operate in lieu of the money received from sale of segregated SW. BBMP does not have to bother about segregation, transportation and disposal. Eighty per cent of city garbage (Municipal waste) is handled in this manner. This leads to substantial savings in the municipal expenditure to the tune of 20-30 per cent.

(3) Dorekere Lake in ward No. 84 of Bangaluru is given to Walkers Association for maintenance. The association has also planted 750 trees (Social forestry), managed lighting and cleaning and development of footpath. Association also promote socialization in the weekends. The association also organize social functions in the weekends and has also improved overall security in the lake and surrounding areas.

appropriate low cost, environment-friendly, pro-poor technology for waste disposal.

Finally, it appears that extra-budgetary resources for improved sanitation are a must to achieve national policy agenda on rapid pace of economic development and structural readjustment. Governments' budget alone cannot meet massive requirements of resources. Extra-budgetary resources, therefore, need to be identified and used to meet colossal requirements of funds to promote improved sanitation in urban and rural areas. At the same time, the huge requirements of funds should be converted into effective demand. Accordingly, outreach of financing should also be expanded to facilitate demand at the level of individual beneficiaries and respective local governments.

References

BBMP, Budget-Brihat Bangaluru Mahanagar Palika (2015).

GoI, Budget Speech, Ministry of Finance, GoI (2015).

GoI, Economic Survey, Government of India (2014).

GoI, Guidelines – Swachchh Bharat Mission – Rural, Government of India (2014).

GoI, Guidelines-Swachchh Bharat Mission – Urban, Government of India (2014).

GoI, Ninth Five Year Plan, Planning Commission, Government of India, (1997).

HPEC, High Power Expert Committee Report on Urban Infrastructure, Government of India (2010).

HSMI, *Status, Potential and Roadmap for Urban Finance* (2006).

Mehta Dinesh and Mehta Meera (November 2014) Financing Sanitation – Ideas for India.

Pandey (2015-a): Potential for Financing City Infrastructure, IIPA, New Delhi.

Pandey (2015-b): City Resource Pool for Sustainable Habitat in India appeared in the Administrator 56(2) (July 2015).

Pandey, Urban Governance Reforms in Ahmedabad and Bangaluru (2016).

UN Habitat Agenda: UN Habitat (1996).

UN, Millennium Development Goals (MDGs) (2001).

UN, *UN Sustainable Development Goals* (2015).

UNICEF, Progress on Drinking Water and Sanitation (2014).

Water Aid India, Drinking Water and Sanitation in India – Coverage, Financing and Emerging Issues (2005).

WDI, *World Development Indicators* (2015).

WUF, Habitat issues in the Pursuit of the Millennium Development Targets for Water Supply and Sanitation (2006).

http://www.mdws.gov.in/

http://www.worldbank.org/watsan/pdf/WSS_Franchise.pdf

http://mhupa.gov.in/Default.aspx?ReturnUrl=%2f

http://moud.gov.in/contactus

http://washfunders.org/Blog/(tag)/Bill%20%26%20Melinda%20Gates%20Foundation

Index